Alexander Osherenko

Opinion mining and lexical affect sensing

Alexander Osherenko

Opinion mining and lexical affect sensing

Computer-aided analysis of opinions and emotions in texts

Südwestdeutscher Verlag für Hochschulschriften

Imprint
Any brand names and product names mentioned in this book are subject to trademark, brand or patent protection and are trademarks or registered trademarks of their respective holders. The use of brand names, product names, common names, trade names, product descriptions etc. even without a particular marking in this work is in no way to be construed to mean that such names may be regarded as unrestricted in respect of trademark and brand protection legislation and could thus be used by anyone.

Publisher:
Südwestdeutscher Verlag für Hochschulschriften
is a trademark of
Dodo Books Indian Ocean Ltd., member of the OmniScriptum S.R.L Publishing group
str. A.Russo 15, of. 61, Chisinau-2068, Republic of Moldova Europe
Printed at: see last page
ISBN: 978-3-8381-2488-9

Zugl. / Approved by: Augsburg, Universität Augsburg, Diss., 2010

Copyright © Alexander Osherenko
Copyright © 2011 Dodo Books Indian Ocean Ltd., member of the OmniScriptum S.R.L Publishing group

Вере Малевой

...нет правды на земле, но правды нет и выше.
Пушкин «Моцарт и Сальери»

ACKNOWLEDGMENTS

Special thanks are owed to Dr. Benjamin Satzger, Dr. Faruk Bagci, Dr. Matthias Rehm and all colleagues for advices.

Many thanks to my parents who supported me in the PhD undertaking and never doubted that I succeed. I am very thankful to them!

I am very indebted to my dear friend, Prof. Dr. Erhard Fähnders, for his support and for his tips inspired through own life experience.

BRIEF TABLE OF CONTENTS

List of Tables viii
List of Figures x
List of Acronyms xii
1   Introduction 1
2   Affective Behaviour 12
3   Related Work on Opinion Mining/Lexical Affect Sensing 24
4   Corpora 59
5   Statistical Opinion Mining 80
6   Semantic Affect Sensing 144
7   Hybrid Emotion Recognition 170
8   Affect Sensing Using Multimodal Fusion 180
9   Conclusion 191
Appendix A: Theoretical Foundations of Linguistics 199
Appendix B: Emotion Recognition as a Data Mining Problem 204
Appendix C: Affective Behaviour As HMMs 214
Appendix D: SPIN Rules 217
Appendix E: Preliminaries of Data Fusion 231
Appendix F: Achievements 234
Bibliography 236
Index 253

COMPLETE TABLE OF CONTENTS

List of Tables viii
List of Figures x
List of Acronyms xii
1 Introduction 1
    1.1 Examples and Challenges 2
    1.2 Motivation 4
        1.2.1   Recognition 5
        1.2.2   Simulation 7
        1.2.3   Modelling 7
    1.3 Basic Notions 8
    1.4 Research Questions 9
    1.5 Thesis Outline 11
2 Affective Behaviour 12
    2.1 Detecting Emotions 13
        2.1.1   Psychological Cues 13
        2.1.2   Linguistic Cues 15
    2.2 Defining Emotions 20
        2.2.1   Types of Emotions 21
        2.2.2   Emotion Dimensions 21
    2.3 Modelling Affective Applications 22
        2.3.1   PSI Model 22
        2.3.2   OCC Model 23
3 Related Work on Opinion Mining/Lexical Affect Sensing 24
    3.1 Word Level 24
        3.1.1   Emotion Words from Manually Composed Dictionaries 24
        3.1.2   Emotion Words With Numerical Appraisal 26
        3.1.3   Automatic Extraction of Emotion Words from WordNet 27
        3.1.4   Automatic Creation of Lists with Emotion Words from the Internet 29
    3.2 Sentence/Phrase Level 30
        3.2.1   Sentence/Phrase Level Using Linguistic Relations 30
        3.2.2   Sentence/Phrase Level Using Heuristic Rules 34
        3.2.3   Sentence/Phrase Level Using Semantic and Grammatical Means 37
    3.3 Document Level 42

    3.3.1 Document Level Using the Naïve Algorithm 42
    3.3.2 Document Level Using Lexical Means 44
    3.3.3 Document Level Using Stylometric Means 49
    3.3.4 Document Level Using Findings in Personality Analysis 51
  3.4 Overview of Previous Approaches to Lexical Emotion Recognition 53
    3.4.1 Sentence/Phrase-level Affect Sensing 53
    3.4.2 Document-level Opinion Mining 55
  3.5 Shortcomings of Previous Approaches to Affect Sensing 56

4 Corpora 59
  4.1 Long Texts 59
    4.1.1 Pang Movie Reviews Corpus 59
    4.1.2 Multimodal Corpus with Spontaneous Dialogues 59
        4.1.2.1 Mapping E/A data onto affect segments 61
        4.1.2.2 Assessing the Mapping 68
    4.1.3 Corpus with Product Reviews 72
    4.1.4 Berardinelli Movie Review Corpus 74
  4.2 Short Texts 74
    4.2.1 Fifty Word Fiction Corpus 75
    4.2.2 Sentences from Berardinelli Movie Review Corpus 75
  4.3 Properties of Studied Corpora 76

5 Statistical Opinion Mining 80
  5.1 Feature Extraction and Evaluation 80
    5.1.1 Lexical Features 81
        5.1.1.1 Extraction of Lexical Features 81
        5.1.1.2 Manipulating Lexical Features 83
        5.1.1.3 Lexical Features' Evaluation 84
    5.1.2 Stylometric and Deictic Features 85
    5.1.3 Grammatical Features 87
    5.1.4 Overview of Utilized Features 88
  5.2 Core Data Mining Questions 89
    5.2.1 Classifier Choice 90
    5.2.2 Lexical Feature Evaluation 93
    5.2.3 Plotting Classification Results 95
    5.2.4 Feature Value Normalization 99
    5.2.5 Optimizing the Feature Space 101
        5.2.5.1 Forward Selection Heuristic 101

		5.2.5.2	Backward Elimination Heuristic	102
5.3	Interpreting Classification Results in Emotional Corpora			105
	5.3.1	Classes-Similarity Evaluation Measure		107
	5.3.2	Cost-Based Evaluation Measure		110
	5.3.3	Classes-number Evaluation Measure		113
5.4	Classification Results			115
	5.4.1	Pang Movie Reviews Corpus		116
		5.4.1.1	Results Using Lexical Features	116
		5.4.1.2	Results Using Stylometric, Deictic, Grammatical Features	118
	5.4.2	Multimodal Corpus with Spontaneous Dialogues		119
		5.4.2.1	Results Using Lexical Features	120
		5.4.2.2	Results Using Stylometric, Deictic, Grammatical Features	123
	5.4.3	Corpus with Product Reviews		125
		5.4.3.1	Results Using Lexical Features	125
		5.4.3.2	Results Using Stylometric, Deictic, Grammatical Features	128
	5.4.4	Berardinelli Movie Review Corpus		131
		5.4.4.1	Results Using Lexical Features	131
		5.4.4.2	Results Using Stylometric, Deictic, Grammatical Features	134
5.5	Discussion			136
	5.5.1	Lexical Features		137
	5.5.2	Optimizing the Space of Lexical Features		139
	5.5.3	Comparison with Other Feature Groups		142
5.6	Further Research			142
6 Semantic Affect Sensing				144
6.1	General Considerations			144
	6.1.1	Prime Examples		144
	6.1.2	Restrictions		145
6.2	Information Sources			145
	6.2.1	Sources of Affect Information		146
		6.2.1.1	Emotion Words from Affect Dictionaries	146
		6.2.1.2	Movie Glossary	147
	6.2.2	Sources of Grammatical Information		147
		6.2.2.1	Affect Analysis in the Linguistic Literature	147
		6.2.2.2	Grammatical Information from Empirical Examples	150
	6.2.3	Differentiated Linking Clauses and Phrases		150
6.3	Implementation of Semantic Affect Sensing			151

- 6.3.1 System Architecture 151
  - 6.3.1.1 SPIN Parser 151
  - 6.3.1.2 Stanford Parser 152
- 6.3.2 Constructing SPIN Rules 154
  - 6.3.2.1 SPIN Rules from Affect Information 154
    - 6.3.2.1.1 Word-spotting SPIN Rules 154
    - 6.3.2.1.2 SPIN Rules from Movie Glossary 157
  - 6.3.2.2 Grammatical SPIN Rules 157
    - 6.3.2.2.1 Grammatical SPIN Rules from Literature 157
    - 6.3.2.2.2 Grammatical SPIN Rules from Empirical Examples 157
  - 6.3.2.3 SPIN Rules for Linking Clauses and Phrases 158
- 6.3.3 Algorithm 159
- 6.3.4 Processing Example 161
- 6.3.5 Implementation Details 163
  - 6.3.5.1 Analyzing Rule Performance and Gathering Statistics 163
  - 6.3.5.2 Implementation of the Strategies of the Word-Spotting 164
  - 6.3.5.3 Choosing SPIN rules 164
- 6.3.6 Results 165
- 6.4 Discussion 167
- 6.5 Further Research 168

7 Hybrid Emotion Recognition 170
- 7.1 Analysis of Long Texts 170
  - 7.1.1 Feature Extraction and Evaluation 170
  - 7.1.2 Results 171
  - 7.1.3 Discussion 171
- 7.2 Analysis of Short Texts 172
  - 7.2.1 Statistical Approach as Leading 172
    - 7.2.1.1 Feature Extraction and Evaluation 172
    - 7.2.1.2 Evaluation Example of Semantic Features 174
    - 7.2.1.3 Results 175
    - 7.2.1.4 Discussion 176
  - 7.2.2 Semantic Approach as Leading 176
    - 7.2.2.1 Empirical Rules 177
    - 7.2.2.2 Results 178
    - 7.2.2.3 Discussion 178
- 7.3 Further Research 178

8	Affect Sensing Using Multimodal Fusion		180
	8.1 Existing Approaches		180
	8.2 Experimental Setting		182
	8.3 Results of Decision-Level Fusion		183
	8.4 Results of Feature-Level Fusion		185
	8.5 Discussion		188
	8.6 Further Research		190
9	Conclusion		191
	9.1 Contributions		191
		9.1.1 Comparison of the Proposed Approaches	191
		9.1.2 Theoretical Contributions	192
		9.1.3 Experimental Contributions	193
		9.1.4 Application-related Contributions	194
		9.1.5 Practical Contributions	195
	9.2 Answers to the Research Questions		195
	9.3 Outlook		197
Appendix A: Theoretical Foundations of Linguistics			199
	A.1 Grammatical Structure		199
	A.2 Sentence Patterns		200
	A.3 Meaning and its Modification		201
Appendix B: Emotion Recognition as a Data Mining Problem			204
	B.1 Data Collection and Inter-annotator Agreement		205
	B.2 Dataset Composition		205
	B.3 Learning		206
		B.3.1 Supervised Learning	207
		B.3.2 Unsupervised Learning (Clustering)	208
	B.4 Classification		209
		B.4.1 Classifier Algorithms	209
		B.4.2 Classification Evaluation	212
	B.5 Optimizing Feature Space		213
Appendix C: Affective Behaviour As HMMs			214
	C.1 HMMs for Affective Behaviour		214
	C.2 HMMs for Affective Behaviour For SAL Characters		215
Appendix D: SPIN Rules			217
	D.1 Grammatical SPIN Rules from Theoretical Sources		217
	D.2 Grammatical SPIN Rules from Empirical Sources		218

- D.3 Scenario-dependent SPIN Rules...............220
- D.4 Application Frequency of SPIN Rules...............221
- D.5 SPIN Rules for Linking Phrases...............224
- D.6 SPIN Rules for Linking Clauses...............225

Appendix E: Preliminaries of Data Fusion...............231

Appendix F: Achievements...............234
- F.1 Publications...............234
- F.2 Reprints...............235
- F.3 Demo...............235
- F.4 Projects...............235

Bibliography...............236

Index...............253

LIST OF TABLES

Table 1: Examples of DAL words and their scores ... 27
Table 2: Extraction pattern types ... 32
Table 3: Corpora for classifying subjective phrases ... 37
Table 4: Overview of sentence/phrase level approaches ... 54
Table 5: Overview of document-level approaches ... 55
Table 6: Inter-annotator agreement values for 6 segments ... 66
Table 7: Counts of affect segments in the SAL corpus ... 67
Table 8: Inter-annotator agreement values for 5 segments ... 68
Table 9: Counts of affect segments for the SAL characters ... 69
Table 10: Properties of the introduced long text corpora ... 78
Table 11: Properties of the introduced short text corpora ... 79
Table 12: Overview of extracted features ... 89
Table 13: 9-classes confusion matrix ... 107
Table 14: 9-classes transformation specification analytically ... 108
Table 15: 9-classes transformation example ... 108
Table 16: 5-classes confusion matrix ... 109
Table 17: 5-classes transformation specification analytically ... 109
Table 18: 5-classes transformation example ... 109
Table 19: Maximal results of opinion mining in PMRC using lexical features ... 116
Table 20: Results of opinion mining in PMRC using stylometric, deictic, grammatical features ... 119
Table 21: Maximal results of emotion recognition in SAL using lexical features (no history) ... 120
Table 22: Maximal results of emotion recognition in SAL using lexical features (history 7) ... 123
Table 23: Results of emotion recognition in SAL using stylometric, deictic, grammatical features ... 123
Table 24: Maximal results of opinion mining in CwPR using lexical features ... 125
Table 25: Results of opinion mining in CwPR using stylometric, deictic, grammatical features ... 128
Table 26: Maximal results of opinion mining in BMRC using lexical features ... 131
Table 27: Results of opinion mining in BMRC using stylometric, deictic, grammatical features ... 134
Table 28: Maximal classification results before applying the optimizing heuristics ... 136
Table 29: Optimizing the space of lexical features ... 141
Table 30: Semantic affect sensing for 3 classes ... 166
Table 31: Semantic affect sensing for 5-classes ... 167
Table 32: Results of hybrid affect sensing ... 175
Table 33: Optimizing maximal results in feature-level fusion for history 7 ... 187

Table 34: Examples of grammatical clause patterns 201
Table 35: Grammatical SPIN rules from theoretical sources 218
Table 36: Grammatical SPIN rules from empirical examples 220
Table 37: Scenario-dependent grammatical SPIN rules 221
Table 38: Frequencies of use of SPIN rules 223
Table 39: SPIN rules for linking phrases 225
Table 40: SPIN rules for linking clauses 230

LIST OF FIGURES

Figure 1: The example of a movie review 2
Figure 2: Emotional chat 3
Figure 3: Taxonomy of applications utilizing emotional awareness 5
Figure 4: Searching positive emotions in texts 6
Figure 5: Osgood profile for the word *adventure* 15
Figure 6: Linguistic factors influencing textual meaning 16
Figure 7: E/A space 22
Figure 8: OCC model 23
Figure 9: The WordNet structure 28
Figure 10: EmpathyBuddy 31
Figure 11: Subsumption hierarchy 33
Figure 12: An example of a review from PMRC, version 2.0 59
Figure 13: A SAL annotation in ANVIL 61
Figure 14: A variant of 3 affect segments in the E/A space 62
Figure 15: Affect segments as divided by the k-means algorithm 63
Figure 16: Segmentation in five segments 64
Figure 17: A variant of 6 affect segments in the E/A space 65
Figure 18: Examples of SAL turns 66
Figure 19: Final affect segmentation in the E/A space 68
Figure 20: Sample dialogue from SAL 70
Figure 21: HMMs for SAL characters 71
Figure 22: An example of a product review 73
Figure 23: Example review in BMRC 74
Figure 24: Extraction of words from DAL 83
Figure 25: Classifier choice in PMRC 91
Figure 26: Classifier choice in BMRC 92
Figure 27: Lexical feature evaluation in PMRC 93
Figure 28: Lexical feature evaluation in BMRC 94
Figure 29: Numbering Grammatical Combinations in PMRC 98
Figure 30: Renumbering Grammatical Combinations in PMRC 99
Figure 31: Normalized/non-normalized values of deictic features 100
Figure 32: Classes-number evaluation function 115
Figure 33: Lexical features in PMRC 117

Figure 34: Stylometric, grammatical, deictic features in PMRC 118
Figure 35: Lexical features in SAL 121
Figure 36: SAL results depending on the history length 122
Figure 37: Classification results for history length 7 124
Figure 38: Lexical features in CwPR 126
Figure 39: Applying BEH in CwPR 127
Figure 40: Feature combinations in CwPR 129
Figure 41: Grammatical combinations in CwPR 130
Figure 42: Lexical features in BMRC 132
Figure 43: Applying BEH in BMRC 133
Figure 44: Grammatical, deictic, stylometric features in BMRC 135
Figure 45: Affect segmentation for emotion words 155
Figure 46: Affect recognition using the whole text 160
Figure 47: Affect recognition using clauses 160
Figure 48: Affect recognition using phrases 161
Figure 49: Rules in hybrid affect sensing 177
Figure 50: Decision-level fusion 183
Figure 51. Decision-level fusion after discretization 185
Figure 52: Feature-level fusion 186
Figure 53. Feature-level fusion after discretization 188
Figure 54: Grammatical sentence structure 199
Figure 55: Ontology of adjuncts 202
Figure 56: Ontology of intensifiers 203
Figure 57: Phases of conventional data mining 204
Figure 58: The k-means algorithm 208
Figure 59: Learning in SVM 210
Figure 60: Decision tree for a weather forecast 212
Figure 61: HMM for affective behaviour 214
Figure 62: Types of high-level feature fusion 231
Figure 63: Consensus patterns in the majority vote 233

LIST OF ACRONYMS

AI	Artificial Intelligence
BDI	Belief-Desire-Intention
BEH	Backward Elimination Heuristic
BMRC	Berardinelli Movie Review corpus
BMRC-S	Sentences from the Berardinelli Movie Review corpus
BNC	British National Corpus
CwPR	Corpus with Product Reviews
EP	Extraction Pattern
FSH	Forward Selection Heuristic
FWF	Fifty Word Fiction Corpus
GI	General Inquirer
HCI	Human-Computer Interaction
HMM	Hidden Markov Model
IG	Information Gain
IMDB	Internet Movie Database
LIWC	Linguistic Inquiry and Word Count
MFCC	Mel Frequency Cepstral Coefficient
MPQA	Multi-Perspective Question Answering
NB	NaïveBayes
OMCS	Open Mind Common Sense
PMRC	Pang Movie Review corpus
PMI-IR	Pointwise Mutual Information – Information Retrieval
POS	Part-Of-Speech
SAL	Sensitive Artificial Listener
SVM	Support Vector Machines
WSJ	Wall Street Journal

1 INTRODUCTION

Human life consists of emotions and opinions; it is hard to imagine the world without them. Emotions and opinions control how humans communicate with each other and how they motivate their actions. Emotions and opinions are omnipresent and play a role in nearly all human actions. Emotions and opinions influence the way humans think, what they do, and how they act.

Certainly, many issues can be mentioned in this regard, and much has been said about emotions and opinions. But how do humans express what they feel, and how can this be detected by others? And who are these others? Aliens? Computers?

In his contribution to *Meaning and Mental Representations*, Umberto Eco describes the way aliens would articulate what they feel ([Eco, 1988]):

The members of Putnam's expedition on Twin Earth were defeated by dysentery. The crew drank as what the natives called so, while the chiefs of staff were discussing rigid designation, stereotypes and definite descriptions.

Next came Porty's expedition. In this case, the native informants, called Antipodeans, were tested in order to discover if they had feelings and/or mental representations elicited by the word water. It is well known that the explorers were unable to ascertain whether or not Antipodeans had a clear distinction between mind and matter, since they used to speak only in terms of their nerves. If an infant neared a hot stove his mother cried: Oh my God, he will stimulate his <u>C-fibers</u>.

Instead of saying "It looked like an elephant, but then it struck me that elephants don't occur on this continent, so I realized that it must be a mastodont, they used to say: I had <u>G-412</u> together with <u>F-11</u>, but then I had <u>S-147</u>..."

When antipodeans speak about their feelings they use specifications of their nerves such as G-412, F-11 or S-147 — therefore it is nearly impossible to misunderstand what they feel. If someone tried to detect emotions in "antipodean" utterances, he would never have doubts. He would seek specifications of nerves and associate the feelings with the found specifications. However, such information about feelings is not humanlike: humans do not convey emotions using specifications of nerves; humans utilize either subtle means for expressing feelings or even mask them.

And how about computers? How can a computer detect emotional meaning[1] of human texts? This thesis explores answers to these questions.

1.1 EXAMPLES AND CHALLENGES

Let us investigate some examples concerning detection of emotional meaning in order to comprehend problems arising in this regard!

For instance, what emotional meaning expresses a movie review? Movie review is a text consisting of the plot of the movie and the opinion of the reviewer ([Reelviews, 2008]). The emotional meaning is expressed through the number of stars (4 stars means an excellent movie and 0 stars means a bad movie). Can a computer analyze the emotional meaning of the movie review and how? (Figure 1).

Wrestler, The

☆☆☆½

A movie review by James Berardinelli

The film with the loudest buzz at the 2008 Toronto Film Festival was Darren Aranofsky's *The Wrestler* - quite a change for the almost universal indifference. *The Wrestler*, on the other hand, excited interest from all corners and, just before its first screening distribution rights. Almost immediately, the studio's publicity department went into overdrive, and for good reason. This is the k Actor), for Marisa Tomei (Best Supporting Actress), for Aronofsky (Best Director), and for the film (Best Picture). It's redem following his debut feature, *Pi* and its forceful follow-up, *Requiem for a Dream*.

Rourke, in what may be the defining performance of a rocky career that appeared to have hit rock bottom, plays Randy "The l of declining health and advancing age to performing in small venues and doing autograph signings. Randy dreams of one day re; "Don't know what you got till it's gone" - tells a different story. When a heart attack fells Randy after a low-level bout, the doct re-assess things. Is life without wrestling - even what passes for "wrestling" at this stage of his career - any kind of life? He gets

Figure 1: The example of a movie review

The *Wrestler* movie review tells a story of a wrestler. It contains details about wrestler's physical and mental suffering expressed through words that have a negative emotional meaning. Maybe, the reviewer did not like the movie and wants to express his negative opinion? Nothing of the kind. The review is rated 3.5 out of 4 stars although it contains both positive laudatory words and negative devastating plot details. Therefore the problem of automatic opinion mining is to infer an emotional meaning of the movie review that consists of words of different emotional meaning: positive, negative, and words without emotional meaning at all. It can be complicated.

---

[1] *Emotional meaning* is the meaning of a text piece (a word, a phrase or a sentence) that expresses an emotion.

Probably, emotional analysis of movie reviews is hard to master, but is the analysis of short utterances, for instance in a chat, easier to perform (Figure 2)? Is the analysis of emotions in utterances such as *Oh, I'm really happy with it and I think it was a really good decision.* simpler?

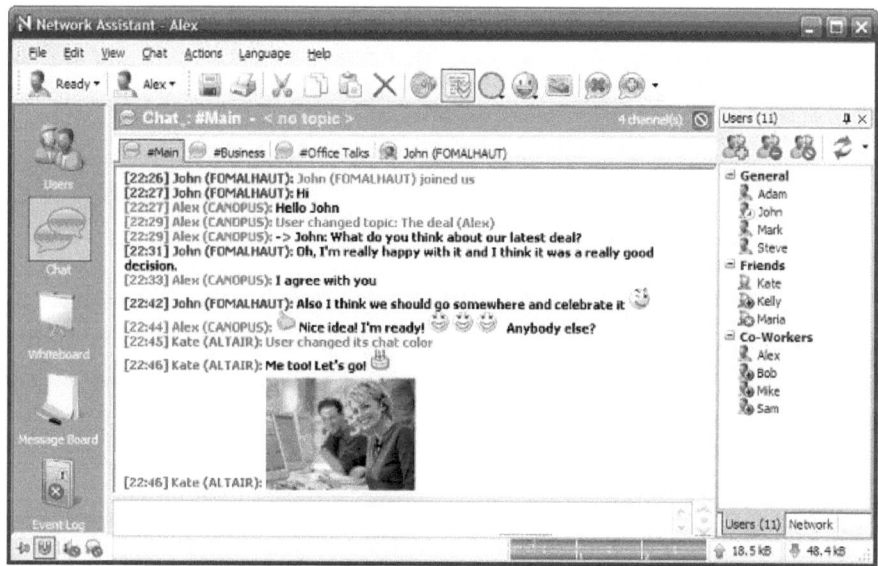

Figure 2: Emotional chat

No, it is not easier. First, analyzed texts can be very different in regard to the contained words. For instance, the utterance *Oh, I'm very happy with it...* means the same as *Oh, I am very satisfied with it...* or *I am very content with it...* although the same emotion can be conveyed using different words *happy-satisfied-content*. That means that emotion recognition should consider the influence of various words in order to obtain a believable emotional meaning of the analyzed utterance. However, a complete list of such words is difficult to compile. Second, particular words in an analyzed utterance influence the meaning of the text in different manner, for example, the word *not* neglects a phrase and the word *very* intensifies the meaning of a phrase. That's why grammatical issues (negations, intensifications) must be considered in emotion recognition to calculate a believable meaning. Furthermore, utterances to analyze can contain connection words such as *although* or *if* that do not have emotional meaning and still influence emotional meaning as in the sentence *Oh, I am very happy with it although it is not ready...* Third, emotional meaning of an utterance is not always humanly evident: what are the emotional meaning of the text *I doubt he is happy* or the text *He seems to be happy but sometimes he looks very sad*? How can a computer sense expressed emotions in such utterances if even humans are not confident of their emotional meaning? What words should be given special consideration in emotional analysis?

Many questions occur in the field of emotion recognition in texts ([Planalp, 1999]). But why is computer-aided emotion recognition in texts so important? What is the motivation?

1.2 MOTIVATION

Technical devices support people in various tasks such as remembering and calculating. Such devices become familiar tools when performing routine repetitive tasks where humans may fail. Devices can undertake a large number of activities and are particularly successful in their work.

However, technical artefacts are usually operated by humans with their vague behaviour and the ambiguous way of thinking. Therefore it would be beneficial for humans if technical artefacts would adapt their exact behaviour to the human nature and provide not only necessary technical functions but also the ability to "understand" human intelligence and human emotions. Such devices have "personality" and behave adequately to human feelings ([Companions, 2009]).

Emotion recognition belongs to the field of study of human-computer interaction (HCI) and comprehensive research is being carried out to this extent focusing on various aspects of affective applications. For instance, [Beale & Peter, 2008] discuss principles and a role that affect and emotions play in building affective applications and report on affective applications that have been developed according to these principles. Tajadura-Jiménez and Västfjäll examine properties of affective sound and state, for example, that a sound is considered to be pleasant if it has a particular frequency or loudness ([Tajadura-Jiménez & Västfjäll, 2008]). The main function of affective applications can be emotion recognition, for example, emotion recognition using speech. [Vogt et al., 2008b] give guidelines on developing such applications and report on a sample application that addresses the major challenges of emotion recognition from speech. User experience and software design constitute a further important field of research. For instance, [Walker & Prytherch, 2008] describe an approach for improving the software design influenced by users' emotional responses, users' attitudes, and expectations and claim that user interaction in the design process is under-recognised. The development of affective applications belongs to the crucial application domains of research. For example, [Zoll et al., 2006] discuss a computer game that can help a student to resolve a complicated emotional psychological problem. They describe a computer system that assists the student by giving an educational advice facilitating coping with this emotional problem.

Furthermore, according to [Jones & Sutherland, 2008], emotionally responsive computer games can help to reduce readiness to use violence and to stimulate "moderate" emotions other than anger, rage or aggression. They discuss a computer game that recognizes emotions of the user in order to enhance gaming.

Evidently, there are many aspects of HCI that need particular consideration and further research. In order to limit the number of such aspects and shed light on the possible use of emotion recognition, this thesis discusses taxonomy of affective applications ([Batliner et al., 2006]) as a starting point for further discussion (Figure 3).

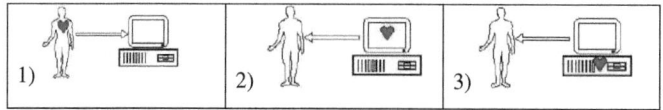

Figure 3: Taxonomy of applications utilizing emotional awareness

Possibility 1 describes recognition of emotions, for example, from texts. Possibility 2 defines applications that simulate human reactions, for example, imitate urgent warnings in an agitated speech style in order to warn users. Possibility 3 describes a modelling possibility where the computer system maintains, for instance, emotional representations of a user or system state.

In the following, this thesis discusses affective applications more exactly focusing on emotion recognition.

1.2.1 RECOGNITION

Emotional applications can detect emotions using texts (the main issue of this thesis). Why is so important to recognize affect automatically?

According to [Liu, 2007], emotion recognition in texts can be utilized for the following reasons:

1. Computer-aided emotion recognition in product reviews is particularly interesting for businesses looking to improve their products on the basis of customer reviews. In this case, it is beneficial to maintain an automatic module to emotion recognition and to avoid not only the stressful but also the time-consuming labour-intensive work of manually acquiring customers' opinions.

2. Some people make their decisions on purchasing a product or using a service according to the opinions of a trustworthy person. In this case, the decision can be made by a module to

automatic emotion recognition, for example, under consideration of features of the product that are preferred by the buyer.

3. Some individuals seek opinions on political topics where a computer can suggest an answer to a certain political question based on political preferences of a particular person.

4. Companies may be interested in automatic emotion recognition for conducting advertising campaigns on the Internet. For example, a module to emotion recognition can find a web page that praises a particular product and offer this page an advert for a particular product. However, if a web page criticizes the product, the advertising company would be more likely to offer an advert for a competing product. In this way, a module to automatic emotion recognition can facilitate conducting advertising campaigns.

5. The option to retrieve/search opinions in texts can be used as a general option in search dialogs. For example, a text editor can provide a search dialog for searching not only for a text, but also for a particular mood, e.g. *positive*[2] or *negative*[3] where emotional meaning of the text is revealed by a module to emotion recognition (Figure 4).

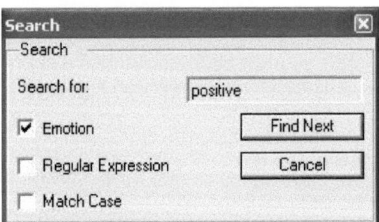

Figure 4: Searching positive emotions in texts

Emotion recognition can be necessary in the house of the future. For instance, artificial artefacts such as vacuum cleaners would "comprehend" affect in utterances of house owner and do not disturb the owner with loud sweeping noises. Or imagine a talk with a CD player that plays (arousing or relaxing) music appropriate to the mood of the owner or a lamp that adjusts illumination according to the psychological state of the owner. In all these cases, it is necessary to recognize affect.

---

[2] *Positive*: hopeful and confident, or giving cause for hope and confidence ([Cambridge, 2008]).
[3] *Negative*: not hopeful, or tending to consider only the bad side of a situation ([Cambridge, 2008]).

Except direct applications of emotion recognition as those listed above, there are also other application fields that are not evident and can be considered concealed since their main function lies in the area of simulation and modelling. Nevertheless, these areas also need emotion recognition as the next sections show.

1.2.2 SIMULATION

Affective applications can simulate emotions in order to imitate affective reactions mimicking a response according to a particular emotion. Why do such applications need a module to automatic emotion recognition?

Here is a possible answer. For example, an affective application can be an emotionally-sensitive environment used for tutoring purposes ([Mello et al., 2008]). The tutoring environment can rely on an intelligent tutoring system that interacts with students using natural language and facilitates learning by composing educational explanations ([Graesser et al., 2005]). In order to construct believable tutoring dialogues, this environment can be endowed with the ability to recognize learner's affective state and provide hereby means for motivating the learner, for detecting the learner's emotional/motivational state, and for responding to that state in an appropriate manner.

1.2.3 MODELLING

An affective system can be utilized for representing virtual humans or their groups. In the simplest case, an affective system can represent a single virtual human. The goal is to develop a virtual human that exhibits emotional behaviour that is similar to the human behaviour in order to enhance its acceptance by human users (cf. section C.1). Human emotions can occur occasionally, from time to time ([Picard, 1997]). For this reason, the virtual human can be based on a model that relies on mathematical means and considers probabilities that a particular emotion occurs in the virtual human. For instance, the virtual human can be in emotional state *joy* and become interested on the basis of emotional observations from a module for emotion recognition.

An affective system can be based on a model that considers the interplay of emotion, cognition, and behaviour ([Marsella & Gratch, 2002]). Such system reacts to different types of emotions (cf. section 2.3): event-based emotions (driven by *desirability*), agent-based emotions (driven by *praiseworthiness*), or object-based (driven by *appealingess*). According to observed emotions the system can plan and perform actions corresponding to its beliefs. Hereby, automatic recognition of emotions can be utilized, for example, for determining the type of emotion that took place and adjusting correspondingly the system behavior.

An affective system can represent a community of virtual humans and consider the needs of real humans like the needs of their body and mind (cf. section 2.3.1). For example, such virtual humans can have emotional needs that can be considered satisfied according to the indications of a module to automatic emotion recognition.

An affective system can be utilized for studying social behaviour in an organization. Every organization consists of groups of persons organized in a particular social structure. According to [dos Lucas et al., 2007], hierarchical importance of a social group is influenced by emotions. Hence, a social affective system needs a module to automatic emotion recognition in order to determine the current social status of a particular social group thus ensuring that the social system behaves comprehensibly.

An affective system can be a believable intelligent robot. [Breazeal, 2002] describes challenges of building believable robots and identifies such issues as personality or empathy. Furthermore, she describes the Kismet robot that maintains an emotion system with a module to emotion recognition that influences the behaviour of the robot. Dautenhahn and colleagues describe socially intelligent agents and claim that emotions influence believability of their behaviour ([Dautenhahn et al., 2002]). Thus, in order to influence this behaviour, socially intelligent agents can utilize a module to emotion recognition.

1.3 BASIC NOTIONS

This thesis discusses approaches to analyzing human emotion, affect, and opinion in texts. But what are opinion, emotion, affect in this thesis? Notion *opinion* is defined in accordance with [Merriam-Webster, 2007] as a view, judgment, or appraisal formed in the mind about a particular matter. Not much different is defined the term *emotion* — the affective aspect of consciousness; a state of feeling; a conscious mental reaction (as anger or fear) subjectively experienced as strong feeling usually directed toward a specific object and typically accompanied by physiological and behavioural changes in the body ([Merriam-Webster, 2007]). Or notion *affect* is defined as a set of observable manifestations of a subjectively experienced emotion. The notions are difficult to differentiate.

Since psychological discussion in regard of the difference between notions *affect*, *emotion* and *opinion* is outside the scope of this thesis, this thesis differentiates between them according to the length of the text that expresses these *emotion*, *affect* or *opinion*: if the analyzed text contains more than empirically revealed 200 words this thesis speaks about *opinion* and *opinion mining*, and about *affect* and *affect sensing*, otherwise. If the length of the analyzed text is unknown, this thesis uses the term *emotion* and the corresponding approach combines both opinion mining/lexical affect sensing under the name *emotion recognition*.

How does this thesis define approaches to opinion mining and approaches to affect sensing? Approaches to *opinion mining* rely on mathematical means to analyze opinion, for example, counts of words. In contrast, approaches to *affect sensing* analyze affect utilizing semantics of occurring opinion words and their grammatical interdependencies.

1.4 RESEARCH QUESTIONS

As already discussed, there are many questions in the area of automatic emotion recognition and this thesis elaborates on some of them:

1. **How do the approaches in this thesis address the challenges of emotion recognition?**

   There are different challenges of emotion recognition that need particular consideration and a reliable approach to emotion recognition should accept them.

2. **Are the approaches to emotion recognition in this thesis general enough to analyze a variety of emotional texts?**

   The analyzed texts express emotions in their own way. These texts can contain specialized words or repetitions or incorrect wordings and still convey an emotional meaning. How do the proposed approaches solve this problem?

3. **The number of existing approaches to emotion recognition is huge. How can the approaches in this thesis contribute to overcoming problems of emotion recognition?**

   The interest in lexical emotion recognition is immense and the research efforts are growing rapidly. Thus, is there a necessity of additional research in this field?

4. **What information and what means should be used in emotion recognition for the analysis of emotional texts?**

   What sources of information should be used for emotion recognition? Should an approach to emotion recognition utilize only counts of words of the analyzed text or it is possible to scrutinize emotional meaning of a text using such data as the average length of sentences or words? What means are of particular importance in emotional analysis, for example, what classification algorithm should be utilized in the statistical approach?

5. **Can the means of approaches in this thesis be utilized for analysis of texts independent of their language?**

   Emotional texts can be composed using a variety of languages. Correspondingly, is it enough to consider only words or symbols in the analyzed texts in order to recognize emotions? Can approaches in this thesis be considered to be general enough in order to perform language-independent analysis?

6. **This thesis investigates in detail emotion recognition using data of the lexical modality[4] (lexical affect sensing). Can data of other modalities be utilized for affect sensing in order to enhance obtained results?**

   Emotions can be deduced from various media — not necessarily from textual data, but, for instance, from acoustic or visual data. Can information from a variety of different sources be joined together in order to improve emotion recognition?

---

[4] *modality* represents a general class of: a sense through which the human can receive the output of the computer (for example, visual modality); a sensor or device through which the computer can receive the input from the human (tactition modality) ([Wikipedia, 2008]).

1.5 THESIS OUTLINE

The remaining chapters of this dissertation are structured as follows:

- Chapter 2 illustrates significant cues of affective behaviour in psychology and linguistics.

- Existing approaches to emotion recognition are discussed in chapter 3. This chapter describes the information resources necessary for understanding these approaches and discusses their shortcomings.

- Chapter 4 describes corpora used for evaluating the proposed approaches and outlines their most remarkable properties.

- Chapter 5 discusses the proposed statistical approach to opinion mining. It describes the utilized information, as well as classification means and results.

- Chapter 6 explores the proposed semantic approach to affect sensing. It describes sources of utilized information, the implemented computer system, and obtained results.

- Chapter 7 investigates the hybrid approach to emotion recognition that combines the statistical approach and the semantic approach. Additionally, this chapter discusses the results obtained.

- Chapter 8 studies emotion recognition using multimodal fusion and discusses classification results.

- The dissertation concludes with contributions of this thesis and discusses future work in chapter 9.

2 AFFECTIVE BEHAVIOUR

A large amount of information has been procured about emotions, and various scientific fields investigate them, highlighting particular aspects of affective information. [Janney, 1996] points out that biology, ethology, and behavioural psychology focus on *body* and interpret feelings as patterns of behaviour. Clinical neurology and neuropsychology concentrate on *brain* and understand feelings as patterns of neural activity. Traditional psychology, experimental psychology, and social psychology analyze *mind*, and feelings are considered as experience. Cognitive psychology studies *thought*, for which feelings are adaptive responses to cognitive appraisals of anticipated or imagined outcomes of situations. Developmental psychology and interactional psychology describe *partnership* as the interactive negotiation of affect.

The influence of emotions is investigated by other sciences. [Budd, 1985] discusses philosophical contents of emotions and describes the relation between emotions and music in Schopenhauer's philosophy. In traditional psychology, [Planalp, 1999] presents a comprehensive study of emotions regarding social, moral, and cultural processes and investigates cues for communicating emotions and describing how emotions communicate moral meaning or how emotional meaning is constructed through communication. In social philosophy, social theory, and branches of psychology and anthropology, emotions are investigated in the context of social constructions that are judged desirable or appropriate in one's group. Cognitive anthropology and anthropological linguistics distinguish cultural variation and functions of affect. In philosophy, emotions are considered to be evidence of consciousness and higher mental functions ([Wertsch, 1985]). Social psychology investigates how emotions are perceived dependent on context and society ([Scherer et al., 2001]). Socio-cultural psychology studies emotions in the context of their influence on human development ([Vygotskij, 1996]). Psychological linguistics discusses the expression of texts using linguistic means. [Kantor, 1977] undertakes a critical analysis of psychological aspects of linguistics and discusses language as a means for expressing thoughts or mental states. Computer science develops tools, techniques, and devices for sensing, interpreting, and processing emotion signals ([Picard, 1997]).

Indeed, many sciences explore emotions, and an exhaustive study of all the issues arising from every field would be outside the scope of this thesis. Therefore, in this thesis, the perspectives only of those sciences considered to be closely related to computer-aided emotion recognition are examined in detail: the perspective of traditional psychology, the perspective of linguistics, and the perspective of computer science.

2.1 DETECTING EMOTIONS

Emotions are everywhere and ever present. They are fluent and irrepressible, but how can they be grasped?

2.1.1 PSYCHOLOGICAL CUES

Psychology investigates a variety of cues for sensing emotions and translates them into a tangible form. For instance, [Planalp, 1996] examines psychological cues for conveying emotions, e.g. using face, gestures/body, activity, physiological, voice, context, trait, other, verbal. The *face* cues include specific posing or movement of the eyes, mouth, brow, or nose, general references to how the "face looked" and eye gaze. The *gestures/body* cues are specific references to posing or movement of the hands, arms, legs, body, or head (excluding face), specific nervous behaviours using hands, arms, legs, body, or head (e.g. pacing, scratching head), descriptions of movements about how the person walked (e.g. walked proudly, walked heavily, ran into room). The *activity* cues are specific descriptions of nonverbal behaviour that can involve an object other than a part of the body and are not repetitive as nervous habits, for instance, throwing a plate, taking a bath, or going dancing. The *physiological* cues are arousal symptoms or uncontrollable reflex actions, for example, blushing, deep breathing, crying. The *voice* cues correspond to references to the pitch, rate, volume, or quality with which words are spoken, vocalizations, for instance, sighs, laughter, back-channeling[5]), phrases prefaced with "sounded like", any description of the voice that does not refer to the actual words spoken or content of discussion, references to amount of talk, for example, talkative or lack of talk, quiet. The *context* cues include reported past, present or future facts or events that are relevant to understanding the experienced emotion. The *trait* cues are references to the traits, predispositions, or habitual behaviours that help to identify the observed emotion. The *other* cues category contains cues that do not fit in the categories above.

Verbal cues are the most significant cues for detecting emotional behaviour, and so merit within the scope of this thesis special consideration. *Verbal* (direct/indirect) cues correspond to textual utterances either made to the respondent or overheard by the respondent. *Indirect verbal* cues mean

---

[5] *Back-channeling* — an acoustic agreement without interrupting speakers's turn, e.g. 'uh-huh' ([Feke, 2003]).

that the emotional behaviour of a human is expressed in verbal form without directly stating the emotion being felt, e.g. *I do have much work to do!* In contrast, *direct verbal* cues directly communicate the emotions being felt, e.g. *I'm angry!* to express anger or *I feel depressed!* to convey depression.

[Langenmayr, 1997] looks at the role of words in natural-language texts, revealing that although words are generally used for communication, they can also be utilized for other purposes such as showing affective reactions.

But how can particular words be emotionally appraised? Psychology presents appropriate means. For instance, the emotional appraisal of words can be undertaken using an Osgood questionnaire ([Osgood et al., 1957]). Correspondingly, the emotional meaning of the studied word is distinguished according to the values of three dimensions (*evaluation, activation, potency* scores[6]). In order to extract the emotional meaning, a respondent estimates a score for the word ranging from 5 (the highest degree) down to 1 (the lowest degree) by answering questions of the form *"Means <word> <bipolar pair>?"*. For instance, the respondent evaluates the *evaluation* score of the word *adventure* to 4.0 by answering the question *Means adventure something good/bad?*; the respondent evaluates the *activity* score of the word *adventure* to 1.0 and answers the question *Means adventure something active-passive?*; the respondent evaluates the *potency* score of the word *adventure* to 2.0 and answers the question *Means adventure something strong/weak?*. The resulting emotional meaning of the word is represented as a triple of Osgood scores, called an Osgood profile (Figure 5).

---

[6] The *evaluation* score stands for assessing the pleasantness of a word (pleasant/not pleasant). The *activation* score corresponds to the activeness of a term a word denotes (active/passive). The *potency* score means the strength of a term a particular word denotes (strong/weak).

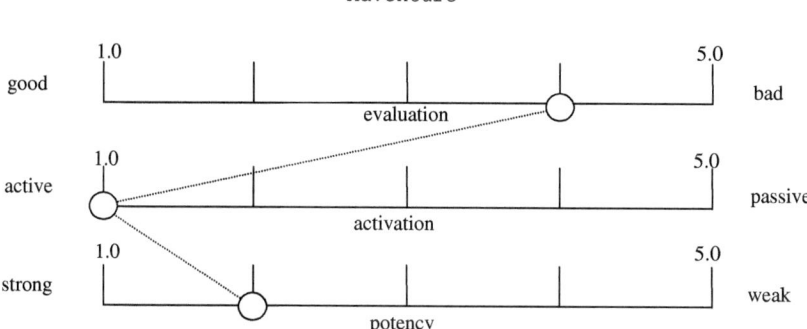

Figure 5: Osgood profile for the word *adventure*

Figure 5 shows the Osgood profile for the word *adventure* using the dimensions *evaluation*, *activation*, and *potency*. The dimension values are defined empirically for the purposes of this thesis.

An Osgood profile defines the emotional meaning of individual words, but not the emotional meaning of a text consisting of many words. [GAF, 2002] explores the means to identify a specific emotion by using a recall and verbal report. For this purpose, a user answers questions about the emotion regarding its occurrence (*How long ago, Where, Who was present*), general evaluation of the emotion (*Pleasant/Unpleasant*), the characteristics of the emotion (*Suddenly/Abruptly, Predicted/Unpredicted, Familiar/Unfamilar*, and so on), and a verbal description of the emotion (*Verbal description, Emotion terms describing the emotion*). Using the provided answers, an expert system deduces the emotion that took place in the past.

Hence, [GAF, 2002] deduces emotions by psychological means. In an analogous manner, this thesis discusses an approach to detecting emotions using verbal means.

2.1.2 LINGUISTIC CUES

Emotions can be expressed in text and linguistics describes the means to identify and to appraise these emotions.

[Fries, 1996a] presents the factors influencing textual meaning, e.g. the verbal expression of emotions (Figure 6).

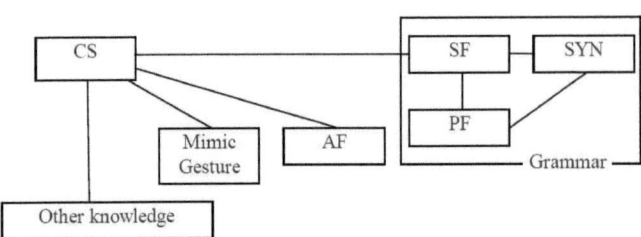

Figure 6: Linguistic factors influencing textual meaning

1. The conceptual structure (CS) distinguishes various aspects of the text:

    a. Emotional meaning;

    b. Thematic organization;

    c. Elocution (the relation between the speaker and the world);

    d. Representational content.

2. The semantic form (SF) defines factors according to their lexical and grammatical structure. For example, interjections can be considered as expressions of emotions.

3. The syntactic form (SYN) defines the syntactic content of a text. For example, the syntactic form influences the emotional content of a text in German:

    a. *Dass du immer soviel trinken musst!* (You drink too much alcohol! – connecting word is missing);

    b. *Feuer!* (Fire! – missing article and governing category);

    c. *Unvorstellbar!* (Unimaginable! – missing governing category);

    d. *Raus!* (Get out! – prepositional phrases without governing category);

4. The articulation (AF) and phonological form (PF) influence the meaning of a text.

Evidently, textual meaning has many facets. However, for simplicity, the meaning of a text is analyzed within the scope of this thesis in connection with CS, SF, and SYN only, and AF is not considered. PF is analyzed in this thesis in regard to multimodal fusion in chapter 8.

What are some concrete examples of the implications of emotions in linguistics? [Fries, 1996b] examines 74 emotions and describes the means for conveying emotions in natural language; for example, *Das Herz bricht* (cry your heart out) for expressing sorrow. Hence, he points out words used for communicating emotions being felt and presents descriptions of corresponding emotional episodes, such as an emotional episode describing a person who feels *fear* in threatening circumstances. Moreover, this study describes metaphors[7] for communicating emotions, such as *Gefühle vergehen* (feelings "go away"), to illustrate that emotions decay.

The approach by [Fries, 2007] defines a formalism for describing emotional scenes in the STRIPS[8] style using preconditions and their consequences. For instance, the emotional scene <*unexpectedness*> can be defined as follows:

Emotional scene <*unexpectedness*>
    precondition π: subject χ thinks ρ;
    state σ:
        experiences ε (<*pleasure*>)
        value ω of emotional state σ: (exp_)
    action:
        precondition π and state σ induce state σ'   (1)

where χ is the subject of the text; ρ is interpreted as emotional stimulus; state σ describes the current state of subject χ, pleasure; the variable ε describes a predicate of the current state; and the variable ω describes the emotional meaning of the state.

Hence, an emotional scene can be described using predicates and dimensions of emotional states. There are four classes of predicates of emotional state that define a value of the variable ε:

1. <pleasure>

2. <empathy>

3. <appreciation>

4. <interest>

---

[7] *Metaphor* is a figure of speech in which a word or phrase literally denoting one kind of object or idea is used in place of another to suggest a likeness or analogy between them (as in *drowning in money*) ([Merriam-Webster, 2007]).

8 STRIPS (Stanford Research Institute Problem Solver) is an automated planer that defines actions using preconditions, goals — situations which the planner is trying to reach (postconditions), a set of actions ([Wikipedia, 2008]).

Emotional value ω is defined using the following dimensions:

1. dimension *polarity* defines if an emotion is positive (pol₊) or negative (pol₋) or neutral (pol₀);

2. dimension *expectedness* defines if an emotion is expected (exp₊) or unexpected (exp₋);

3. dimension *intensity* defines the intensity of an emotion (aroused — int₊, relaxed — int₀).

Emotional value ω in a description of an emotional scene is defined by a triple:

$$\omega = <\alpha, \beta, \gamma> \mid \alpha \in \{pol_+, pol_-, pol_0, a\}$$
$$\beta \in \{exp_+, exp_-, exp_0, a\}$$
$$\alpha \in \{int_+, int_0, a\} \qquad (2)$$

Hence, emotional value ω has three dimensions where {pol₊, pol₋, pol₀, a} defines values of the dimension *polarity* (a positive, a negative, a neutral emotional value or absent); {exp₊, exp₋, exp₀, a} defines values of the dimension *expectedness* (expected, unexpected or absent); {int₊, int₀, a} describes values of the dimension *intensity* (aroused, relaxed or absent). Note that the last dimension (intensity) has only three values defining an emotion as having positive intensity, having no intensity or this dimension is absent in the proposed emotional value — there is no negative intensity. The dimensions *polarity* and *intensity* are very similar to the descriptions of *evaluation/activation* dimensions in the E/A space (cf. section 2.2.2).

Using descriptions such as in (1), a text can be categorized as reflecting a particular emotional scene. However, an exact, numerical appraisal of an emotion in the proposed formalism is given only by at most three discrete values of dimensions.

How else can emotions be numerically appraised using linguistic means? [Jahr, 2000] examines means for appraising the intensity of emotions. Emotions by themselves are revealed empirically. Adapted for this thesis, intensity of emotion *E* is calculated using the formula:

$$E_l = \frac{B\ (M + \sum F_{E_x}) \sum V_a}{W} \qquad (3)$$

where *B* is a personal interest in the dialogue topic (usually 1); *M* is the number of linguistic means, e.g. number of stylistic figures (metaphors, etc.); ΣF_{Ex} is a sum of empirical weights of the linguistic means; ΣV_a is a sum of the weighted variables that influence emotional concernment; *W* is the number of words in the appraised text.

For instance, this approach analyzes the intensity of emotion *Unmut (resentment)* in an article from a juristic magazine:

Kaiser: Strafen statt Erziehen? (Zeitschrift für Rechtspolitik 30 (1997), 451-458.)
Im Rückblick von einhundert Jahren fällt es daher die Bilanz im sanktionsrechtlichen Umgang mit jugendlichen Straftätern *nicht uneingeschränkt positiv* oder *ermutigend* aus. Offenbar waren die Erwartungen der Reformväter *zu hoch gesteckt* und es ist *Bescheidenheit* angezeigt. Denn Jugendstrafrecht und Jugendgerichtsbarkeit weisen *gravierende Gebrechen* auf. Trotz des skizzierten *Mängelprofils* empfiehlt es sich, ebenso am Erziehungsgedanken wie an Verfahrensgrundsätzen und Interventionssystem des Jugendstrafrechts festzuhalten. *Freilich* läßt *es sich nicht leugnen*, daß es sich hierbei *nicht nur* um unterschiedliche und zum Teil gegenläufige Ideen und Strategien handelt, *sondern daß auch* unterschiedliche Handlungsstile durch *Konflikte* zwischen miteinander *rivalisierenden Professionen fest angelegt* sind. Sonst stehen den mehr *bewahrenden Jugendpädagogen* im *wachsenden Umfang experimentierfreudige Sozialpädagogen* und sonstige Sozialwissenschaftler gegenüber, die Ihnen *das Feld* im Umgang mit jungen Straffälligen *streitig machen*. Die unterschiedliche Beteiligung der verschiedenen Berufsgruppen an Fachveranstaltungen, etwa der Deutschen Vereinigung für Jugendgerichte und Jugendgerichtshilfen, lässt dies darüber hinaus die *„vested interests"* erkennen. Die Verrechtlichung und der Informalismus haben aber in gleicher Weise international für einen *Reformschub* im Jugendrecht der Gegenwart gesorgt.

Emotional figures (empirical weights F_{Ex} are provided in brackets):

nicht uneingeschränkt positiv (+0.5) - ermutigend (0)- offenbar (−0.5) - Reformväter (0) - zu hoch gesteckt (0) - Bescheidenheit angezeigt (0) - gravierende Gebrechen (+1) - Mängelprofil (0) - freilich (−0.5) - läßt es sich nicht leugnen (0) - nicht nur… sondern auch (−0.5) - Konflikte… fest angelegt (+0.5) - bewahrende Jugendpädagogen (0) - wachsender Umfang (0) - experimentierfreudige Sozialpädagogen (0) - rivalisierende Pädagogen (0) - Feld streitig machen (0) - „vested interests" (0) - Reformschub (0).

Emotional intensity of emotion *Unmut (resentment)* is calculated as

$$E_l = \frac{1*(19+0.5)*1}{166} = 0.117 \qquad (4)$$

where $B=1$; $M = 19$; $\Sigma F_{Ex} = 0.5$; $W = 166$, $\Sigma V_a = 1$.

Hence, it is possible to determine the intensity of emotion by linguistic means. However, the emotion itself must be revealed empirically.

What additional means can be employed additionally for appraising emotions? According to [Fussell, 2002], the verbal appraisal of emotions depends on literal and figurative[9] expressions and, moreover, on emotional metaphors and the role of the conversational partner in creating emotional meaning. The emotional meaning is influenced by culture.

[Hunston & Thompson, 2000] describe methods for appraising an author's opinion. Correspondingly, opinion is influenced by its functions, for example, such as expressing opinion, or maintaining relations with other persons, or organizing the discourse. Hence, its appraisal is influenced by the importance of communicating opinion, by a value of building a relation between writer and reader, and by the significance of choosing the subject of discourse. Hunston and Thompson examine lexical items that express opinion and explore corresponding grammatical means. In this way, they focus on adverbs, adjectives, verbs indicating affect, certainty, doubt, vague language; and on modals indicating possibility, necessity, and prediction.

[Leech & Svartvik, 2003] describe grammatical means to express emotions (the code of a mean referred to hereafter is designated in brackets): interjections (299), e.g. *Oh, what a beautiful present!;* exclamations (300a), e.g. *What a wonderful time we've had!*; emphatic *so* and *such* (300b), e.g. *I'm so afraid they'll get lost!*; repetitions (300c), e.g. *This house is 'far, 'far too expensive!*; intensifying adverbs and modifiers (301), e.g. *We are utterly powerless!*; emphasis (302), e.g. *How ever did they escape?*; intensifications of negative sentences (303a), e.g. *She didn't speak to us at all*; negative noun phrases beginning with *not a* (303b), e.g. *We arrived not a moment too soon*; fronted negations (303c), e.g. *Never have I seen such a crowd of people!*; exclamatory and rhetorical questions (304, 305), e.g. *Hasn't she grown!* and *What difference does it make?*. Note that this thesis uses findings by [Leech & Svartvik, 2003] for appraising emotions.

2.2 DEFINING EMOTIONS

There are four different approaches to defining emotions ([Cornelius, 1996]): the Darwinian approach, which focuses on universal, instinctive, and natural functions of humans; the Jamesian approach, which declares that emotions are bodily responses; the cognitive approach, which concentrates mainly on the appraisal of emotions; and the social approach, which affirms that emotions are constructions that serve social purposes.

---

[9] *Figurative*: used not with their basic meaning but with a more imaginative meaning. For instance, in sentence *Of course, she was using the term massacre in the figurative sense* the word *massacre* has a

Within the scope of this thesis, the cognitive approach needs special consideration.

2.2.1 TYPES OF EMOTIONS

The simplest way to define emotions is to define the categories to which these emotions belong to. For instance, the text *I'm very happy!* expresses intuitively an emotion within the category *joy*. Since there are many emotions and it is difficult to find a category in which the emotion would fit, psychologists elaborate on various sets of emotion categories. For instance, Ekman defines six categories of emotions: *anger, disgust, fear, joy, sadness, surprise* ([Ekman, 1993]). According to Izard, emotions belong to ten categories: *anger, disgust, fear, guilt, interest, joy, sadness, (distress), shame, surprise* ([Izard, 1977]). Numerically, emotional meaning can be expressed as a vector containing six elements that represent emotional loads of Ekman emotions (Ekman vector); emotional meaning can be defined by an Izard vector containing ten values representing emotional loads of Izard emotions (Izard vector).

2.2.2 EMOTION DIMENSIONS

No matter which emotion categories are beneficial for describing a particular scenario, what dimensions of emotions should be distinguished? As there is no consensus about emotion categories, there is also no consensus about emotion dimensions ([Schröder, 2004]). Some distinguish between pleasure, arousal, and dominance dimensions. Others identify evaluation, activation, potency, and evaluation dimensions or the evaluation, activity, potency dimensions. However, the dimensions essentially define the answers to questions such as: how good or bad, how aroused or relaxed, and how powerful or weak a particular emotion is. Thus, the dimensions have a great deal in common, and their particular names can be considered to be synonymous.

This thesis uses the dimensions of *evaluation* (synonymous to valence or pleasure) and *activation* (synonymous to arousal and activity). Graphically, different approaches suggest that emotional appraisals can be represented circularly in a 2D-form in the Evaluation/Activation space ([Cowie et al., 2000]). This thesis denotes the Evaluation/Activation space as simply the E/A space (Figure 7).

figurative meaning ([Cambridge, 2008]).

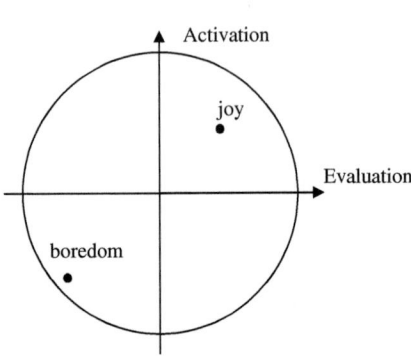

Figure 7: E/A space

Figure 7 shows the E/A space representing the emotion *joy* (a state of happiness or felicity) and the emotion *boredom* (the state of being weary and restless through lack of interest). The E/A values of emotions lie in the circle. Note that *joy* has a high value within the dimension *evaluation* and a high value for the dimension *activation*, whereas the emotion *boredom* is characterized by a low value for the dimension *evaluation* and a low value within the dimension *activation*.

2.3 MODELLING AFFECTIVE APPLICATIONS

2.3.1 PSI MODEL

The PSI theory is based on psychological theories of human action regulation, intention, and behaviour. It describes a comprehensive model of the human brain, its cognitive processes, emotion and motivation and relies on the informational structure of an intelligent, motivated, emotional agent (called PSI) which is able to survive in arbitrary domains of reality ([Bartl & Doerner, 1998]). The PSI agent is driven by several motives (the need for food, water, certainty, competence, affiliation, and the avoidance of pain). The cognitive processes in PSI are influenced by emotional states and processes.

The most significant components of a PSI agent are motivators, pleasure system, motor system ([Dörner, 2001]). The motivators define the agent's intentions; for example, they express the agent's need to life support and to retain some resource within particular boundaries, such as the resource defining the supply for water and energy. The PSI agent has a pleasure system that changes the intentions of the agent according to its wishes and emotions. If the agent has to renew some resource, it can initiate a particular action and move using its motor system to the location where it can obtain this resource.

2.3.2 OCC MODEL

[Ortony et al., 1988] defines a comprehensive model of emotions (OCC model) that is often used in computer systems. This model describes a detailed psychological model of emotions that relies on cognitive, appraisal issues of emotions (Figure 8).

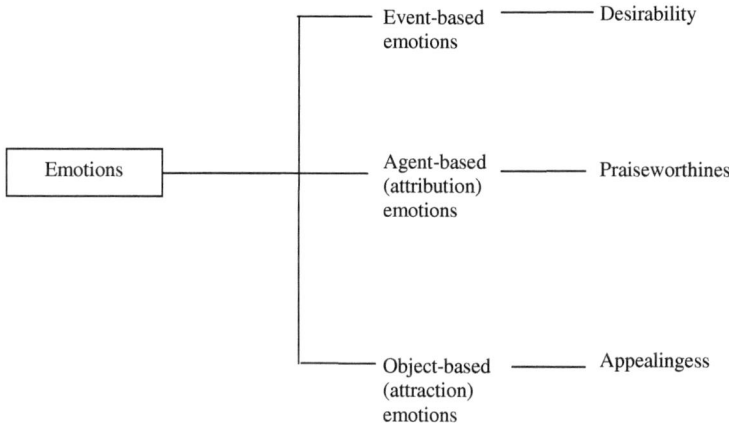

Figure 8: OCC model

The OCC model highlights three groups of emotions: event-based emotions (driven by *desirability*: pleased/displeased), agent-based (attribution) emotions (driven by *praiseworthiness*: approving/disapproving), or object-based (attraction) emotions (driven by *appealingess*: liking/disliking). OCC introduces global and local variables influencing the intensity of emotions — global variables, e.g. *unexpectedness*, define emotional intensity independent of the group to which the corresponding emotion belongs; in contrast, local variables influence the intensity of emotions of particular groups, e.g. the local variable *desirability-for-other* influences the intensity of *event-based emotions*.

3 RELATED WORK ON OPINION MINING/LEXICAL AFFECT SENSING

Related work in the lexical emotion recognition can be distinguished mainly by the granularity of analysed entities in the studied texts:

- *Word level.* The main entity of emotional meaning are particular words (cf. section 3.1);

- *Sentence or phrase level.* The main entity of emotional meaning is a sentence or a phrase of a text (cf. section 3.2);

- *Document level.* The main entity of emotional meaning represents the text itself (cf. section 3.3).

This thesis outlines the existing approaches to emotion recognition emphasizing its most significant findings in section 3.4 and discusses their shortcomings in section 3.5.

3.1 WORD LEVEL

Human languages define different words and affect sensing at the word level aims at identifying their emotional meaning. Most words do not have affective background or express an affective meaning only in a specific context, but some words (emotion words) convey emotional information independently of the context of their use. Emotion words are especially important in this thesis since the proposed semantic approach relies on them.

3.1.1 EMOTION WORDS FROM MANUALLY COMPOSED DICTIONARIES

Affect sensing at the word level can use manually composed affect dictionaries that contain emotion words which emotional meaning is ascribed by a human.

[Stone et al., 1966] introduces the General Inquirer dictionary (GI) containing 13,000 words and 34,914 word senses. Since a word can have different senses in GI, the word can occur several times in the dictionary. For instance, verb *admit* occurs three times in GI according to 3 senses as: 1) To acknowledge, confess, agree; 2) To grant entry, membership or access to something; 3) "Admittedly" — adverbial form of sense 1.

GI groups words in different ontologies, for instance, words in the *tag* ontology and words in the *marker* ontology. Most significant words of the *tag* ontology in the context of emotional analysis belong to the following categories: 1,635 words in the category *Positiv* containing 1,915 positive word senses, 2,005 words in the category *Negativ* containing 2,293 negative word senses. 17 words are ambiguous[10] and annotated dependent on a sense both as a word in the category *Positiv* and as a word in category *Negativ*. For instance, word *fun* is specified contradictory as a positive noun with the meaning *Enjoyment, enjoyable*, and as a negative verb with the meaning *Make fun (of)"— to tease, parody*.

Besides words in the *tag* ontology, words in GI can be grouped according to the *marker* ontology. The *marker* ontology distinguishes 182 syntactic and semantic categories the most significant from which in the context of emotional analysis are *Emotions* (*anger, fury, distress, happy...*) and *Evaluative Adjective* (*good, bad, beautiful, hard, easy...*). Clearly, all words in the categories *Emotions* and *Evaluative Adjective* category of the *marker* ontology also belong to the discussed above categories of the *tag* ontology, *Positiv* and *Negativ*.

Affect sensing at the word level can be performed using the Linguistic Inquiry and Word Count dictionary (LIWC) ([Pennebaker et al., 2001]). LIWC contains 2,251 word patterns representing words of different inflection, for example, pattern *abandon** represents all inflections[11] of word *abandon*. Moreover, LIWC groups words in 68 categories, most interesting of which in the context of emotional analysis is the category *Affective or Emotional Processes* (*Affect*) that contains 617 patterns referring to affective or emotional processes. The category *Affect* is subcategorized into positive emotions (*Posemo*) and negative emotions (*Negemo*). The category *Posemo*, in its turn, has 2 subcategories: *Posfeel* representing words that express positive feelings and *Optim* representing words that convey optimism and energy. The category *Negemo* has three subcategories: subcategory *Anx* that represents words of anxiety or fear, subcategory *Anger* that represents words of anger, subcategory *Sad* that represents words of sadness. For instance, word *afraid* belongs to categories *Affect*, *Negemo* and *Anx*. Patterns in LIWC are annotated additionally with the part-of-speech tags[12] (POS) associated with the corresponding pattern.

---

[10] 17 ambiguous words: even, hit, help, deal, matter, make, particular, mind, hand, arrest, board, laugh, pass, fun, fine, order, hustle

[11] *Inflection* represents a change in or addition to the form of a word which shows a change in the way it is used in sentences.

[12] *POS tagging* is the process of marking up words according to their linguistic category, e.g. marking up the verb defined as an inflected verb.

[Levin, 1993] describes English verbs of different semantic meaning and among others 113 verbs conveying positive/negative emotions. 34 verbs are found neither in the positive nor in the negative GI (hereafter referred to as *Levin verbs*).

EQI is a list of emotion words and phrases (mainly adjectives and adverbs) that currently contains over 3,000 entries ([Myrick & Erney, 1984]). Emotion words are stored in the EQI dictionary without an exact emotional annotation and, hence, entries in this dictionary must be annotated manually in order to use them for sensing affect.

3.1.2 Emotion Words With Numerical Appraisal

The above dictionaries contain emotion words *without* numerical appraisal of affective meaning. However, numerical appraisal is sometimes necessary, for example, for automatic assessing emotional meaning of a text.

[Whissell, 1989] introduces Whissell's Dictionary of Affect (DAL), a dictionary of affective language that can be used insofar. DAL words are extracted from a corpus of 1,000,000 words. The current version of DAL contains 8,742 words of different inflection. DAL words can have equal lemmata[13], for instance, verb *abandon* and its inflected form *abandoned*; they can be stopwords[14]. DAL words are scored along three dimensions: *evaluation*, *activation*, and *imagery* that are determined by human judgement. For the purpose of evaluating scores, over 200 human raters (both men and women) evaluated each word for the *evaluation* score and the *activation* score in average 8 times and for the *imagery* score in average 5 times. Based on the yielded scores, the mean value is stored as a final score of the corresponding word in DAL. where scores for the *evaluation* dimension range from 1 (unpleasant) to 3 (pleasant), for the *activation* dimension range from 1 (passive) to 3 (active), for *imagery* dimension range from 1 (difficult to form a mental picture of this word) to 3 (easy to form a mental picture).

In this thesis, the original scale is mapped from the range [1 to 3] onto the range [−1 to 1] for better readability (Table 1).

---

[13] *Lemma* represents a canonical form of a word, for instance, the canonical form of the verb *is* is represented by infinitive *be*.

[14] *Stopword* defines a very frequent word of a language, e.g., the articles *the* or *a* in the English language.

Word	Evaluation	Activation	Imagery
a	0.0	−0.62	−1.0
abandoned	−0.86	0.1	1.0
accepted	−0.33	−0.67	−0.2

Table 1: Examples of DAL words and their scores

The word *a* (usually considered as neutral) represents in DAL a word with the neutral meaning: its *evaluation* score has a value of 0.0 expressing no evaluation; the *activation* score has a value of −0.62 expressing the passive meaning; the *imagery* score is −1.0 meaning a high difficulty to form a mental picture. The DAL word *abandoned*, usually considered as negative, has an *evaluation* score value of −0.86 expressing high unpleasantness; the *activation* score is −0.67 denoting the passive meaning; the *imagery* score has a value of 1.0 indicating the easiness to form a mental picture.

Indeed, major score values of DAL words can be explained using commonsense. However, not all score values are humanly comprehensible. For instance, the *evaluation* score for the DAL word *accepted* has the value −0.33 and should thereby represent a negative word although it is usually considered as positive. There are also other examples of DAL words which emotional appraisal is not comprehensible. Hence, the DAL scores are not always humanly plausible and therefore need particular consideration.

3.1.3 AUTOMATIC EXTRACTION OF EMOTION WORDS FROM WORDNET

Emotion words can be extracted using linguistic relations in the WordNet database ([Fellbaum, 1998]). WordNet is a lexical database of English words. The current version of WordNet contains 147,249 words and 207,016 word-sense pairs (Figure 9).

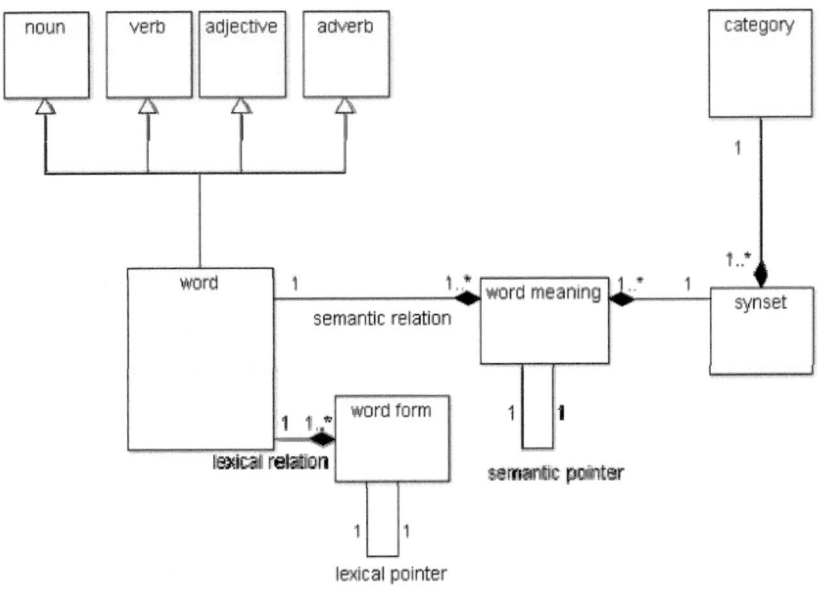

Figure 9: The WordNet structure

WordNet contains nouns, verbs, adjectives and adverbs grouped in sets of cognitive synonyms (synsets). For instance, WordNet contains noun *table*, verb *wish*, adjective *tedious*, and adverb *happily*. Words in WordNet can have different meanings that are described in glosses, for example, adjective *tedious* has 2 meanings: *so lacking in interest as to cause mental weariness* and *using or containing too many words*. Synsets in WordNet are organized in a network and interlinked by means of semantic and lexical relations represented by pointers. Semantic relations as synonymy or hypernymy/hyponymy (hierarchical relations) hold between word meanings, for instance, between word *human* and word *primate*. In contrast, lexical relations apply to word forms, for example, verb *be* and its inflected form *is* have a lexical relation. Word meanings in WordNet belong to different categories, for instance, noun *distress* belongs to the category *[noun, feeling]*.

WordNet relations can be used for calculation of semantic similarity, for instance, between an emotion word and other words. [Budanitsky et al., 2001] presents an overview of approaches to calculating semantic similarity and discusses the [Rada et al., 1989] approach that utilizes hierarchical relations in WordNet; the [Hirst & St-Onge, 1998] approach that makes use of path lengths between words in WordNet; the [Leacock & Chodorow, 1998] approach that utilizes the path length of hyponymy relations in WordNet; the [Resnik, 1995] approach that considers the notion of information content to detect emotion words; the [Lin, 1998a] approach that refines the Resnik's approach.

WordNet can be used not only for calculating semantic similarity but specifically for calculating affective orientation of words. [Kamps & Marx, 2002] describe an approach to computationally calculating scores of WordNet words that map onto Osgood's scores. [Kamps et al., 2004] introduce an approach that relies on the synonymy relation in WordNet and propose measures for estimating emotional orientation of words. [Andreevskaia et al., 2006a], [Andreevskaia et al., 2006b] estimate the emotional orientation of words in WordNet and describe an approach that uses not only the semantic relations in WordNet, but also utilizes the corresponding word glosses. [Esuli et al., 2006] introduce SentiWordNet, in which WordNet synsets are labelled with three numerical scores representing objective, positive and negative estimations.

[Valitutti et al., 2004] compose the WordNet-Affect database that makes use of emotion words stored in WordNet. Hence, WordNet-Affect contains 1,903 terms that are 539 nouns, 517 adjectives, 238 verbs, 15 adverbs. Note that WordNet-Affect contains only emotion words (items in the database) and no information on their emotional meaning.

3.1.4 AUTOMATIC CREATION OF LISTS WITH EMOTION WORDS FROM THE INTERNET

Emotion words' lists, e.g. DAL are not exhaustive and do not contain every emotion word that can occur in an affect expression. To bridge this gap, lists of emotion words can be composed automatically using Internet search engines, e.g. Google or Altavista. For instance, [Turney, 2001] and [Taboada et al., 2006] describe approaches to automatic creation of emotion word lists using the PMI-IR measure. The main idea of PMI-IR is to count co-occurrences of a hypothetical emotion word (target word) and a seed emotion word within a particular word frame, for instance, in the same Internet document. Consequently, the target word can be considered to be an emotion word if it co-occurs significantly often in the same document as the seed emotion word. Mathematically, the PMI-IR score is calculated as

$$PMI\text{-}IR(target, seed) = \frac{hits(target \text{ AND } seed)}{hits(target)} \qquad (5)$$

where *hits(target AND seed)* is the number of hits where the word *target* and the word *seed* co-occur significantly often within a particular word frame, *hits(target)* is the overall number of hits of word *target* in the analyzed texts.

3.2 SENTENCE/PHRASE LEVEL

Affect sensing at the sentence/phrase level identifies emotional phrases or emotional sentences[15] in a text. Typically, affect sensing in sentences/phrases is performed by semantic approaches to affect sensing considering, hereby, meanings of words and grammatical interdependencies between them.

3.2.1 SENTENCE/PHRASE LEVEL USING LINGUISTIC RELATIONS

[Liu et al., 2003] describes an approach to affect sensing at the sentence/phrase level based on facts from the Open Database Common Sense database (OMCS). OMCS contains 400,000 commonsense facts, e.g. *Some people find ghosts to be scary* ([Singh, 2002]). The approach assumes that the emotional meaning of an analyzed text is conveyed by a concept, that is, a verb, a noun, an adjective phrase participating in the analyzed text. The proposed approach extracts all sentences from OMCS that contain emotional facts (affective common sense) by using seed words with the known Ekman vector, for example, emotional adjectives *happy, sad, frightening*, or emotional nouns *depression, delight, joy*, or emotional verbs *scare, cry, love*. Then, the approach generates sentence models. Such model can be the Subject-Verb-Object-Object (SVOO) model known from linguistics; or the Concept-Level Unigram Model (CLU) extracted for each sentence as an Ekman vector; or the Concept-Level Valence Model extracted for each concept as a scalar value between −1.0 and 1.0 indicating that the word contained in the sentence implies positive or negative emotional meaning; or the Modifier Unigram Model assigning an Ekman vector to each modifier in a sentence (modifiers are called in this thesis intensifiers). By propagating emotional meaning of the analyzed sentences from the generated models, the sensing engine calculates the Ekman vector representing the emotional meaning of the analyzed text.

The approach by Liu and colleagues is evaluated using the affectively responsible email program called EmpathyBuddy (Figure 10).

---

[15] *Emotional phrase, emotional sentence* is a phrase, or a sentence respectively that expresses an emotional meaning.

To: mom@foobar.com
Subject: my car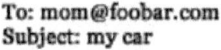

hi mom!

guess what? i bought a new car last week.

i got into an accident and I crashed it.

But please know that I wasn't hurt
and that everything is okay.

Wait... I meant

Figure 10: EmpathyBuddy

EmpathyBuddy accompanies composition of emails by making suggestions on how to extend the typed email text with emotional elements, e.g. emoticons[16]. Evaluation of the prototyped system is done by a usability test[17] with 20 users that assess the system qualities as entertainment, interactivity, intelligence, adoption and confirm a satisfactory system performance.

From the approach by Liu and colleagues, this thesis can utilize the fact that affect sensing relies on concepts that can be seen as anchors of emotional meaning surrounded by additional words. Moreover, this thesis can use the fact that affect sensing relies on emotion words and utilizes different models of texts that can be considered as prototypes of rules used in the proposed semantic approach to affect sensing.

[Riloff et al., 2006] use a statistical approach to identifying emotional phrases based on the subsumption hierarchy that determines the most significant features for affect sensing utilizing grammatical information on particular text patterns. The proposed approach utilizes extraction patterns (EP) generated by the AutoSlog package ([Riloff & Phillips, 2004]) that contain

---

[16] *Smiley* or *emoticon* is a symbol or combination of symbols used to convey emotional content in written or message form.

[17] *Usability test* is a technique used to evaluate a software or a hardware product by testing it on users ([Wikipedia, 2008]).

grammatical information on particular words and also lexico-syntactic information about phrases (Table 2).

Pattern Type	Example Pattern
<subj> PassVP	<subj> is satisfied
<subj> AuxVP Dobj	<subj> has position
<subj> AuxVP Adj	<subj> is happy
ActVP <dobj>	endorsed <dobj>
InfVP <dobj>	to condemn <dobj>
ActInfVP <dobj>	get to know <dobj>
PassInfVP <dobj>	is meant to be <dobj>
NP Prep <np>	opinion on <np>
InfVP Prep <np>	to resort to <np>
<possessive> NP	<noun>'s speech

Table 2: Extraction pattern types

<subj> denotes the subject of a sentence, *<dobj>* and *Dobj* denote a direct object, *<np>* and *NP* is a noun phrase, *<possessive> NP* is a concatenation of a genitive and a noun phrases, *<noun>* is a noun, *ActVP* is a verb in the active voice, *ActInfVP* is a concatenation of a verb in the active voice and an infinitive verb, *PassInfVP* denotes a concatenation of a verb in the passive voice and an infinitive verb, *AuxVP* denotes an auxiliary verb, *ActVP* is an active verb, *Prep* is a preposition, *InfVP* is an infinitive verb. For a thorough description of the grammatical terms above, see [Wikipedia, 2008] and [Quirk et al., 1985]).

Besides EPs, the [Riloff et al., 2006] approach uses unigrams and bigrams extracted by the NSP package ([Banerjee & Pedersen, 2003]).

In order to limit the huge amount of utilized features (unigrams, bigrams, EPs), the subsumption hierarchy is utilized to extract features (Figure 11).

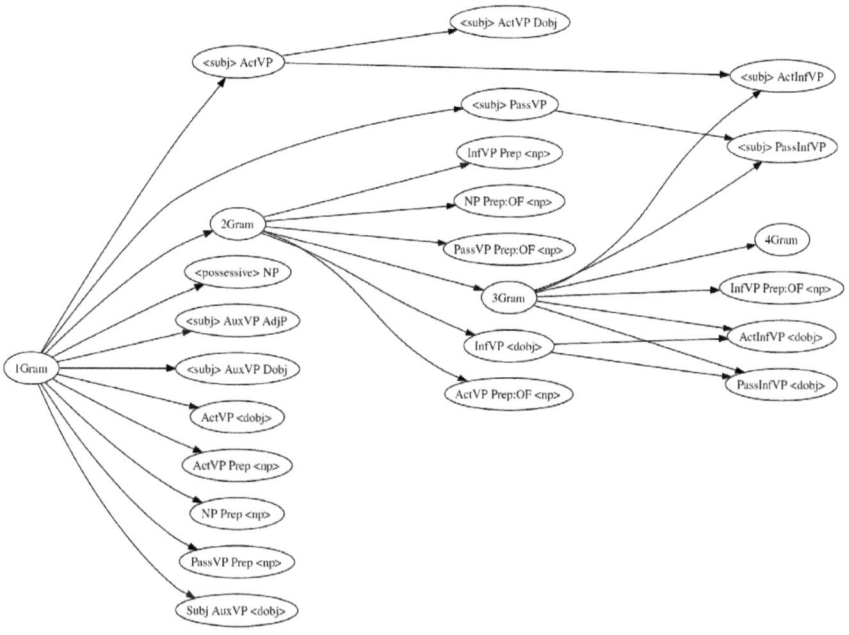

Figure 11: Subsumption hierarchy

Figure 11 shows how the subsumption hierarchy defines relations between words patterns. For instance, the unigram *happy* (unigram — 1Gram) subsumes the bigram feature *very happy* (bigram — 2Gram) since every unigram *happy* occurs in every bigram *very happy*.

Features are extracted using two ranking methods: one method ranks features using the traditional IG and utilizes the N best features, the second method ranks features using the subsumption hierarchy. The feature extraction method using IG selects from 1,000 to 10,000 features (hereafter the N value) in increments of 1,000. Feature selection using the subsumption hierarchy extracts features using three threshold values $\delta=0.0005$, $\delta=0.001$, $\delta=0.002$ that meet the following requirements: feature a subsumes feature b, and $IG(a) \geq IG(b)-\delta$ where a, b are features.

The approach by Riloff and colleagues is evaluated using three corpora (MPQA at the sentence level, and PMRC, version 1.0, OP at the document level). In this section, the classification of MPQA at the sentence level is discussed thoroughly. For the description of classification in PMRC and OP at the document level see section 3.3. The Multi-Perspective Question Answering (MPQA) corpus contains 535 news articles consisting of 9,289 sentences from a wide variety of news sources. The news articles are manually annotated for beliefs, emotions, sentiments, speculations, etc. using a comprehensive annotation scheme that considers subjective/objective[18] states ([Wiebe et al., 2005b]).

Classification results of datasets with ranked features are evaluated using 4 baseline datasets: a dataset with unigrams, a dataset with unigrams and bigrams, a dataset with unigrams and EPs, and a dataset with unigrams and bigrams and EPs. The approach uses the SVMlight classifier for classifying the extracted datasets utilizing a three-fold cross-validation ([Joachims, 1999]).

Performed experiments confirm that the datasets with features extracted by IG are classified worse than the baseline in some cases and virtually never when using the datasets with the features according to subsumption. Furthermore, the combination of two feature selection methods, the subsumption feature selection prior to the IG feature selection generally performs best of all. Hence, the best accuracy value of 75.4% yields the dataset with features extracted using the threshold $\delta=0.0005$ where features are extracted using the subsumption feature selection and IG using $N=4,000$ features.

This thesis assumes that unigrams, bigrams, EPs play a significant role in affect sensing. Hence, affect sensing can rely, first, on features consisting of, e.g. emotion words and intensifiers that participate in the patterns; second, EPs can be considered as prototypes of rules used in the proposed semantic approach to affect sensing.

3.2.2 Sentence/Phrase Level Using Heuristic Rules

[Wiebe & Riloff, 2005a] describe an approach to automatically classifying sentences as subjective/objective using an *unannotated* corpus that consists of 298,809 sentences from a world press collection. Using two rule-based classifiers (subjective/objective), they create an *initial training set* on the basis of empirical knowledge about emotion words, N-grams[19] and EPs.

---

[18] *Objective*: based on real facts and not influenced by personal beliefs or feelings ([Cambridge, 2008]).

[19] *N-gram* is an adjacent subsequence of N-elements from a given sequence of words. Unigram contains one word, for instance, *emotion word*. Bigram is an adjacent sequence of two words, for instance, an intensifier and an *emotion word*.

The empirical knowledge distinguishes strong and weak clues of subjectivity[20] in emotional expressions where strong subjective clues have subjective meanings with high probability, and weak subjective clues have subjective meanings with lower probability. A sentence is considered to be subjective if it contains two or more strong subjective clues. In contrast, a sentence is considered to be objective if there are either no subjective clues in the current sentence, or there is at most one strong subjective clue in the previous and next messages combined, or the sentence contains at most two weak subjective clues in the current, previous, and next sentences together.

MPQA is used for testing the subjective and objective rule-based classifiers. Hereby, the subjective rule-based classifier yields the recall value of 34.2% and the precision value of 90.4%. The objective rule-based classifier calculates the recall value of 30.7% and the precision value of 82.4%.

To improve these recognition rates, an additional subjective NaïveBayes (NB) and an additional objective NB are used. The subjective NB is trained using the initial training set and yields the recall value of 70.6% and the precision value of 74.7%. Next, it is trained unsupervised using as the training set the dataset obtained after the first classification. Classification rates improve to the recall value of 86.3% and the precision value of 78.1%. Analogous to the subjective NB, the objective NB is trained using the initial training set yielding the recall value of 77.6%, and the precision value of 68.4%. However, in contrast to the performance improvement in subjective NB, the performance of the objective NB reduces in the second training (unsupervised) stage to the recall value of 57.6% and the precision value of 77.5%.

From the approach by Wiebe and Riloff, this thesis utilizes the fact that affect sensing relies on empirical cues that can be considered as prototypes of rules in the proposed semantic approach.

[Wiebe et al., 2004] describe an approach to identifying subjective phrases using three types of subjective clues: unique words' clues (hapax legomena[21]), collocation[22] clues, and clues of distributional similarity of occurring adjectives and verbs.

---

[20] *Subjectivity* is a state modified or affected by personal views, experience, or background according to [Merriam-Webster, 2007].

[21] *Hapax legomena* are words found only once in a corpus.

[22] *Collocation* is a noticeable arrangement or conjoining of linguistic elements (as words), for instance, an emotional phrase can be a collocation of emotion words.

Unique words provide the first kind of clues to subjectivity in the proposed approach. Performed experiments study influence of the low-frequency words in a corpus and confirm that such words are an important clue of subjectivity.

The second kind of subjective clues provide collocations. The proposed approach extracts N-grams in the analyzed texts, in particular all unigrams, bigrams, trigrams, and 4-grams and transforms them in pairs of the form *(word_stem;POS)*. For instance, the text *in the can* is transformed to the pairs' trigram *in-prep the-det can-noun* where a trigram starts with a preposition pair *in-prep*, followed by a determiner pair *the-det*, and ending with a noun pair *can-noun*. N-grams can also contain information on the frequency of a word. For example, the bigram, *U-adj as-prep*, that matches the phrase *perverse as* is defined as a pattern containing a unique adjective (*U-adj*) and the preposition *as* (*as-prep*). The approach defines a measure for evaluating N-gram contribution to subjectivity as the ratio between the number of the N-grams considered as subjective and the total number of N-grams.

The third kind of subjective clues in the proposed approach is measured using the distributional similarity ([Lee, 1999]). Accordingly, adjectives and verbs are considered to be emotional if their distributional similarity is similar to the distributional similarity of seed emotion words.

Corpora of two kinds are used for conducting experiments in identifying subjective phrases: a small corpus containing sentences manually annotated as subjective/not-subjective from the Wall Street Journal (WSJ) and newsgroups; a large corpus with existing document-level categories from WSJ (OP1 and OP2). Although the latter corpus is annotated at the document level it is used for evaluation of the proposed approach at the phrase level due to its large size and the independent composition outside the laboratory.

Documents in OP1 and OP2 belong to six categories: *News, Business, Editorial, Letter to the Editor, Arts & Leisure reviews*, and *Viewpoints*. They are labeled as non-opinion if they belong to the categories *News*, and *Business*. In contrast, the documents are labeled as opinionated if they belong to the categories *Editorial, Letter to the Editor, Arts & Leisure reviews*, and *Viewpoints*.

Table 3 shows the statistics of utilized corpora.

Name	Source	Number of words	Type of
WSJ-SE	WSJ	18,341	Sentences
NG-SE	Newsgroup	15,413	Sentences
OP1	WSJ	640,975	Documents
OP2	WSJ	629,690	Documents

Table 3: Corpora for classifying subjective phrases

The *Name* column shows the corpus name; the *Source* column describes the source of the corpus, e.g. WSJ; the *Number of words* column presents the number of words in the corresponding corpus; the *Type of* column shows the granularity of the studied corpus.

The approach by Wiebe and colleagues extracts features using the aforementioned kinds of subjective clues and calculates increase or decrease of precisions in identifying subjective phrases.

From the approach by Wiebe and colleagues, two findings can be used in this thesis: first, semantic affect sensing can utilize empirical knowledge about subjective cues as prototypes of rules; second, affect sensing in the proposed statistical approach can consider the frequency of extracted features.

The approach by Choi and Cardie ([Choi & Cardie, 2008]) considers compositional semantics to analyze affect in sentences: the meaning of a compound expression is a function of its parts and of the syntactic rules by which they are combined. In order to assess the polarity of sentiment-bearing expressions they apply a two-step process: assess the polarity of the constituents of the expression by splitting it and deriving emotional meaning of constituents from a system database; apply a set of rules that infer the emotional meaning of a compound expression from emotional meanings of its constituents. The approach uses negators and emotion words from GI. The approach evaluated using MPQA yields the accuracy value of 90.7%

This thesis can utilize from the approach by Choi and Cardie the fact that semantic affect sensing can use rules containing emotional meaning of constituents in order to analyze the emotional meaning of compound expressions.

3.2.3 Sentence/Phrase Level Using Semantic and Grammatical Means

Affect sensing at the sentence/phrase level can make use of semantic and grammatical means from linguistics. For instance, [Neviarouskaya et al., 2007] describe a semantic approach to affect sensing in 160 sentences from a corpus with weblogs ([NielsenBuzzMetrics, 2008]). The sentences are annotated by three annotators as an Izard vector.

The approach utilizes a database that comprises of 1,627 emotion words extracted from WordNet-Affect, as well as 362 emoticons, 337 most popular acronyms and abbreviations. The entries in the database are manually annotated as Izard vectors. The proposed classification algorithm uses 112 modifiers of emotional meanings, e.g. *very* (called in this thesis, intensifiers), and negations, e.g. *not*.

The proposed algorithm calculates the emotional meaning of a sentence in five stages:

1. *In the first stage*, the sentence is tested for occurrences of symbols as emoticons, abbreviations, acronyms, interjections, exclamatory or question marks, repeated punctuation and capital letters. If a corresponding symbol is detected, the algorithm makes a simplifying assumption that the emotional meaning of this symbol determines the emotional meaning of a whole sentence, extracts the emotional meaning of the symbol from the system database and finishes the algorithm. Otherwise, the system goes to the second stage.

2. *In the second stage*, the algorithm scrutinizes syntax of the analyzed sentence using the Connexor parser ([Connexor, 2008]) and identifies grammatical relations, words' lemmata or POS tags.

3. *In the third stage,* for each encountered emotion word the system extracts its emotional vector from the system database. If a modifier is encountered, the system utilizes its modifying coefficient from the system database. If a word is in the comparative or in the superlative form, the emotional meaning of the corresponding text is multiplied by 1.2 or 1.4 respectively. For instance, the emotional meaning of the text containing *worse* (in comparative form of word *bad*) is multiplied by 1.2 or by 1.4 if the text contains the superlative form *worst* of word *bad*.

4. *In the forth stage*, the system calculates an emotional vector of the extracted phrases. The phrase-level analysis is performed under consideration of emotional meaning of symbols found in the system database. Hereby, the system distinguishes the following types of phrases:

    a. adjective phrases, e.g. *extremely sad*;

    b. noun phrases, e.g. *brotherly love*;

    c. verb phrases, e.g. *enjoy bad weather*.

The emotional meaning of a sentence in the proposed approach is influenced by:

a. adverbs of degree, e.g. *almost*;

b. negations, e.g. *no* or *never*;

c. prepositions, e.g. *without* or *except*.

The following phrases are disregarded:

a. phrases beginning with, e.g. *think*;

b. phrases beginning with modal verbs, e.g. *can*;

c. conditional phrases beginning with, e.g. *if* or *even if*.

The calculated emotional vector is processed in the fifth stage.

5. *In the fifth stage*, the system outputs the emotional meaning of the sentence considering detected patterns of the sentence structure.

The system output is assessed by 3 annotators: the output agrees with one annotator in 79.4% sentences, and with at least 2 annotators in 70% sentences.

This thesis can utilize the findings of the approach by Neviarouskaya and colleagues as follows: first, affect sensing can rely on emotion words and intensifiers; second, classification result can be obtained by analysis of meanings of text parts and not the whole text where the integral meaning is inferred from the affective meanings of the parts.

[Strapparava & Mihalcea, 2007] describes classification of news headlines regarding expressed emotions and their valence. Headlines are extracted from major newspapers such as New York Times, CNN, BBC News, as well as Google News. The corpus is annotated independently by six annotators in two ways: by emotions and by valence.

The emotion annotation and the valence annotation each are done according to a fine-grained and a coarse-grained scale. A fine-grained emotion annotation is defined by a sequence of numbers that represent emotional load of a headline in the format:

$$id \ anger \ disgust \ fear \ joy \ sadness \ surprise \qquad (6)$$

where *id* describes the number of the headline and the following values represent the emotional load of Ekman emotions. A fine-grained emotion annotation is made in the interval from [0, 100] where 0 means that the emotion is not expressed in the given headline and 100 represents the maximal emotional intensity of the emotion. For instance, the first headline in the training set (*Mortar assault leaves at least 18 dead*) is represented by the annotation row:

$$1\ 22\ 2\ 60\ 0\ 64\ 0 \tag{7}$$

where *1* at the beginning is the number of the headline, the following *22* represents the load of the emotion *anger*, *2* represents the load of the emotion *disgust*, and so on.

A coarse-grained emotion annotation is calculated by mapping the fine-grained emotion annotation onto 0/1 (0 = [0,50), 1 = [50,100]).

The fine-grained valence annotation is significantly simpler than the fine-grained emotion annotation and uses the format:

$$id\ valence \tag{8}$$

where *id* describes the number of the headline and *valence* shows the emotional valence of a headline.

Fine-grained valence annotations are defined in the interval [–100, 100] where 0 represents a headline with neutral emotional load, a highly negative headline is defined by a value of –100, and a valence value of 100 corresponds to a highly positive headline. For instance, the headline *Mortar assault leaves at least 18 dead* is annotated as:

$$1\ –98 \tag{9}$$

where number *1* corresponds to the number of the headline and *–98* represents its emotional valence, in this case, a negative emotional valence.

A coarse-grained valence annotation is calculated by mapping the fine-grained valence annotation onto the values –1/0/1 (–1 = [–100, –50], 0 = (–50,50), 1 = [50,100]).

5 competitive teams developed systems to affect sensing in the aforementioned headlines (UPAR7, SICS, ClaC, UA, SWAT). All systems utilize a training dataset consisting of 250 headlines and a testing dataset containing 1,000 headlines.

UPAR7 is a rule-based system that uses word-spotting[23] and a dependency graph obtained from a syntactic parser. The approach utilizes WordNet-Affect, SentiWordNet and the Stanford Parser ([Klein & Manning, 2003]).

The SICS team developed an approach to classifying the valence annotation based on a word-space model and a set of seed words. This approach analyses emotional valence using a geometric distance to two points: to a point defining the negative valence, and to a point defining the positive valence. The final valence orientation of a headline is determined by the point that is geometrically closer to the negative/positive valence points.

The ClaC team submitted two systems: the rule-based semantic ClaC system; the statistical ClaC-NB system. Both systems calculate the valence of headlines in the range [−100, 100]. The semantic ClaC system uses a list of emotion words, valence shifters (negations and intensifiers), and a set of rules. A list of emotion words is composed from WordNet, as well as the words from the categories *Positiv* and *Negativ* of GI. The list of empirically extracted valence shifters includes 450 words and expressions. The set rules is composed on the basis of empirical knowledge. The grammatical parsing of the headlines is done by the MiniPar parser ([Lin, 1998b]). The statistical ClaC-NB system utilizes NB for classification. A description of extracted features is not provided.

UA classifies emotions utilizing Internet resources and works similarly to PMI. Consequently, the approach calculates the ratio of documents from the Internet that contain all headline words and emotion words in a close proximity divided through the number of documents containing all headline words and all emotion words.

The SWAT system description in the aforementioned approach is not received on time and will be added later.

Classification results yielded by the proposed systems show that the most promising approaches to valence classification (both fine-grained and the coarse-grained annotation) is calculated by the semantic ClaC. In contrast, UPAR7 yields better results in classification of emotions for both annotation scales.

This thesis can utilize the findings of Strapparava and Mihalcea in different ways: first, analysis of short texts as headlines is more benefical when performed by semantic and not by statistical

---

[23] *Word-spotting* describes a method for deducing the emotional orientation of texts based on detecting emotion words occurring in a classified text.

methods; second, affect analysis in short texts can be done according to the scheme introduced by the semantic CLAC, i.e. by using emotion words, intensifiers, negations, and grammatical rules; third, semantic rules can be deduced on the basis of empirical knowledge as in the semantic ClaC approach.

[Balahur & Montoyo, 2008] describe an approach to classifying emotions and valence of the headlines in [Strapparava & Mihalcea, 2007]. The approach uses emotion words from WordNet-Affect and own valence shifters (negations and intensifiers). An amount of the utilized shifters is not specified. The approach calculates the overall valence of a text using empirically extracted weights of intensifiers utilizing a culture-dependent lexical database emerging from humanities: from the theory of pragmatic relevance ([Sperber & Wilson, 2004]), from Maslov's theory of human needs ([Maslov, 1943]) and from Neef's theory of human needs ([Max-Neef, 1991]).

Evaluation of the approach is performed using the test data from [Strapparava & Mihalcea, 2007] and the corresponding Spanish translation. The best result of the valence classification in English texts yields the recall value of 65.01% whereas the best result of the valence classification in Spanish texts is 66.13%. The best result of sensing the emotion *fear* in English texts is the recall value of 45.37%. In Spanish texts, the recall value for sensing the emotion *fear* is 44.89%.

The findings by Balahur and Montoyo confirm that an approach to semantic affect sensing in short texts should use emotion words and intensifiers to detect the expressed emotion.

3.3 DOCUMENT LEVEL

Opinion mining at the document level aims at classification of documents according to their emotional meaning. Typically, opinion mining is performed by statistical approaches to opinion mining. In the following, existing approaches to emotion recognition at the document level are discussed thoroughly.

3.3.1 DOCUMENT LEVEL USING THE NAÏVE ALGORITHM

A naïve algorithm to classify expressed opinion in a document makes use of counts of text pieces that are classified, for instance, as positive or negative:

1. Extract all subjective text pieces[24] from the processed document;

2. Classify the extracted text pieces as positive/negative;

3. If the number of positive text pieces exceeds the number of negative pieces the document is considered to express a positive opinion; otherwise, it is considered to express a negative opinion.

Many approaches use this naïve algorithm. For instance, [Turney, 2002] describes the following approach to classifying reviews: the approach uses the PMI-IR measure to detect the semantic orientation of subjective phrases; a review is considered as *recommended* if the most subjective phrases are classified as *positive*, and *not recommended*, otherwise. The approach achieves the average accuracy value of 74% on 410 reviews from [Epinions, 2008] sampled from four different domains (reviews of automobiles, banks, movies, and travel destinations).

[Yi et al., 2003] introduce an approach to opinion mining that classifies subjective phrases as positive/negative in topic or non-topic documents[25]. The positive/negative orientation of documents is evaluated similarly to the naïve algorithm above as the count of the exceeding affective votes.

To assess the emotional orientation of text pieces, the approach detects phrases that match the pattern

<predicate> <sentiment_category> <target>   (10)

where <predicate> is a verb, <sentiment_category> is a relation between the source and the target of the emotional phrase (either positive, or negative, or opposite), <target> refers to the target of an emotional phrase. 120 patterns of the proposed form are collected automatically and adjusted manually. For instance, using the proposed pattern the approach extracts the phrase <impress> <positive> <by;with object> that occurs in the sentence *I'm impressed by the picture quality* describing a camera. Emotion words necessary for opinion mining, e.g. *impress*, are extracted from GI, DAL, or WordNet.

---

[24] A *subjective text piece* is defined in accordance with [Wiebe, 1994] as: Subjective text pieces... are ...states of an experiencer holding an attitude, optionally toward an object. These states include intellectual ones, such as someone believing, wondering, or knowing something; emotive ones, such as someone hating something or being afraid; and perceptual ones, such as someone seeing or hearing something.

[25] A *topic document* is a document describing a topic, for instance, a camera.

The approach by Yi and colleagues is evaluated in experiments on reviews from the digital camera domain: using 485 manually annotated as topic documents and 1,838 annotated as non-topic documents. The documents are collected on the Internet. A review is considered as *recommended* if the number of positive patterns in review's text pieces exceeds the number of negative patterns and as *not recommended*, otherwise. This classification algorithm yields the recall value of 56% and the precision value of 87%.

The approach by Yi and colleagues calculates high results. However, this thesis does not use corresponding findings since it has a significant drawback: it uses patterns that are adjusted manually although the sought statistical approach to opinion mining should work preferably completely automatically.

3.3.2 Document Level Using Lexical Means

This section describes opinion mining in documents using lexical means (words of the analyzed document).

[Pang et al., 2002] classify documents using unigrams, bigrams, the POS tags' features. The approach does not apply stemming[26] to extracted unigrams/bigrams or removes stopwords. Since performed experiments reveal no classification improvement using datasets with bigrams in comparison to the datasets with unigrams, the approach extracts only unigrams as features. Combinations of unigrams and their POS tags also do not improve classification results. In summary, the approach extracts 16,165 unigrams and evaluates them either as frequency vector[27] or as presence vector[28]. The approach tested a method of the feature evaluation that considers the position of the corresponding unigram in a review text as a word occurring in the first quarter, or the last quarter, or in the middle of a document assuming hereby that a review text begins with an overall sentiment statement, followed by a plot discussion, and ends with author's conclusions. However, such evaluation method did not reveal significant improvement of classification rates.

---

[26] *Lemmatization* or *stemming* is a process of transforming a word to its canonical (uninflected) form, e.g., the inflected verb *abandoned* in the past tense is transformed to canonical form *abandon*.

[27] A *frequency vector* of feature values is defined in the case of unigrams as a vector of unigram counts in the analyzed text (cf. a mathematical definition in section 5.1.1.3).

[28] A *presence vector* of feature values is defined in the case of unigrams as a vector of binary values 1/0 expressing if a unigram is present/absent in the analyzed text (cf. a mathematical definition in section 5.1.1.3).

The approach by Pang and colleagues evaluates PMRC, version 1.0 (700 positive reviews and 700 negative reviews) using the SVMlight classifier ([Joachims, 1999]) and the three-fold cross-validation. The composed dataset yields better classification results calculating the best accuracy value of 82.9% where utilized features are evaluated as a presence vector in comparison with features evaluated as a frequency vector.

This thesis utilizes the findings of the [Pang et al., 2002] approach as follows: first, an approach to opinion mining can analyze emotional meaning by utilizing non-lemmatized unigrams that can be stopwords evaluated as a presence vector; second, consideration of *position* features does not bring about significant improvement of results.

[Pang & Lee, 2004] describe an approach to classifying documents of PMRC. Following [Pang et al., 2002], the approach extracts unigram features and evaluates them as a presence vector and not as a frequency vector. Pang and Lee also consider the context information hypothesizing that nearby sentences tend to have the same subjectivity.

Hereby, a two-stage scheme evaluation scheme is used: in the first stage, the approach detects and evaluates subjectivity of document sentences using NB; in the second stage, it classifies *only 30 most subjective text parts* of the whole document where the subjectivity of a part is the probability value calculated by NB. The approach uses SVMlight and yields the accuracy value of 87.2% on the ten-fold cross-validation.

This thesis utilizes the revealed findings as follows: an approach to opinion mining can extract unigrams; second, the extracted unigrams can be evaluated as a presence vector; third, the approach can consider the context of analyzed texts.

[Yu & Hatzivassiloglou, 2003] describe an approach to opinion mining that classifies documents from WSJ. It maps documents in the categories *News*, *Business*, *Editorial*, and *Letter to the Editor* onto two classes: opinion (*Editorial, Letter to the Editor*) and non-opinion (*News, Business*). The approach extracts unigrams without stemming or the stopword removal. Evaluation is performed using 8,000 articles: 4,000 articles are used for learning, testing is done on other 4,000 articles. The approach utilizes NB and yields the F-measure value of 97%.

This thesis utilizes the revealed findings in two ways: first, the extracted features are unigrams that are not lemmatized (but yet potentially); second, the extracted unigrams can be stopwords.

[Finn & Kushmerick, 2006] describe an approach to classifying documents as *subjective/objective*, or *positive/negative*. The documents for the subjective/objective classification (351 football articles, 289 politics articles, 156 finance articles) are extracted automatically from the chosen Internet pages. For the positive/negative classification, the approach uses 723 movie reviews from [MRQE, 2008], and 631 restaurant reviews from [Zagat, 2008].

The approach uses three datasets for classifying affect: a dataset with unigrams applying stemming and the stopword removal (without specifying their number), a dataset with 36 POS tags, and a dataset with 152 stylometric features. The unigrams are evaluated as a presence vector; the POS tags features as a frequency vector normalized through the number of words in the document; the stylometric features, e.g. average sentence length or average word length, are evaluated corresponding to their names.

The approach by Finn and Kushmerick is evaluated using two algorithms: the C4.5 algorithm chosen for the reason of its comprehensibility for a human observer and an ensemble meta-classifier relying on the C4.5 algorithm. The ensemble meta-classifier uses a combination of three classifiers trained using the datasets described above. Note that the ensemble meta-classifier utilizes all three datasets and hereby uses implicitly all features.

To evaluate the approach, a one-domain experiment and a cross-domain experiment are performed. The one-domain experiment measures the ability of the approach to classifying documents of a single domain. In contrast, the cross-domain experiment estimates the ability of the approach to generalize to new domains: documents of one domain are used for learning, documents of another domain for testing. For instance, movie reviews are used for learning and restaurant reviews for testing.

Performed experiments utilize the ten-fold cross-validation. In the one-domain experiment, the best average accuracy value for the positive/negative review classification is 82.7% calculated using the unigram features and the C4.5 classifier. The best average accuracy value of 90.5% for the subjective/objective article classification is yielded using the ensemble meta-classifier (all features). In the cross-domain experiment, the best average accuracy value of 49.1% for the positive/negative review classification is calculated using the ensemble meta-classifier (all features). The best average accuracy value of 78.5% for the subjective/objective article classification is yielded using the POS features and the C4.5 classifier whereas all results are comparable.

This thesis utilizes the findings of the approach by Finn and Kushmerick as follows: an approach to opinion mining can use unigrams; the choice of the utilized classifier plays a secondary role.

[Dave et al., 2003] examines classification of product reviews from Clnet. The studied corpus consists of 10 randomly selected sets of 56 positive and 56 negative reviews from 4 largest categories of Clnet (in total, 448 reviews). A review is annotated as *positive* if it is rated in Clnet with three or more stars, and as *negative*, otherwise.

Before feature extraction, reviews' texts are preprocessed as follows:

1. Unique words are substituted with the string *_unique*, product names are substituted with the string *_productname*, product specific words are substituted with the string *_producttypeword*;

2. Ambiguous words are disambiguated using POS tags and substituted with their distinct similarities using WordNet. POS tagging is done by the MiniPar parser ([Lin, 1998b]);

3. Negations are identified by the words *not*, and *never*. Negation phrases are substituted with artificial terms resulting from the combination of the corresponding negation and the following word. For instance, the phrase *not good* becomes the *NOTgood* string.

After making the above changes, the approach extracts N-grams (unigrams, bigrams, trigrams) that are evaluated as frequency vectors. The SVMlight classifier is used for classification and yields the accuracy value of 85.8% using ten-fold cross-validation without stratification.

This thesis can utilize the findings by Dave and colleagues as follows: first, a statistical approach can make use of the frequency of unigrams; second, a statistical approach can consider grammatical issues as negations in a statistical approach although such consideration is typical for semantic approaches. Unlike Dave and colleagues that consider names of products and product types, the statistical approach in this thesis does not distinguish extracted unigrams semantically.

In section 3.2, the [Riloff et al., 2006] approach was discussed for affect sensing at the sentence level. In this section, opinion mining in documents from PMRC, version 1.0, and classification of documents from OP is described thoroughly utilizing the same classification approach.

PMRC, version 1.0 contains 700 positive and 700 negative movie reviews. OP consists of 2,452 articles from WSJ mapped onto opinion/non-opinion classes as follows: articles labeled as

Editorial, Letter to the Editor, Arts & Leisure Review, or *Viewpoint* are considered as opinionated, documents labeled as *Business* and *News* are labeled as non-opinionated.

The feature extraction and the feature evaluation in OP and PMRC are performed similarly to MPQA; two feature selection methods are used: the conventional IG feature selection and the subsumption feature selection. IG extracts best features (the N value) from 1,000 to 10,000 in increment of 1,000. In both corpora, unigrams that have frequency less than five are discarded. The subsumption feature selection extracts features using three threshold values $\delta=0.0005$, $\delta=0.001$, $\delta=0.002$ that meet the following requirements: feature a subsumes feature b, and $IG(a) \geq IG(b)-\delta$ where a, b are features.

The approach is evaluated using SVMlight and a three-fold cross-validation. To facilitate comparison of classification results, 4 baseline datasets are composed: a dataset with all unigrams, a dataset with unigrams and bigrams, a dataset with unigrams and EPs, a dataset with unigrams and bigrams and EPs. The combination of two feature selection methods, the subsumption feature selection prior to the feature selection using IG, yields the best result value, higher than the baseline values. For OP, the best accuracy value is 99% (the threshold $\delta=0.0002$ for subsumption and $N=3,000$, $N=4,000$, $N=5,000$ unigrams for IG). For PMRC, the best accuracy value is 83.1% (the threshold $\delta=0.0002$ for subsumption and $N=7,000$ unigrams for IG).

This thesis can utilize the findings by Riloff and colleagues as follows: since the approach claims implicitly that individual features contribute to significant improvement of classification results, such improvement can be expected using optimization of the feature space.

[Whitelaw et al., 2005] describe an approach to opinion mining in the documents of PMRC. The approach is based on extracting appraisal groups (groups of words that evaluate some issue). These groups comprise of an adjective and an optional list of modifiers, for instance, *very good* or *not terribly funny*. Appraisal groups can have the following properties:

1. The *Attitude* property is evaluated as the type of appraisal (either as *affect*, e.g. 'happy', 'angry', or as *appreciation*, e.g. 'slender', 'ugly', or as *judgement*, e.g. 'heroic', 'idiotic').

2. The *Orientation* property indicates whether the group is positive or negative.

3. The *Graduation* property estimates the intensity of the group in terms of force (or 'intensity') expressed mainly via modifiers such as, for instance, *very*, or *slightly*.

4. The *Polarity* property is evaluated as *marked* if the group modifies other appraisal attributes and *unmarked*, otherwise. For example, the group containing word *very* is *marked* since it increases the intensity of an emotional text, the group containing word *not* is also *marked* since it marks the opposed meaning.

Properties of appraisal groups found in the studied text are extracted from a system lexicon. The system lexicon is compiled using a semi-automated technique utilizing WordNet. Note that not every sequence of words has all properties above, for instance, appraisal group *not happy* has the property *Attitude* (*affect*), the property *Orientation* (*positive*), the property *Polarity* (*marked*), but no property *Graduation*.

The approach composes datasets containing unigrams and features on the basis of detected appraisal groups and classifies these datasets using the SVM classifier and the ten-fold cross-validation. The maximal accuracy value of 90.2% is yielded by the dataset containing unigrams and appraisal groups' features with the *Attitude* property and the *Orientation* property. Note that the [Whitelaw et al., 2005] approach yields a high recognition result (90.2%) but has a remarkable drawback: it relies on a manually and not automatically composed lexicon of appraisal properties.

This thesis can utilize the findings by Whitelaw and colleagues in the same way as the findings by Riloff and colleagues: individual features can contribute to significant improvement of classification results.

3.3.3 DOCUMENT LEVEL USING STYLOMETRIC MEANS

The classification approaches discussed above are developed especially for emotional analysis. There are though other approaches from a related science (stylometry or *authorship attribution*[29]) that are similar to the approaches to opinion mining since they also classify texts. Even if classification aims at identifying text author, not at identifying the emotional class of the text, this thesis can examine stylometric approaches in order to reveal their appropriateness for opinion mining. Hereafter, this thesis refers to approaches to authorship attribution as stylometric approaches.

---

[29] *Authorship attribution* is defined as an approach to determining the author of a textual piece on the basis of the virtue of the text, e.g. length of words or sentences.

Typically, stylometric approaches make use of information in texts that, at the first glance, can not be considered as emotional, e.g. lengths of words or the average length of text sentences. How can these means be used for opinion mining and is it generally possible?

Surely, the applicability of stylometric means for opinion mining is not evident. However, affect has a multifold nature and can be conveyed using different ways of expression. Probably, stylometric means could not contribute to opinion mining and they cannot be used for emotion recognition. However, [Planalp, 1996] only examines 9 psychological cues for expressing emotions and not every cue can be understood as emotional. For instance, Planalp's activity cue — *taking a bath* — expresses literally a physical activity without emotional characterization: the emotional characterization is ascribed by persons interpreting this activity.

Why do not give stylometric means a try? [Pennebaker et al., 2003] present an overview of psychological aspects of natural words and draws, at first, an unexplainable conclusion that the words, people use, convey psychological information over and above their literal meaning; words are diagnostic for the social, mental, and even physical state although they do not primarily express affect from the point of view of commonsense as linking pronouns, prepositions, and other particles. [Chung & Pennebaker, 2007] point out that unemotional, function words[30] have psychological functions.

But how can function words (words without an emotional meaning) influence emotional interpretation of a text? Evidently, by the fact of their presence: a human uses words of particular length or function only under very special emotional circumstances. This statement can be proved exactly by calculating corresponding results using stylometric means in different corpora (see section 5.4.1.2, section 5.4.2.2, section 5.4.3.2, section 5.4.4.2).

First, let's take a look at means that can be utilized insofar! [Diederich et al., 2000] introduces an approach to identifying the author of an article from a daily newspaper *Berliner Zeitung*. The approach uses a text corpus consisting of 2,652 articles (the training set contains 2,121 and the testing set contains 531 articles from 150 authors). The articles are extracted from the domains: politics, economy, and local affairs and annotated as texts of a particular author.

---

[30] *Function words (or grammatical words)* have almost no literal meaning and are used in texts primarily to express grammatical relationships with other words within a sentence, e.g., article *a* or auxiliary verb *be*.

The utilized features include tagwords (combination of function words and corresponding POS), bigrams of tagwords, and word lengths. Tagwords and tagwords' bigrams are evaluated as a frequency vector. Evaluation of the approach is performed using SVMlight and the 5-fold cross-validation without stratification yielding the recall value of 51.4% and the precision value of 100%.

The approach uses features extracted from texts for the purpose of determining authorship attribution. Similarly, this thesis can utilize the findings by Diederich and colleagues as follows: unigrams extracted from texts can be utilized not for the purpose of authorship attribution but also opinion mining.

3.3.4 Document Level Using Findings in Personality Analysis

Probably, personality is an issue that is nearly impossible to measure numerically. At least, it is highly problematic to do, but not more problematic than measuring emotions. And what is actually the difference between emotions and personality from the point of view of commonsense? Actually, there is no difference: they are both fuzzy and hard to grasp numerically. Why not adopt findings in personality analysis to measure emotions?

The personality can be defined using the Big Five personality traits ([McCrae & Costa, 1999]):

1. The *extraversion* personality trait is described by the words *sociable, assertive, playful* vs. *aloof, reserved, shy*. Extraverts are full of energy, and often experience positive emotions. In contrast, introverts tend to be quiet.

2. The *emotional stability* personality trait is described by the words *calm, unemotional* vs. *insecure, anxious*. Emotionally unstable people respond expressively to events that would not affect most people, and their reactions tend to be more intense than normal.

3. The *agreeableness* personality trait is described by the words *friendly, cooperative* vs. *antagonistic, faultfinding*. Agreeable persons are generally friendly and helpful, and always seek a compromise with others; they also have an optimistic view of human nature. Disagreeable individuals are selfish and unconcerned with others' well-being.

4. The *conscientiousness* personality trait is described by the words *self-disciplined, efficient* vs. *inefficient, careless*. This personality trait influences controlling, regulating, and directing spontaneity in person's behaviour. Conscientious individuals avoid trouble and achieve success through purposeful planning; they can be perfectionists and workaholics.

5. The *openness to experience* personality trait is described by the words *intellectual, insightful* vs. *shallow, unimaginative*. This personality trait distinguishes between imaginative, creative people and down-to-earth, conventional people. Open people are intellectually curious, appreciative of art, and sensitive to beauty and tend to be, compared to closed people, more aware of their feelings.

[Mairesse et al., 2007] present a study of human personality that has a strong resemblance with the study in this thesis: the proposed approach also uses linguistic means to recognize psychological issues that are, in this case, personality traits.

First, this approach studies personality markers in language and confirms that, for instance, the *extraversion* trait can be estimated using linguistic categories of used words. The numerical assessment is done using a formula that relies on word frequencies (Was ist F):

$$F = (noun\ freq + adjective\ freq + preposition\ freq + article\ freq - pronoun\ freq - verb\ freq - adverb\ freq - interjection\ freq + 100)/2 \quad (11)$$

Empirical formula (11) defines a value to measure the *extraversion* trait based on the frequency of nouns (*noun freq*), on the frequency of adjectives (*adjective freq*), on the frequency of prepositions (*preposition freq*), on the frequency of articles (*article freq*), on the frequency of pronouns (*pronoun freq*), on the frequency of verbs (*verb freq*), on the frequency of adverbs (*adverb freq*), and on the frequency of interjections (*interjection freq*).

Claiming that personality traits can be identified using numerical means, [Mairesse et al., 2007] state that the Big Five traits can be assessed using statistical means. Hereby, they extract the following feature subsets: LIWC features, MRC features, the *utterance type* features, Prosodic features.

The LIWC features correspond to words of 88 categories in LIWC that are evaluated as a frequency vector. The approach extracts additionally 14 MRC features evaluated according to the MRC statistics, for example, as the number of syllables per word ([Coltheart, 1981]).

The *utterance type* features specify 5 features of the type of the classified utterance (assertion, command, command, prompt). These features are evaluated using the following heuristic: if an utterance uses the imperative form (has a command verb, for instance, *must* or *have to*) or an utterance is a yes/no second person question with a modal verb like *can*, the utterance is a command; if an utterance is a single word utterance used for back-channelling, the utterance is a

Prompt; a *Question* utterance is an interrogative text which is not a command; *Assertion* is any other utterance.

The prosodic features are based on values of voice's pitch and intensity represented by the minimum, maximum, mean, standard deviation.

Evaluation of the [Mairesse et al., 2007] approach is performed using data of two corpora: an essays corpus and EAR ([Mehl et al., 2001]). For simplicity, this thesis discusses only classification of the EAR corpus.

The EAR corpus contains 15,269 conversation extracts from 96 participants. Personality traits of the participants are rated by 18 independent observers. The approach calculates classification results as a 5-classes problem where it uses NB and 10-fold cross-validation. The recognition of all five personality traits yields the average accuracy value of 27.42%.

This thesis can utilize the findings of the approach by Mairesse and colleagues similar to the findings by Diederich and colleagues: the proposed approach extracts unigrams to measure personality so this thesis assumes similarly that unigrams are suitable to measure emotions. Moreover, unigrams can be used for classifying texts of many classes (2 classes vs. 5 classes).

3.4 OVERVIEW OF PREVIOUS APPROACHES TO LEXICAL EMOTION RECOGNITION

3.4.1 SENTENCE/PHRASE-LEVEL AFFECT SENSING

Table 4 outlines the approaches to the sentence/phrase-level affect sensing.

Approach	Corpus	Resources	Classes	Result
[Liu et al, 2003]	—	Commonsense facts, sentence models	Ekman emotions	Satisfactory system performance
[Riloff et al., 2006]	MPQA	Unigrams, bigrams, EPs ranked using IG and subsumption hierarchy	subjective/ objective	Accuracy value of 75.4% using SVMlight
[Wiebe & Riloff, 2005a]	298,809 sentences from a world press collection	Emotion words, N-grams, EPs	subjective/ objective	Unsupervised: recall value of 86.3% and the precision value of 78.1% using subjective NB; recall value of 57.6% and the precision value of 77.5% using objective NB
[Wiebe et al., 2004]	Sentences from WSJ and newsgroups	Three clues of subjectivity	subjective/not-subjective	Comprehensive summary of means for detecting subjectivity
[Choi & Cardie, 2008]	MPQA	negators, emotion words from GI, rules based on compositional semantics	subjective/ objective	Accuracy value of 90.7%
[Neviarouskaya et al, 2007]	Sentences from a corpus with weblogs	Emotion words from WordNet-Affect, intensifiers, negations	Izard emotions	The system output agrees with at least 2 annotators in 70% sentences
[Strapparava & Mihalcea, 2007]	1,250 annotated headlines	A rules-based approach, a PMI approach, a statistical approach	3 valence classes (positive/negative/ neutral); 2 emotion classes (positive/negative)	Best results are achieved by the semantic ClaC for sensing valence or UPAR7 for sensing emotions
[Balahur & Montoyo, 2008]	Data from [Strapparava & Mihalcea, 2007]	Emotion words from WordNet, Sperber's theory of pragmatic relevance, Maslov's theory of human needs, Neef's theory of human needs	3 valence classes (positive/negative/ neutral); 2 emotion classes (positive/negative)	Recall value of 65.01% for classification of the valence of English sentences, recall value of 66.13% for classification of the valence of Spanish sentences. Recall value of 45.37% for classification of emotions in English sentences, recall value of 44.89% for classification of emotions in Spanish sentences.

Table 4: Overview of sentence/phrase level approaches

The *Approach* column contains a bibliographic reference to the approach being discussed; the *Corpus* column defines the corpus used for evaluation; the *Resources* column describes resources used for affect sensing; the *Classes* column contains labels of classes the analyzed texts belong to; the *Result* column shows the yielded result of affect sensing.

In summary, an approach to lexical affect sensing at the sentence/phrase level can utilize the findings of existing approaches as follows:

1. The most semantic approaches rely on emotion words either extracted from the manually composed dictionaries with emotion words or automatically using PMI.
2. The semantic approaches consider grammatical interdependencies between words and can be seen as protypes of rules. The rules can be composed on the basis of empirical commonsense.

3.4.2 DOCUMENT-LEVEL OPINION MINING

Table 5 outlines the document-level approaches to opinion mining.

Approach	Corpus	Resources	Classes	Result
[Turney, 2002]	410 reviews from [Epinions, 2008]	PMI-IR	Recommended/not-recommended	74% precision
[Yi et al., 2003]	485 topic or 1,838 non-topic digital camera documents	Naïve algorithm	Recommended/not-recommended	87% precision, 56% recall
[Pang et al., 2002]	PMRC, v. 1.0	Unigrams features evaluated as a presence vector	Negative/positive	82.9% precision
[Pang & Lee, 2004]	PMRC, v. 2.0	Unigrams evaluated as a presence vector	Negative/positive	87.2% precision
[Yu & Hatzivassiloglou, 2003]	WSJ	Unigrams	Opinion/Non-opinion	97% F-measure
[Finn & Kushmerick, 2006]	Movie and restaurant reviews; football, politics, finance articles	Unigrams, POS tags, stylometric features	Negative/positive, subjective/objective	Avg. 82.7% precision with C4.5, or avg. 77.3% precision with ensemble meta-classifier
[Dave et al., 2003]	1120 reviews from Cnet	Unigrams, bigrams, trigrams	Negative/positive	85.8% precision
[Riloff et al., 2006]	PMRC, v. 1.0	Unigrams, bigrams, EPs	Negative/positive	82.7% precision
	OP	Unigrams, bigrams, EPs	Negative/positive	98.7% precision
[Whitelaw et al., 2005]	PMRC, v. 2.0	Unigrams and appraisal groups	Negative/positive	90.2% precision
[Diederich et al., 2000]	2,652 articles from Berliner Zeitung	Tagwords, bigrams of tagwords, word length	Author/Not author	100% precision, 51.4% recall
[Mairesse et al., 2007]	15,269 conversation extracts	LIWC, MRC, utterance type features, prosodic features	5-classes problem	27.42% accuracy using NB

Table 5: Overview of document-level approaches

The *Approach* column contains a bibliographic reference to the approach being discussed; the *Corpus* column defines the corpus used for evaluation; the *Resources* column describes resources used for opinion mining; the *Classes* column contains labels of classes the classified texts belong to; the *Result* column shows the yielded result of opinion mining.

Note that the most document-level approaches use statistical means to perform opinion mining. Moreover, the overwhelming number of approaches extract unigrams; second often are the features extracted on the basis of POS tags. Particular noteworthy is an attempt to utilize the position of unigrams as in the [Pang et al., 2002] approach. Although the proposed approach did not discover possible advantages of position consideration, the possibility of improving results arising insofar should not be underestimated.

In summary, an approach to opinion mining at the document level can utilize the findings of existing approaches as follows:

1. Lexical features can be used for opinion mining. These features can be lemmatized words or stopwords. Lexical features can be evaluated as presence or frequency vectors. Hereby, texts that build the basis for composed datasets can have any origin and labeled using arbitrary number of emotion classes. Specific filtering of words, for example, according to product names is not necessary.

2. POS features are less relevant for approaches to opinion mining.

3. Influence of the context of texts can be tested.

4. Applicability of stylometric features such as the lengths of words can be tested.

5. Optimization of the feature space can be expected to provide significant improvement of results of emotion recognition.

3.5 SHORTCOMINGS OF PREVIOUS APPROACHES TO AFFECT SENSING

The previous approaches to affect sensing have the following shortcomings:

1. *Generality:* Previous approaches to statistical opinion mining described classification results for a particular domain/corpus or limited number of corpora that raised the questions of their general applicability to emotional classification. Furthermore, prior work did not consider the properties of analyzed texts, e.g. the text length.

2. *Thorough examination of data-mining issues in opinion mining:* Prior approaches to statistical opinion mining rarely studied data mining issues as the choice of classifier, feature evaluation and normalization of their values although it can significantly influence the classification results. Furthermore, the prior approaches did not study the methods to improve classification using optimization of the feature space.

3. *Consideration of grammatical findings in statistical opinion mining:* Past work in statistical opinion mining rarely addressed applicability of grammatical findings to the statistical opinion mining considering this research area as a typical application field of semantic approaches.

4. *Composition of many datasets for comprehensive study of the proposed statistical approach:* Previous approaches to statistical opinion mining described classification results only for a limited number of datasets, e.g. a dataset with unigrams, a dataset with 36 POS tags, and a dataset with 152 stylometric features, in total, 3 datasets, although a thorough study of classification results is more reliable when undertaken using many datasets with many features.

5. *Consideration of the authorship attribution:* Past work to statistical opinion mining used stylometric approaches to detect the author and not to classify affect although the classification task in both cases is very similar in that it analyzes and classifies a text.

6. *Results interpretation:* Existing approaches to statistical opinion mining evaluate their results using data mining measures, e.g. the recall value, and do not describe humanly comprehensible means for interpreting classification results. However, interpretation of results is highly beneficial especially in the field of opinion mining since it can be utilized for improving comprehensibility of results, for example, in believable software programs or dialogue systems.

7. *Plotting results:* Previous approaches did not describe a method to visualize yielded results although it can be used for studying classification results (cf. shortcoming 4).

8. *Differentiated semantic approach and its evaluation:* Previous approaches to semantic affect sensing classified texts without maintaining differentiated grammatical interdependencies in form of linking rules. However, such explicit interdependencies can facilitate comprehensibility of the classification results.

9. *Hybrid approach:* Previous approaches to emotion recognition considered either statistical or semantic methods, but never both. However, results of emotion recognition can consider a

hybrid solution that combines the flexibility of the statistical approach and the comprehensibility of the semantic approach.

10. *Multimodal fusion:* Prior approaches to emotion recognition did not provide a thorough study of multimodal fusion in emotion recognition.

4 CORPORA

This chapter describes emotional corpora that were used in the performed experiments and outlines properties of their texts.

4.1 LONG TEXTS

This section introduces corpora containing long texts. Long texts are defined in this thesis as texts consisting of more than 200 words.

4.1.1 PANG MOVIE REVIEWS CORPUS

Pang Movie Review Corpus (PMRC), version 2.0 contains 2000 movie reviews ([Pang & Lee, 2004]) that are annotated according to sentiment polarity. It consists of 1000 positive movie reviews and 1000 negative movie reviews.

Movie reviews are extracted from the *rec.arts.movies.reviews* newsgroup of [IMDB, 2008] and annotated by their authors using a star notation. The yielded star notation is mapped by Pang and Lee onto positive/negative classes although an exact mapping method is not specified.

Figure 12 shows an example of a negative review from PMRC (cv000_29416.txt)

plot : two teen couples go to a church party , drink and then drive .
they get into an accident .
one of the guys dies , but his girlfriend continues to see him in her life , and has nightmares .
what's the deal ?
WATCH THE MOVIE AND " SORTA " FIND OUT . . .
critique : a mind-fuck movie for the teen generation that touches on a very cool idea , but presents it in a very bad package .
which is what makes this review an even harder one to write , since I generally applaud films which attempt to break
...

Figure 12: An example of a review from PMRC, version 2.0

The review is a weblog with its typical properties, i.e. it contains slang words (underlined words) or unclear wordings. Moreover, it contains a grammatically incorrect text (the text in small capitals).

4.1.2 MULTIMODAL CORPUS WITH SPONTANEOUS DIALOGUES

Affect sensing in spontaneous dialogues is indispensable for many applications and is studied therefore thoroughly within this thesis. Possible candidates for corpora with spontaneous emotional dialogues are the Switchboard corpus containing spontaneous conversations, Rochester Marriage

Counseling Corpus with dialogues between married couples ([Chambers et al., 2004]), and SAL ([Kollias, 2007]). However, the use of SAL is more beneficial for two reasons: first, it is freely available; second, it is multimodal and can be thus utilized in experiments to emotion recognition using multimodal fusion (see chapter 8).

The Sensitive Artificial Listener corpus (SAL) contains audio-visual data of four users each communicating with one of four psychologically different characters: optimistic and outgoing (Poppy), confrontational and argumentative (Spike), pragmatic and practical (Prudence), depressing and gloomy (Obadiah) that try to draw the user into their own emotional state.

Affective meaning of dialogue turns in SAL is annotated by 4 annotators *dr*, *em*, *jd*, *cc* using FEELTRACE[31] data ([Cowie et al., 2000]): 27 dialogues (672 turns annotated by the annotators *dr*, *em*, *jd*), 23 dialogues (569 turns annotated by the annotator *cc*). Affect annotation in FEELTRACE contains numeric E/A data that are supplied continuously on all length of a turn. Particularly important that the annotation considers besides turn texts other information as mimics, gestures or acoustics in the user behaviour.

Annotations of turns as well as their texts can be visualized using ANVIL. ANVIL is a free video annotation tool allowing frame-accurate, hierarchical multi-layered annotation that manages an annotation board showing annotation tracks in time-alignment ([Kipp, 2003]). It was originally developed for annotating gestures but it is also suitable for research in many other fields (Figure 13).

---

[31] *FEELTRACE* is an instrument for dynamically tracking the emotional content of an emotional stimulus as it is perceived over time. The tracking logs the scores as coordinates in the E/A space.

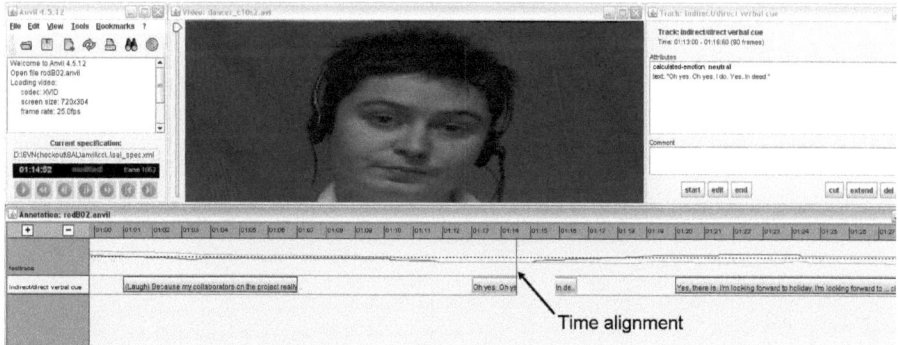

Figure 13: A SAL annotation in ANVIL

Figure 13 shows an ANVIL annotation of a SAL turn containing (from left to right, from top to bottom) the ANVIL system console, the window for a video (*dancer_*), the track window (*indirect/direct verbal cue*) with the text *calculated-emotion*... There is the ANVIL annotation board below these windows showing the most significant tracks in a particular scenario. Time alignment in the dialogue is shown by a vertical line.

In the given scenario to opinion mining, the ANVIL annotation contains two tracks: the *FEELTRACE* track visualizing E/A data where the red line corresponds to the values of the *activation* dimension and the green line corresponds to the values of the *evaluation* dimension; the track *indirect/direct verbal cue* contains the turn text, e.g. *Oh yes. Oh yes, I do. Yes. In deed.* and its affect segment[32] *calculated-emotion* calculated on the basis of data in the *FEELTRACE* track.

Note that turns in SAL dialogues can be seen as a continuous stream of information where dialogue turns are semantically connected with each other: one turn is caused by the previous turn, or the current turn reasons the following turn.

4.1.2.1 Mapping E/A data onto affect segments

Exact emotional meaning, for example, provided by coordinates in the E/A space is not required in the most scenarios of opinion mining: what is the use of affect annotation of a turn given by numerical E/A coordinates, e.g. (0,0) where the only useful information about this turn is the name of its affect segment, e.g. neutral? Even worse, numerical data can complicate emotion recognition:

---

[32] *Affect segment* is a geometric segment in the E/A space.

emotional meaning of a text is easier to detect if this meaning corresponds to a limited number of affect classes and not to a continuous range of values.

To get an idea of how to obtain realistic affect segmentation, this thesis explores different variants of segmentation (Figure 14).

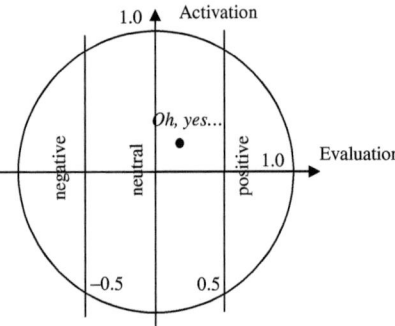

Figure 14: A variant of 3 affect segments in the E/A space

Figure 14 shows a possible affect segmentation of dialogue turns (points in the E/A space) that maps the E/A data onto three affect segments (*negative*, *neutral*, *positive*) ([Osherenko, 2006]). The point corresponds to the affect segment *neutral* of the dialogue turn *Oh yes. Oh yes, I do. Yes. In deed.*

Is the mapping in Figure 14 realistic? The mapping does not differentiate between high and low evaluation or high and low activation what is preferable in emotion recognition in natural-language dialogues. Thus, this segmentation cannot be applied to emotion recognition in natural-language dialogues and has to be dropped.

A desirable, however, more challenging affect segmentation provides the segmentation using five affect segments. To get an idea, how affect annotations of turns can be organized in five groups, the k-means clustering algorithm is used (Figure 15).

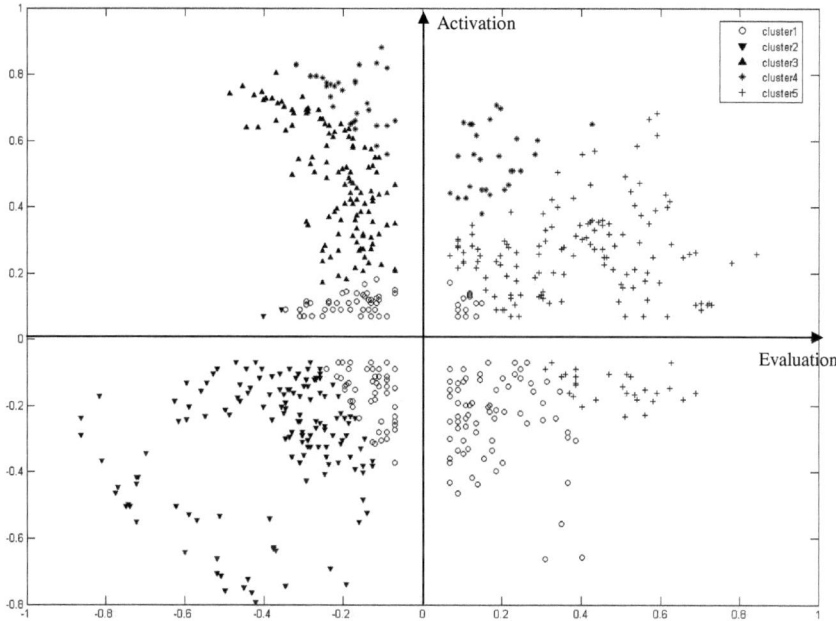

Figure 15: Affect segments as divided by the k-means algorithm

Figure 15 shows automatic grouping of points in 5 clusters using the k-means algorithm. The points (+, ○, •, ▲, ▼) correspond to the E/A annotation made by the majority of annotators at the turn end. Note that the empty areas around the E/A axes are assumed to be characteristic for the provided FEELTRACE data.

The first idea of possible affect segmentation presented in Figure 16 stems from the clustering in Figure 15.

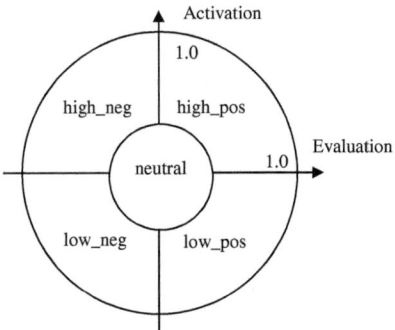

Figure 16: Segmentation in five segments

The *high_neg* affect segment annotates high negative turns (turns with low evaluation and high arousal), the *high_pos* affect segment annotates high positive turns (turns with high evaluation and high arousal), the *low_neg* affect segment annotates low negative turns (turns with low evaluation and low arousal), the *low_pos* affect segment annotates low positive turns (turns with high evaluation and low arousal). The *neutral* affect segment represents neutral turns (turns with evaluation and arousal around zero). Radius 1.0 is predetermined by FEELTRACE.

The affect segmentation in Figure 16 can be used as a rough approximation of the sought affect segmentation. However, the following questions have to be answered: first, how to handle long turns that are annotated in FEELTRACE by a particular annotator contradictory (the corresponding E/A coordinates indicate psychologically contradictory affect segments at different moments of a turn, for instance, *high_neg* and *high_pos*, meaning that an annotator considered a turn as negative at the beginning and as positive at the end); second, how to handle turns where different annotators do not agree, for example, 2 annotators annotate a turn as *high_neg* and 2 annotators as *high_pos*; third, what is the radius of the *neutral* circle; fourth, provides the proposed annotation credible annotation of turns bearing in mind psychological properties of the SAL characters.

In order to solve the problem of long turns and considering that a turn can be represented by several affect segments, the following heuristic is applied: the *neutral* segment has the lowest priority so that if a turn is annotated using several segment labels, the *neutral* segment is excluded from further consideration; the higher emotional annotation has the higher priority, for instance, a turn annotated using the sequence of affect segments *high_pos*, *low_pos*, *neutral* is annotated finally as *high_pos* and a turn annotated with the affect sequence *high_neg*, *low_neg*, *neutral* is annotated as *high_neg*. If the heuristic did not detect a final affect segment because participating segments are psychologically implausible such as *low_neg*, *high_pos*, the turn is annotated as *undefined*. Hence, the heuristic adds a sixth *undefined* segment to the affect segmentation.

The problem of credible annotation (second question) is resolved by using the majority of pair-wise votes of SAL annotators. If the majority cannot be calculated, the ambiguous turns are annotated as *undefined* (Figure 17).

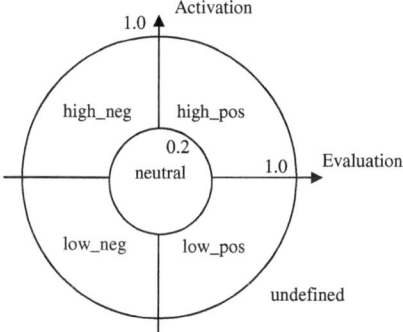

Figure 17: A variant of 6 affect segments in the E/A space

The *high_neg* affect segment annotates high negative turns, the *high_pos* affect segment annotates high positive turns, the *low_neg* affect segment annotates low negative turns, the *low_pos* affect segment annotates low positive turns. The *neutral* affect segment represents neutral turns that are annotated in FEELTRACE within the empirical 0.2 circle (evaluation and activation less than 0.2). The *undefined* segment annotates contradictory turns. Radius 1.0 is predetermined by FEELTRACE.

Radius 0.2 is chosen empirically (third question) in order to calculate an acceptable number of dialogue turns of all affect segments.

Figure 18 shows sample SAL turns which E/A values are mapped onto affect segments in Figure 17.

[1 - Affect segment: 'neutral']
- *Oh I'm pretty good I guess. It's nice to hear a cheery voice though.*

[2 - Affect segment: 'high_pos']
– *(Breath intake) Ah, it's just nice, erm, chatting to somebody who does look on the bright side of life. Most of the people around here are a bit <u>misery</u> guts really.*

[3 - Affect segment: low_pos]
– *No I really am.*

[4 - Affect segment: 'high_neg']
– *Well, that's <u>fine</u>. That's a <u>good</u> state of mind for you to get into.*

[5 - Affect segment: 'low_neg']
– *Erm, that's possible. Why don't you lighten up?*

[6 - Affect segment: 'undefined']
– *Yes, I do and I was angry this morning and I really, really, really hate being woken up in the middle of the night and then I can't sleep again and then you get tired and then you're not ready for the next day and so it goes on and, you know, and I've so much to do at the minute and there's no reason why I should have to do it and people are fighting with people everywhere in Departments and ... Oh, just bad.*

Figure 18: Examples of SAL turns

Note that the turn 1 is annotated *neutral* although it contains the words *pretty*, *good*, *cheery* that are typically considered to convey the positive affect; the turn 2 is annotated *high_pos* despite word *misery* typically considered to convey the negative affect; the turn 3 is annotated *low_pos* despite no emotion words at all; the turn 4 is annotated *high_neg* despite the words *fine* and *good*; the turn 5 is annotated *low_neg*, and not *low_pos* despite its resemblance to the turn 3; the turn 6 is annotated as *undefined* since it was annotated at the beginning *low_pos* and at the end *low_neg*. The reason of such discrepance can be stated as follows: as already mentioned, the annotators relied while annotating not only on the turn text, but also on other issues such as mimics of the user participating in a dialogue.

Does the segmentation in Figure 17 meet all requirements of the sought affect segmentation? What are the inter-annotator agreements averaged over classes for particular annotator pairs (Table 6)?

Annotator pair	Number agreeing co-occurrences	Pair agreement
cc, em	282	41.96%
cc, dr	274	40.77%
cc, jd	264	39.29%
em, dr	359	53.42%
em, jd	395	58.78%
dr, jd	330	49.11%

Averaged inter-annotator agreement: 47.22%

Table 6: Inter-annotator agreement values for 6 segments

The agreement values calculated for annotator pairs are shown in the column *Annotator pair*; the number of agreeing turns is shown in the column *Number agreeing co-occurrences*; the corresponding value in percent is shown in the *Pair agreement* column; the inter-annotator value averaged over 6 annotator pairs is shown in the last row.

Table 7 shows counts of affect segments as annotated by a particular annotator.

Annotator	Number of turns	Count
cc	569	*high_neg*: 135, *low_neg*: 103, *low_pos*: 83, *high_pos*: 132, *neutral*: 80, *undefined*: 36
dr	672	*high_neg*: 210, *low_neg*: 142, *low_pos*: 51, *high_pos*: 177, *neutral*: 27, *undefined*: 65
jd	672	*high_neg*: 278, *low_neg*: 82, *low_pos*: 0, *high_pos*: 148, *neutral*: 110, *undefined*: 54
em	672	*high_neg*: 229, *low_neg*: 98, *low_pos*: 16, *high_pos*: 236, *neutral*: 31, *undefined*: 62

Table 7: Counts of affect segments in the SAL corpus

The *Annotator* column presents the annotator of dialogues; the *Number of turns* column shows the overall number of turns annotated by *Annotator*; the *Count* column represent an affect segment and the number of turns of this segment in the SAL dialogues according to the segmentation in Figure 17.

Obviously, the proposed affect annotation can not be used in the current scenario of emotion recognition as it is evidenced by the low value of the averaged inter-annotator agreement (47.22%) and the high number of turns annotated as *undefined* although the segment *undefined* can be considered merely as an interim solution.

To resolve these problems, the annotation method is changed: the final affect segment is represented now only by the affect segment at its temporal end. Moreover, the *undefined* segment is excluded from the affect segmentation (Figure 19).

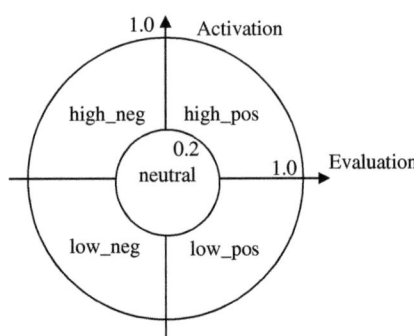

Figure 19: Final affect segmentation in the E/A space

The *high_neg* affect segment annotates high negative turns, the *high_pos* affect segment annotates high positive turns, the *low_neg* affect segment annotates low negative turns, the *low_pos* affect segment annotates low positive turns. The *neutral* affect segment represents neutral turns that are annotated in FEELTRACE within the empirical 0.2 circle. Radius 1.0 is predetermined by FEELTRACE.

4.1.2.2 Assessing the Mapping

This thesis assesses the final affect segmentation in the following manner: the inter-annotator agreement should be high (more than 80% in accordance with [Craggs, 2004]); psychological properties of SAL characters (given by counts of affect segments) and the corresponding affective behaviour (given by HMMs for affective behaviour) should correspond to psychological properties of the SAL characters (optimistic and outgoing, confrontational and argumentative, pragmatic and practical, depressing and gloomy).

Table 8 shows inter-annotator agreement values for the final affect segmentation.

Annotator pair	Number agreeing co-occurrences	Pair agreement
cc, em	537	79.91%
cc, dr	527	78.42%
cc, jd	514	76.49%
em, dr	544	80.95%
em, jd	531	79.02%
dr, jd	519	77.23%

Average inter-annotator agreement: 78.67%   Majority vote: 85.42%

Table 8: Inter-annotator agreement values for 5 segments

Particular annotator pairs are shown in the column *Annotator pair*; the number of agreeing turns is shown in the column *Number agreeing co-occurrences*; the corresponding value in percent is shown in the *Pair agreement* column. The last row shows an inter-annotator agreement value averaged over 6 annotator pairs and the yielded value of the majority vote.

Hence, 98 turns out of 672 turns had to be discarded from further consideration due to the contradictory segments or to the missing agreement between annotators. The remaining 574 turns are annotated as follows: 176 turns as *high_neg*, 103 turns as *low_neg*, 123 turns as *neutral*, 24 turns as *low_pos*, 148 turns as *high_pos*.

The SAL characters try to draw the user in their own emotional state. In order to get evidence thereof and, thus, if the proposed 5-segment affect segmentation can be used for further experiments, the counts of affect segments in dialogues are calculated (Table 9).

Character	Utt. #	Count
Poppy	147	*high_neg*: 21, *low_neg*: 10, *neutral*: 24, *low_pos*: 5, *high_pos*: 87
Spike	159	*high_neg*: 103, *low_neg*: 12, *neutral*: 22, *low_pos*: 1, *high_pos*: 21
Prudence	160	*high_neg*: 43, *low_neg*: 34, *neutral*: 42, *low_pos*: 6, *high_pos*: 35
Obadiah	108	*high_neg*: 9, *low_neg*: 47, *neutral*: 35, *low_pos*: 12, *high_pos*: 5

Table 9: Counts of affect segments for the SAL characters

The name of a SAL character that took part in a dialogue with the user is shown in the column *Character*; numbers of affect segments as annotated using the proposed annotation method are presented in the column *Utt. #*; the column *Count* shows pairs of numbers (an affect segment and the number of turns of this segment in the SAL dialogues). Note that since an affect segment can not be always calculated due to the aforementioned reasons, the total sum of numbers in the column *Utt. #* is 574 and not 672 as the total number of SAL turns.

Table 9 gives a numerical evidence of conformity of the chosen segmentation with the psychological properties of the SAL characters: the highest number of *high_pos* turns (87) is counted in dialogues with the optimistic and outgoing (Poppy); the highest number of *high_neg* turns (103) is counted in dialogues with the confrontational and argumentative Spike; turns are distributed almost uniformly among affect segments in dialogues with pragmatic and practical Prudence; dialogues with depressing and gloomy Obadiah have a noticeably high sum 56=47+9 of negative states (segments *low_neg*, *high_neg*).

The proposed affect segmentation is assessed additionally using the HMMs for affective behaviour (cf. section C.1). However, in contrast to [Osherenko, 2008] where HMMs are used for composing a credible model for affective behaviour, this thesis has a less ambitious intention: it uses HMMs for segmentation assessment and not for acquiring a model of affective behaviour. Hereby, the proposed affect segmentation is supposed to be appropriate if probabilistic transitions between affect segments in a HMM for affective behaviour are psychologically plausible and can be explained using commonsense.

The HMMs for affective behaviour contain five affect states *high_neg*, *high_pos*, *low_neg*, *low_pos*, *neutral* corresponding to the affect segments. Initially, all transition probabilities in the examined HMMs are initialized with a value of 0.2. Then, the transition probabilities are adjusted by the Baum-Welch algorithm using 27 training sequences from the SAL dialogues (equal to the number of the SAL dialogues). The training sequences are composed from affect annotations in consecutive SAL turns. For instance, the training sequence *low_pos neutral low_neg neutral low_pos neutral* is acquired from a dialogue with the depressing and gloomy Obadiah shown in Figure 20 resulting from the first, second, ..., sixth turn (the annotation segments is specified in the square brackets).

...

[1 - Affect segment: low_pos] Well, I can see that, but you're a very gloomy character.

[2 - Affect segment: neutral] Erm, that's possible. Why don't you lighten up?

[3 - Affect segment: low_neg] Well that's true too, but if you dwell on that your not gonna get by life in a very (laugh) positive frame of mind.

[4 - Affect segment: neutral] Sometimes it does, that's true.

[5 - Affect segment: low_pos] Erm, I guess it changes over time, you have ... good days and you have bad days.

[6 - - Affect segment: neutral] Erm, well, you just happen to have caught me on a good day.

...

Figure 20: Sample dialogue from SAL

The resulting HMMs are shown in Figure 21. For better readability, the arcs containing probabilities less than 0.01 are omitted. The complete adjacency matrices of HMMs are presented in section C.2.

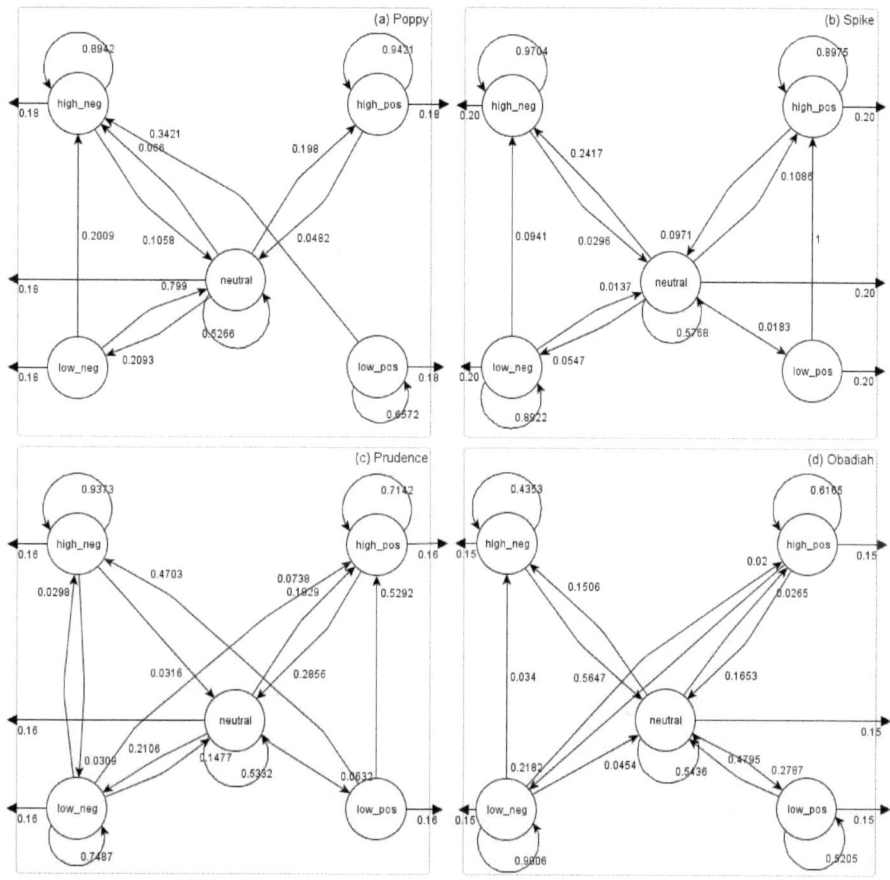

Figure 21: HMMs for SAL characters

The HMMs contain five affect states (*high_pos, low_pos, neutral, high_neg, low_neg*) connected with transitional arcs. The name of a SAL character involved in the dialogue with a user is shown at the top of the corresponding HMM. The observations and their values are shown only for illustrative purposes.

The SAL characters have their own psychological characteristics and dialogues with their participation should be reflected in the composed HMMs. Thus, this thesis studies the probabilities of calculated HMMs. Figure 21 (a) representing dialogues with the optimistic and outgoing Poppy the *high_pos-high_pos* transition has the highest probability value of 94.21% that can be intuitively considered to reflect the optimistic nature of the Poppy's character. Figure 21 (b) shows a HMM for dialogues with the confrontational and argumentative Spike where the probability of the *high_neg-high_neg* transition is 97.04%, the *low_pos-high_pos* probability is 100% that can be considered as aforementioned properties of Spike's character. The HMM in Figure 21 (d) with depressing and gloomy Obadiah indicates a passive behaviour with relative low transition probabilities: the *high_pos-high_pos* transition has a probability value of 61.65% and the HMM in the *high_pos* state can transit either to the *low_neg* state with a low probability value of 21.82% or to the *neutral* state with a probability value of 16.53%, the *high_neg-neutral* transition has a probability value of 56.47%, the highest *low_neg-low_neg* transition has a probability value of 90.06%.

The discussed HMMs for dialogues with three SAL characters (Poppy, Spike, and Obadiah) are psychologically plausible. However, dialogues with pragmatic and practical Prudence yield a HMM in Figure 21 (c) with unexpected probabilities: the *high_pos-high_pos* transition probability is 71.42%, the probability of the *high_neg-high_neg* transition is 93.73%, the *low_neg-low_neg* transition is 74.87%. Such high transitions are attributed though to the small size of the SAL corpus and can be therefore neglected in this thesis.

Hence, the affect segmentation in Figure 17 meets all requirements of the sought affect segmentation: the majority vote yields a value of 85.42% greater than the desirable 80%, counts of affect segments for dialogues with characters as well as the probabilities in the proposed HMMs are psychologically plausible.

4.1.3 CORPUS WITH PRODUCT REVIEWS

This thesis extracted an own corpus with product reviews (CwPR) from [Epinions, 2008] (Figure 22).

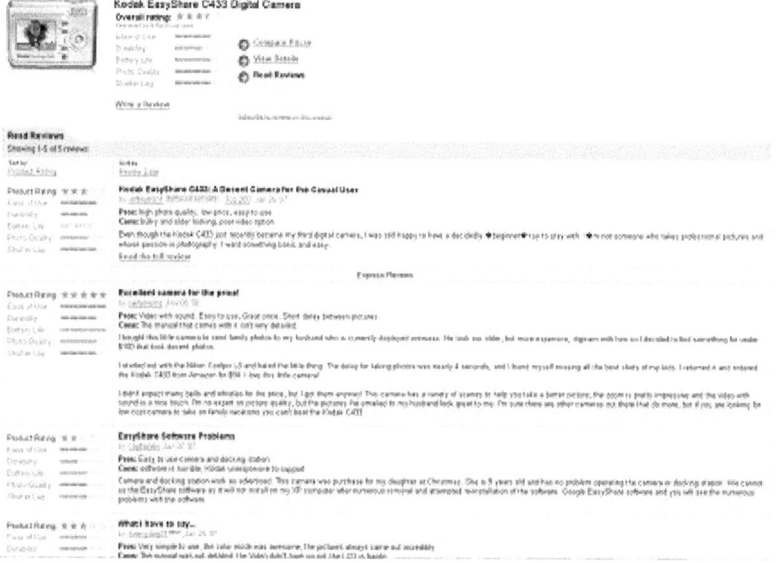

Figure 22: An example of a product review

Collected product reviews are 11,198 reviews on 1,266 digital cameras from 9,567 reviewers. Each product reviews contains 6 ratings for different product categories: the *overall, ease of use, durability, battery life, photo quality, shutter lag* ratings. Ratings are expressed in the star range between 1 star (poor) and 5 stars (excellent). A review can be a full review (more than 200 words) that thoroughly discusses all properties of the reviewed product. It can be also an express review, a brief description of the product. A full review is labeled as *Not Helpful, Somewhat Helpful, Very Helpful, Helpful, Very Helpful, Most Helpful, Off topic* (the review is written on a wrong product); an express review is rated using only two labels *Show* and *Don't Show* in order to recommend showing or hiding the review on the Internet. Review authors can be also rated as being trusted or blocked.

This thesis used an excerpt from CwPR that contains 300 most helpful product reviews consisting of 5 groups of 60 reviews annotated with the *overall* rating in star notation from 1 to 5 stars in the 1 star increment.

4.1.4 BERARDINELLI MOVIE REVIEW CORPUS

Berardinelli Movie Review Corpus (BMRC) contains 215 movie reviews from [Reelviews, 2008] rated with 9 star scores in the range from zero stars (poor) to four stars (excellent) in the half star increment. Hence, BMRC contains 10 movie reviews with the zero rating, 30 movie reviews with the half-star rating, 25 movie reviews each rated using the other 7 ratings in a half-star increment. Reviews are supposed to be written and rated by the same person, James Berardinelli (Figure 23).

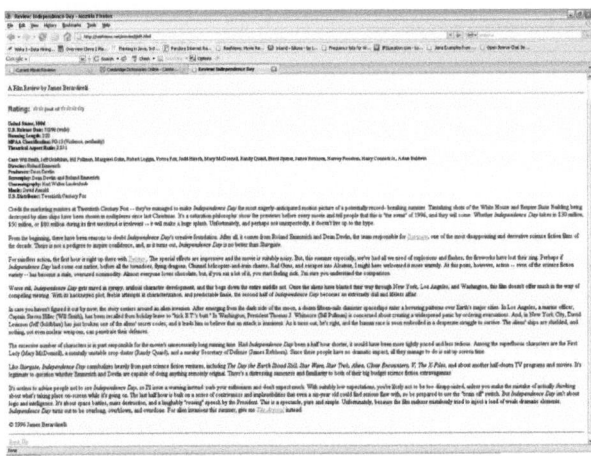

Figure 23: Example review in BMRC

Note that the example review contains a review text annotated with two stars.

BMRC is given special consideration in this thesis since it can be seen as a complete opposite of PMRC and SAL in regard of the following issues: the annotated reviews in BMRC are long texts (on average, reviews consist of 200 words) conveying a clearly expressed opinion of the author on a movie; the movie reviews are supposed to be grammatically correct text pieces without ambiguous wordings and containing only intentional repetitions.

4.2 SHORT TEXTS

The corpora described above contained either long texts (PMRC, CwPR, BMRC) or short texts that can be supposed to be long because they are semantically connected, e.g dialogue turns in SAL. However, this thesis aims to present a complete solution of lexical emotion recognition and discusses hereafter also corpora containing short emotional texts (emotional sentences).

4.2.1   FIFTY WORD FICTION CORPUS

The Fifty Word Fiction corpus (FWF) is a corpus containing 759 English sentences that are manually annotated in terms of their sentiment and affect ([Read, 2004]). FWF contains 82 sentences labeled as *positive*, 171 sentences as *negative*, and 506 sentences as *unclassifiable*, for instance, the sentence *Underneath, they wore turtlenecks.* is annotated as *unclassifiable*, the sentence *We all laughed and ordered beers.* is annotated as *positive*, the sentence *I start to cry because I know I lost you forever.* is annotated as *negative*.

FWF was collected online and available to the general public for one month, during which some 3,301 annotations were made by 49 annotators. The overall inter-annotator agreement in FWF (65%) is calculated as the mean of inter-annotator agreements between an annotator and an expert vote where an expert vote is a vote by the majority of annotators. This value is less than the desirable inter-annotator agreement of 80%. However, despite this low value, FWF is examined in the experiments in this thesis for the reason of its free availability.

4.2.2   SENTENCES FROM BERARDINELLI MOVIE REVIEW CORPUS

This thesis analyses affect sensing in an own corpus containing sentences from 13 randomly chosen movie reviews of the Berardinelli Movie Review Corpus (BMRC-S) (cf. BMRC in section 4.1.4). The compilation of BMRC-S is performed by splitting a movie review in sentences; each sentence is annotated manually using a 5-class annotation scheme (*high negative, low negative, neutral, low positive, high positive*). The resulting BMRC-S contains 1,010 emotional sentences: 173 sentences are annotated as high negative, 432 sentences as low negative, 169 sentences as neutral, 65 sentences as high positive, 171 sentences as low positive. On the basis of this annotation, a 3-classes annotation (*negative, neutral, positive*) is calculated that maps a more detailed 5-classes annotation onto a less detailed 3-classes annotation by changing low/high positive annotation in positive annotation; low/high negative annotation is changed in negative annotation; the *neutral* annotation remains *neutral*. Thus, after such transformation 605 sentences are annotated as *negative*, 169 sentences as *neutral*, 236 sentences as *positive*.

Noteworthy that sentences in BMRC-S are annotated standalone and independent from adjacent sentences (contextual independence). For instance, the four stars (high positive) review of the movie review *21 Grams* can be erroneously supposed to hold only high positive sentences. However, this review contains, for example, the sentence *It's difficult to provide any kind of plot summary that doesn't give away crucial details...* that is annotated standalone as *negative* although in its context this sentence should be understood as *positive*. Similarly, the question *How many other films from the early '70s can make this statement?* refers to a judgement made in previous sentences and should be annotated as *positive*, but following the statement of contextual independence this sentence is annotated as *neutral*.

BMRC-S includes sentences that can be either plot sentences with movie details or subjective sentences that convey opinion. For instance, the corpus contains both a sentence *A Clockwork Orange is told in three acts* that describes a film (*Clockwork Orange* is a movie title) and also a sentence *In this role, Léaud is fantastic* that expresses an opinion about the performance of the actor Léaud.

4.3 PROPERTIES OF STUDIED CORPORA

Above, this thesis described different emotional textual corpora. Here, follows an outline of their most remarkable properties:

1. *Length of emotional texts.* Analyzed texts can be differently long. The length of reviews in PMRC, CwPR and BMRC is on average over 200 words whereas a turn in SAL can contain a single word only. FWF and BMRC-S contain only short texts (sentences).
2. *Verbal intensity of emotional expression.* Emotional corpora do not have to contain evident verbal signs of emotions (emotion words or emotional phrases) and still convey emotional meaning using subtle means. Hence, reviews in PMRC, CwPR and BMRC include evident verbal signs that substantiate the opinion of the author. In contrast, SAL turns as well as as sentences in FWF and BMRC-S do not necessarily include evident verbal signs of experienced emotions.
3. *Grammatical correctness.* Analyzed texts can be grammatically correct or incorrect. However, this thesis assumes that reviews in BMRC consist of grammatically correct sentences whereas reviews in PMRC/CwPR and the dialogues from SAL can be grammatically incorrect, contain repairs, repetitions and inexact wordings. Sentences in FWF and BMRC-S are supposed to be grammatically correct.
4. *Consistency.* Analyzed texts can be consistent/inconsistent regarding author's opinion. For instance, a product review in CwPR can be inconsistent if it expresses at the beginning a positive opinion on a product and a negative opinion at its end. Hence, the reviews from BMRC are supposed to be consistent whereas reviews from PMRC, CwPR as well as turns in SAL can

be inconsistent. Sentences in FWF and BMRC-S are considered to be consistent due to their shortness.

5. *Continuity.* Parts of analyzed text can be semantically connected. Hence, turns in SAL dialogues can be seen as a continuous stream of adjacent turns. In contrast, there is no connection between particular reviews in PMRC, CwPR and BMRC. Sentences in FWF are not continuous; sentences in BMRC-S are intentionally not continuous remembering that they are annotated using the assumption of contextual independence, their "incontinuity".

6. *Author of the emotional text and its annotator.* Various people comprehend a particular text differently. Since an author of a text can mean to convey another emotion by his text than the person who annotates it, this thesis distinguishes the persons who authored a text and its annotator. Hence, a review in PMRC, CwPR and BMRC is considered to be composed and rated by the same person whereas characters and annotators in SAL dialogues are various people; a sentence in FWF is authored and annotated by different persons; a sentence in BMRC-S is authored and annotated by the same person.

Table 10 outlines the corpora containing long texts.

Corpus/ Property	PMRC	SAL	CwPR	BMRC
Length of emotional texts	Rather long	Dialogue turns are differently long	Rather long	Long
Verbal intensity of emotional expression	Can be ambiguous	Ambiguous	Can be ambiguous	Distinct
Grammatical correctness	Can be grammatically incorrect, contain repetitions, and repairs	Can be grammatically incorrect, contain repetitions, and repairs	Can be grammatically incorrect, contain repetitions, and repairs	Does not contain grammatically incorrect phrases, or unintentional repetitions, and repairs
Consistency	Emotional meaning can change	Emotional meaning can change	Emotional meaning can change	Emotional meaning is consistent
Continuity	Separate texts	Continuous stream of turns	Separate texts	Separate texts
Author/annotator of emotional text	Same person[33]	Different persons	Same person[33]	Same person

Table 10: Properties of the introduced long text corpora

The names of analyzed corpora are shown in the title row and the names of their properties in the most left row.

Table 11 outlines the corpora containing short texts.

---

[33] The text author annotates his text and hence the text comprehension and the text annotation can be considered to be equal. Another text in a corpus has a different author that annotates his text. Therefore the text comprehension and the text annotation differ from those of the first text.

Corpus/ Property	FWF	BMRC-S
Length of emotional texts	Short	Short
Verbal intensity of emotional expression	Can be vague	Distinct
Grammatical correctness	Rather grammatically correct	Grammatically correct
Consistency	Emotional meaning is consistent	Emotional meaning is consistent
Continuity	Separate texts	Separate texts
Author/annotator of emotional text	Different persons	Same person

Table 11: Properties of the introduced short text corpora

The names of different corpora are shown in the title row and the names of their properties in the most left row.

This thesis refers to the properties of corpora in Table 10 and Table 11 while discussing results of statistical opinion mining in section 5.5.

5 STATISTICAL OPINION MINING

This chapter describes the statistical approach to opinion mining and concretizes the conventional data mining analysis procedure in Appendix B. Hence, this chapter discusses composition of data mining datasets (section 5.1); answers core data mining questions (section 5.2); explores possibilities for interpreting classification results in emotional domain (section 5.3); shows classification results (section 5.4); discusses these results (section 5.5) and presents future work (section 5.6).

5.1 FEATURE EXTRACTION AND EVALUATION

This section discusses feature extraction and feature evaluation for all analyzed corpora. Specific adjustments are necessary only for emotion recognition in SAL and will be discussed directly in section 5.4.2. Note that the proposed approach lemmatizes analyzed texts but does not perform any other text modification. Possible modification of the text could consider text abstracts (similar to classification of the 30 most subjective text abstracts in the [Pang & Lee, 2004] approach in section 3.3). Moreover, the text structure is not considered in feature extraction (as the position feature in the [Pang et al., 2002] approach). The proposed approach does not alter the classified text according to its genre although there are different studies on the spoken English, the language of newspapers, the language of advertising, the language of literature – narrative prose, the language of literature – poetry, the language of law, the language of religion, the language of politics, the language of broadcasting, the language of humour in [Thorne, 1997]. Also not considered is the genre consideration in [Hillier, 2003] according to the written texts (literary narrative, newspaper reporting), spoken texts (women's talk, children's talk), written texts having spoken features (political speeches, fictional narrative in a regional dialect, television advertisements). General observations on specialized texts in [Bhatia, 2004] or observations on the structure of academic papers in [Swales, 2002] and email correspondence in [Murray, 1991] or examinations on specialized genres in [Bhatia & Gotti, 2006], [Gotti, 2003]), or findings in [Bednarek, 2006] concerning the evaluation in the media discourse are also not taken into account. Findings in natural-language dialogues, called *stances* as in [Biber et al., 1999] as well as typical exchanges[34] between dialogue participants in [Greenbaum, 1996] are not considered in this thesis.

5.1.1 LEXICAL FEATURES

Text consists of words that are called in statistics "lexical features"[35]. This section discusses extraction and evaluation of lexical features in the proposed approach.

5.1.1.1 Extraction of Lexical Features

Six sources of lexical features are explored in this thesis: unigrams from the classified corpus ordered by their frequency (hereafter referred to as corpus frequency list), unigrams from the BNC frequency list, emotion words from DAL, and three corresponding lists containing unigrams' lemmata (hereafter referred to as lemmatized corpus list).

49 datasets containing s/n most frequent lexical features (including stopwords) are used for classification of each particular corpus. s is the length of the corpus frequency list. n is the number of the dataset where $0 < n \leq 10$ in increment 1; from $n > 10$ in increments from 2 to 89. For BMRC, the frequency list consists of $s=15,170$ unigrams. Thus, the first dataset ($n=1$) contains *15,170* features; the second dataset ($n=2$) consists of *7,585* words; the third dataset ($n=3$) contains *5,056* unigrams; ...; the 49th dataset ($n=89$) contains 170 unigrams. For SAL, the frequency list consists of $s=2,033$ unique words. Hence, the first dataset ($n=1$) contains *2,033* features; the second unigram dataset ($n=2$) consists of *1,019* words; the third unigram dataset ($n=3$) contains *679* unigrams; ...; the 49th dataset ($n=89$) contains 22 words.

The word frequency list of BNC can be used for extracting lexical features. The British National Corpus (BNC) corpus is a 100 million word collection of samples of written and spoken language from a wide range of sources, representing current British English, both spoken and written ([Kilgarriff, 1997]).

The BNC frequency list, freely available on the Internet from [BNC, 2008], contains rows in the format

---

[34] *An exchange* is an utterances' pair in a dialogue (question/reply), for instance, an exchange is an utterance requesting for *yes/no* information that is typically replied with an *yes/no* answer, or an exchange is a suggestion of one dialogue participant that is accepted or rejected by another dialogue participant.

[35] In statistics, a word is referred to as a lexical feature or unigram. The set of lexical features is called sometimes Bag-of-Words.

$$\textit{frequency word POS-tag} \tag{12}$$

where *frequency* is the frequency of the word *word*, *POS-tag* denotes the POS tag of the word *word*, e.g. NN as the POS tag of a noun. The BNC tagset contains 61 POS elements ([Leech et al., 1994]).

The BNC frequency list contains words of different inflection and not only lemmata. For instance, it contains three inflections of the verb *approve*: *approve*, *approved*, and *approving*. Moreover, the BNC frequency word list contains word duplicates specified with different POS tags, for instance, the article *a* is specified five times: as the article *at0*, as the unclassified item *unc*, as the noun *np0*, as the personal pronoun *pnp*, as the determiner *dt0*.

In this thesis, unigrams are extracted from the BNC frequency list whereas occurring duplicates are discarded and only the first encountered occurrence and its frequency is considered for extracting. Hence, 62 datasets with lexical features are composed from the BNC frequency list: BNC-10, BNC-30, ..., BNC-72800 where *BNC-n* contains words with at least *n* occurrences in BNC. The values of *n* are selected in the manner that facilitates comparison with the number of features in other corpora. For example, BNC-425 ($n = 425$) contains 11,360 unigrams corresponding to DAL-1 with 8,742 features; BNC-2700 ($n = 2,700$) contains 3,029 unigrams corresponding to DAL-3 with 3,088 features.

Another source of lexical features provides DAL. 40 datasets are composed using DAL words: DAL-1, DAL-2, ..., DAL-40. The dataset DAL-*n* contains all words from DAL with words corresponding to the inequality $\sqrt{activation^2 + evaluation^2} \geq \frac{n-1}{n}$. *n* can be interpreted graphically as a circle in the E/A space. Figure 24 shows the E/A space and the circles corresponding to the datasets with emotion words from DAL. For example, the complete set of the DAL word features lies within the outmost circle while the dotted area corresponds to the dataset DAL-3 containing words corresponding to $n = 3$, for instance, the feature word *brutality*.

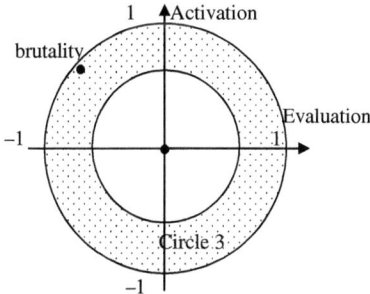

Figure 24: Extraction of words from DAL

5.1.1.2 Manipulating Lexical Features

This section investigates means to manipulate the set of lexical features.

Lexical features can be extracted according to their frequency and seldom words can be discarded (cf. the [Riloff et al., 2006] approach in section 3.3.2). However, the uniqueness of particular words has shown beneficial effect on affect sensing (cf. unique words in the [Wiebe et al., 2004] approach in section 3.2.2). Since filtering lexical features considering their frequency is not evident, the proposed approach does not distinguish words according to their frequency and utilize not only very frequent words such as stopwords, but also very seldom words as hapax legomena.

Words can be extracted according to their POS tags. Batliner and colleagues ([Batliner et al., 2003]) consider six POS group features (NOUN, API, APN, VERB, AUX, PAJ) representing particular groups of words. The NOUN feature counts nouns, the API feature counts inflected adjectives/participles, the APN feature counts not inflected adjectives/participles, the VERB feature counts verbs, the AUX feature counts auxiliary elements and copula[36], the PAJ feature counts particles, pronouns, articles, interjections. This thesis examined if it is beneficial to group lexical features according to their POS tags. However, this grouping did not improve classification results and was therefore excluded from further consideration.

POS tags and their combinations of different lengths can be used not only for extracting unigrams, but also themselves as features. For example, a dataset can contain the feature *NN* counting noun occurrences in a classified text; or a dataset can contain the feature, *JJ_NN*, that counts phrases

---

[36] *Copula* is a type of verb (the most common is 'be'), which joins the subject of the verb with a complement (= word that describes the subject).

tagged as *JJ* and *NN* like *great book*. However, since the POS features worsened classification results in the performed experiments, they are excluded from further consideration.

5.1.1.3 Lexical Features' Evaluation

Lexical features can be evaluated differently. For instance, [Pang et al., 2002] introduces evaluation of lexical features as frequency counts

$$f_w^1 \tag{13}$$

where f_w is the number of occurrences of unigram w in the studied text. The vector that contains features evaluated as frequency counts is referred to hereafter as a frequency vector.

Alternatively, a lexical feature can be evaluated as a binary presence value (1/0) containing elements

$$f_w^0 \tag{14}$$

where f_w is the number of occurrences of unigram w in the studied text. The vector that contains features evaluated as presence values is referred to hereafter as a presence vector.

The formulae (13) and (14) can be summarized as follows:

$$f_w^i \tag{15}$$

where power $i = 0, 1$.

Adding the power $i=-1$ for symmetry, the lexical features can be evaluated using a reciprocal frequency vector (inversed frequency of word occurrences) as follows:

$$f_w^{-1} \tag{16}$$

where $f_w^{-1}|_{f_w=0} = 0$ (if a word is not found in a text, the inverse evaluation equals 0). The vector that contains features evaluated as reciprocal frequency counts is referred to hereafter as a reciprocal or inversed frequency vector.

Noteworthy that lemmatized lists of lexical features contain inflected words but the value of such features is always 0 since the lemmatized texts contain only lemmata. For instance, the lemmatized corpora frequency lists or the lemmatized BNC frequency list contains inflected words which evaluation is always 0. In other words, the lemmatized word lists contain words of different inflection, but only the words that correspond to lemmata can evaluate to a value different from 0.

In section 5.2.2, the application of the introduced evaluation methods will be explored thoroughly.

5.1.2 STYLOMETRIC AND DEICTIC FEATURES

This section describes stylometric features and deictic features that can be utilized for opinion mining. Note that it does not draw, on any account, a conclusion whether it makes sense to utilize such features in opinion mining or not: this conclusion will be discussed in section 5.5.

Stylometric features represent shallow text information, for instance, the mean length of its words. Deictic features correspond to words in a language that are utilized for pointing or specifying function of some words, for example, referencing time (*on that day*) or referencing place (*there*).

In the following, this section describes extracted stylometric and deictic features and the method of their evaluation. Hence, from the stylometric features in [Ramyaa & Rasheed, 2004], this thesis considers the following features:

- Standard deviation of sentence lengths:

    The conventional formula for calculating the standard deviation is adjusted to a population of sentences' lengths. A sentence detector necessary for the feature evaluation uses the following heuristic: sentences are identified using the assumption that a sentence is a text abstract between two adjacent *SENT* tags. Sentence length is the number of sentence words. Standard deviation σ of sentence lengths is calculated as

    $$\sigma = \sqrt{\frac{1}{N}\sum_{i=1}^{N}(x_i - \bar{x})^2} \qquad (17)$$

    where N is the number of sentences in a text, x_i is the length of the current sentence in the sentence lengths' population, and $\bar{x}$ is the average value of sentences' lengths.

- Standard deviation of word lengths (numbers of characters in words):

    The standard deviation feature is evaluated using the formula (17) by replacing sentences' lengths with word lengths.

From [Kjell, 1994]:

- Digrams (letter pairs):

    The classified text is considered to be a sequence of letter pairs. Hereby, non-letters such as "," are dropped. A letter pair feature (26 letters × 26 letters) is one of 676 features whose name corresponds to a pair of adjacent letters evaluated as a frequency vector.

From [Forsyth & Holmes, 1996]:

- Letters:

    The classified text is considered as a sequence of 26 letters of English alphabet (special characters and spaces are omitted). The resulting 26 letter features are evaluated as a frequency vector.

Deictic features from [Hillier, 2003]:

- Demonstratives, e.g. *this*, *that*, *these*, *those* that are tagged as determiners or pronouns:

    1 demonstratives' feature is evaluated as a frequency vector.

- Time references, e.g. *yesterday, now, at the moment, today, now, at present, nowadays, at the present moment*;

    1 time references' feature is evaluated as a frequency vector.

- Place references *here, there*:

    1 place references' feature is evaluated as a frequency vector.

- Forms of the third person, e.g. *it, her, theirs*:

    12 features (*he, him, his, she, her, hers, it, its, they, them, their, theirs*) are evaluated as a frequency vector of the corresponding form.

[Uzuner & Katz, 2005] examines negations *not* and uncertainty markers such as *can, could* for classification.

This thesis assumes that deictic words are per se stopwords. Hence, a set of 526 stopwords from the WEKA toolkit is used as a set of deictic features that are evaluated as a frequency vector ([Witten & Frank, 2005]).

5.1.3 GRAMMATICAL FEATURES

This thesis described in section 2.1.2 grammatical means for expressing emotions using linguistic means. In the following, the same cues are described differently, from the point of view of data mining:

- Interjections (299), e.g. *Oh, what a beautiful present!*:

    The feature is evaluated as the number of occurrences of words tagged as *UH* (interjection).

- Exclamations (300a), e.g. *What a wonderful time we've had!*:

    The feature is evaluated as the frequency of text pieces starting with words tagged as *WP*, *WP$*, *WRB* tags (wh-pronouns and wh-adverbs) and ending with an exclamatory mark.

- Emphatic *so* and *such* (300b), for instance, *I'm so afraid they'll get lost!*:

    This feature is evaluated as the frequency of words *so* and *such*.

- Repetition (300c), e.g. *This house is 'far, 'far too expensive!*:

    The feature is evaluated as the frequency of repetitions of words tagged as adverbs or adjectives. Note that repetitions can be used not only for expressing affect but also factual as in the example: *I can take two carry-ons: a book bag and a light sports bag* where repetition of *bag* conveys no emotional meaning.

- Intensifying adverbs and modifiers (301), e.g. *We are utterly powerless.*:

    The feature value, initially 0, is incremented if positive intensifiers *utterly, absolute, terrific, tremendous, great, grand, fantastic, good, nice, really, definitely, truly, literally* are encountered in the classified text and decremented if negative intensifiers *tremendous, awfully, terribly, bad* are found in the classified text.

- Emphasis (302), e.g. *How ever did they escape?*:

The feature is evaluated as the frequency of words tagged as *WP*, *WP$*, *WRB* followed by either *ever*, or words *ever*, or phrases *on earth*, or *in heaven's earth*.

- Intensifying a negative sentence (303a), e.g. *She didn't speak to us at all!*:

    The feature is evaluated as the frequency of phrases *at all*, *a bit*, *by any means*, *a wink*, *a thing*, or the frequency of the word *whatever*.

- A negative noun phrase beginning with *not a* (303b), e.g. *We arrived not a moment too soon.*:

    The feature is evaluated as the frequency of the phrase *not a* within a noun phrase, for instance, within the phrase *not a moment*.

- Fronted negation (303c), e.g. *Never have I seen such a crowd of people*:

    The feature is evaluated as the frequency of the phrase *not a*, or as the frequency of the word *never* at the beginning of the analyzed text.

- Exclamatory and rhetorical questions (304, 305), e.g. *Hasn't she grown!* and *What difference does it make?*:

    There is an assumption that every question in studied texts is either exclamatory or rhetorical by default. Hence, special consideration of this issue is not necessary and the feature is evaluated syntactically as the frequency of exclamations marks or questions marks respectively.

5.1.4 OVERVIEW OF UTILIZED FEATURES

Table 12 outlines features used for statistical opinion mining.

Group	Features	Number of datasets
Non-lemmatized lexical features	Words from the corpus frequency list, words from the BNC frequency list, words from DAL; words are evaluated as a frequency vector, or a presence vector, or a reciprocal frequency vector	49 datasets with the s/n most frequent lexical features where s is the overall size of a corpus in unigrams and n is the number of the dataset, 62 datasets with words from the BNC frequency list where n is a threshold frequency value, 40 datasets with words from DAL where each unigram meets the requirement $\sqrt{activation^2 + evaluation^2} \geq \frac{n-1}{n}$.
Lemmatized lexical features	Words from the lemmatized corpus frequency list, words from the the lemmatized BNC frequency list, words from lemmatized DAL evaluated as a frequency vector, or as a presence vector, or a reciprocal frequency vector	49 datasets with the s/n most frequent lexical features where s is the overall size of a corpus in unigrams and n is the number of the dataset, 62 datasets with words from the BNC frequency list, 40 datasets with words from DAL where each word meets the requirement $\sqrt{activation^2 + evaluation^2} \geq \frac{n-1}{n}$.
Deictic features	Demonstratives as determiners, demonstratives as pronouns, time references, place references, forms of the third person, stopwords. All features are evaluated as a frequency vector	Datasets with combinations of 6 features (63 datasets)
Stylometric features	Stylometric features (letters, word length, digrams, standard deviation of word length, or sentence word length). Feature evaluation is discussed in section 5.1.2	Datasets with combinations of 5 features (31 datasets)
Grammatical features	The 299, 300a, 300b, 300c, 301, 302, 303a, 303b, 303c, 304-305 features. Feature evaluation is discussed in section 5.1.3	Datasets with combinations of 10 features (1,023 datasets)

Table 12: Overview of extracted features

The column *Group* contains a brief description of the group of features used for classification; the column *Features* outlines the extracted features; the *Number of datasets* column describes the number of datasets participating in the performed experiments.

5.2 CORE DATA MINING QUESTIONS

This thesis elaborates on questions frequently occurring in the statistical opinion mining:

1. What classifier should be used for opinion mining (SVM, InfoGain or NB)? See: section 5.2.1.

2. How should lexical features be evaluated (as a frequency vector, as a presence vector, as a reciprocal frequency vector)? See: section 5.2.2.

3. How should classification results of datasets with combinations of stylometric, grammatical, and deictic features be visualized? See: section 5.2.3.

4. Does normalization of lexical features significantly improve results of opinion mining? See: section 5.2.4.

5. Is it possible to improve classification results using approaches to optimizing the feature space? See: section 5.2.5.

Since PMRC and BMRC can be seen as opposites (cf. their properties in section 4.3), they are considered to provide credible answers to the questions above.

5.2.1 CLASSIFIER CHOICE

A classifier algorithm is chosen using datasets containing only lexical features. Hereby, the intention is the following: if classification results using a particular classifier are significantly higher than classification results using other classifiers this classifier should be used for opinion mining. PMRC datasets and corresponding BMRC datasets are composed in the same manner: a PMRC dataset and its BMRC pendant contain an equal number of features evaluated as a presence vector.

Three classifiers are considered as possible candidates for classification due to their frequent use in emotion recognition: SVM (SMO in the WEKA toolkit), NB, and InfoGain. The InfoGain classifier uses lexical features which IG value is greater than 0.

Figure 25 and Figure 26 show the classification results using different classifiers (SMO, InfoGain, NB).

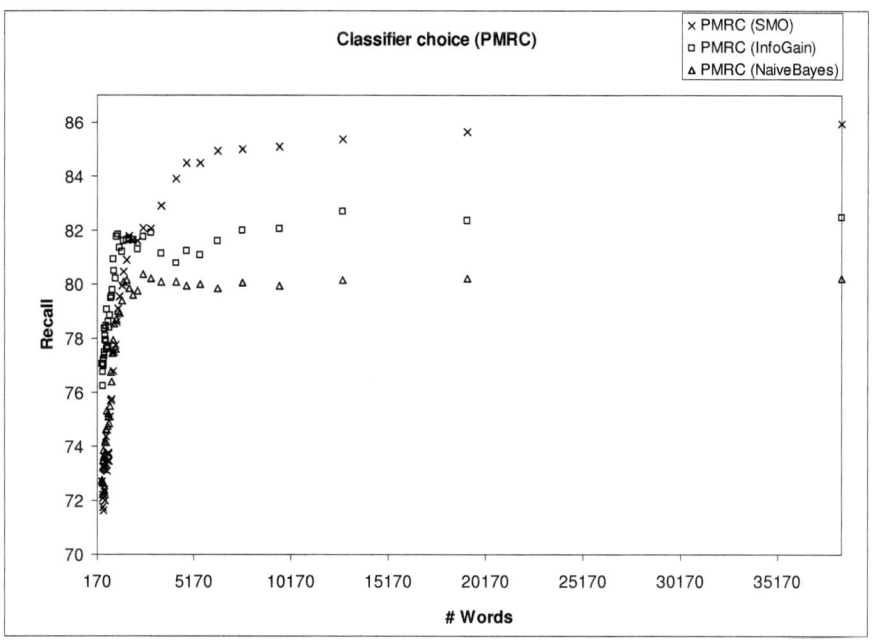

Figure 25: Classifier choice in PMRC

The *#Words* axis shows the number of unigrams extracted from the PMRC frequency list; the *Recall* axis presents the calculated recall value (%).

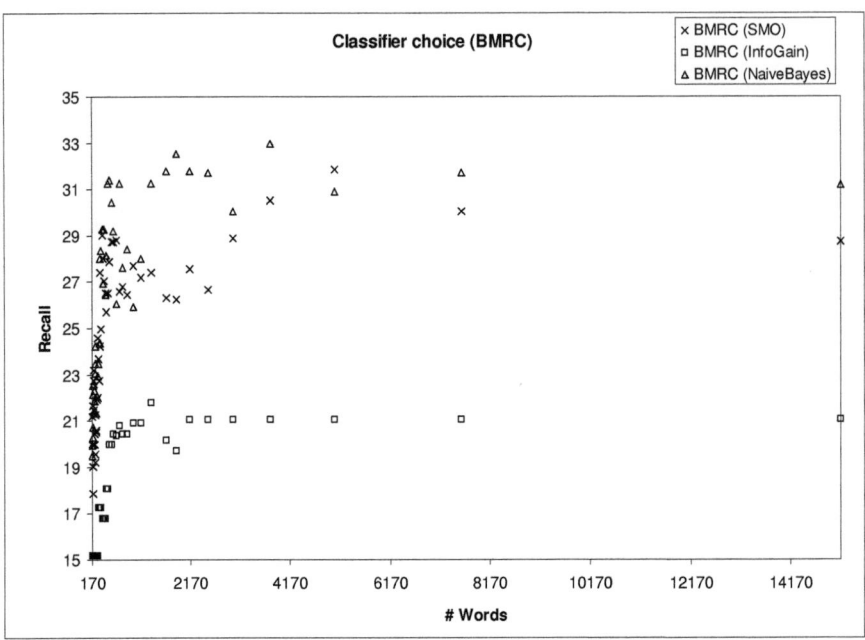

Figure 26: Classifier choice in BMRC

The *#Words* axis shows the number of unigrams extracted from the BMRC frequency list; the *Recall* axis presents the calculated recall value.

There is no clear vote on what classifier calculates the best results: in PMRC, the recall value of 86% is yielded using SVM; the recall value of 82.7% is yielded using InfoGain; the recall value of 80.35% is yielded using NB. Hence, the maximal recall value corresponds to SVM. In BMRC in contrast, the recall value of 31.85% is yielded using SVM, the recall value of 21.78% is yielded using InfoGain, the recall value of 32.96% is yielded using NB. The maximal recall value corresponds to NB.

What classifier is more beneficial for sensing affect? There is no consensus. However, this thesis decided in favour of SVM since it yields high classification results in both corpora and the data mining issues as the classifier choice are outside the scope of this thesis.

5.2.2 LEXICAL FEATURE EVALUATION

The lexical features can be evaluated as a frequency vector, as a presence vector and as a reciprocal frequency vector (cf. section 5.1.1.3). This thesis chooses a particular evaluation method that will be applied in further experiments in order to reduce computational complexity. Hereby, the intention is the following: if classification results using a particular evaluation method are significantly higher than other evaluation methods then the feature values should be evaluated using this method.

Figure 27 compares methods of feature evaluation methods using PMRC.

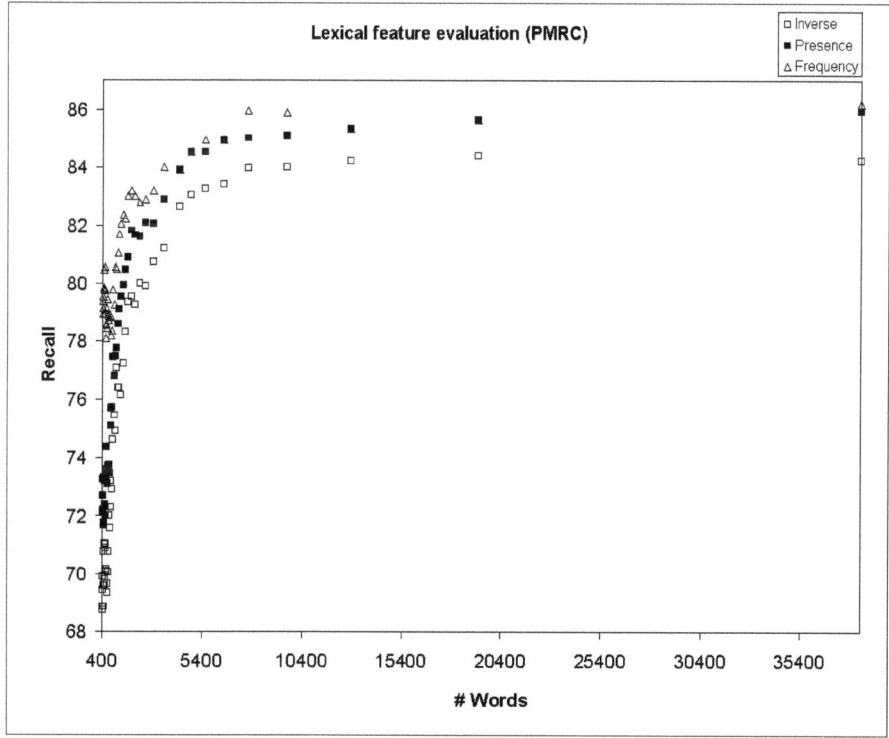

Figure 27: Lexical feature evaluation in PMRC

The *#Words* axis shows the number of unigrams extracted from the PMRC frequency list, the *Recall* axis presents the calculated recall value (%). The maximal recall value of 84.4% is obtained using datasets with features evaluated as an inverse frequency vector, the maximal recall value of

85.95% is calculated using datasets with features evaluated as a presence vector, the maximal recall value of 86.2% is yielded using datasets with features evaluated as a frequency vector. Hence, the best feature evaluation method is the frequency method.

Figure 28 compares methods of feature evaluation using BMRC.

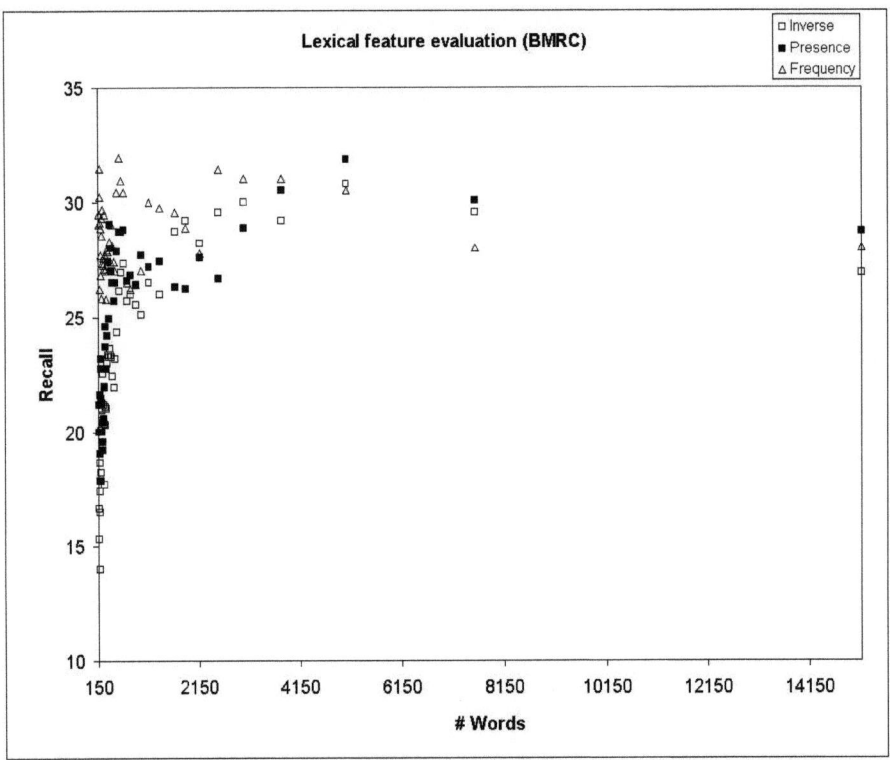

Figure 28: Lexical feature evaluation in BMRC

The *#Words* axis shows the number of unigrams extracted from the BMRC frequency list, the *Recall* axis presents the calculated recall value (%). The maximal recall value of 30.81% is yielded using datasets with features evaluated as an inverse frequency vector, the maximal recall value of 31.85% is obtained using datasets with features evaluated as a presence vector, the maximal recall value of 31.93% is calculated using datasets with features evaluated as a frequency vector. Hence, the best feature evaluation method is also the frequency method.

Hence, lexical features should be evaluated as a frequency vector: in PMRC, the best result of classification is 86.2%; in BMRC, the best result of classification is 31.93%. However, we should bear in mind the following: first, the yielded results using the different evaluation methods differ only insignificantly from each other; second, the presence evaluation method has a remarkable advantage over the frequency evaluation method, that is, there is no need to choose a normalization factor such as the length of sentences in words; third, the [Pang et al., 2002] approach claims that the presence evaluation method is superior to opinion mining than the frequency evaluation.

Thus, the presence feature evaluation method is used in this thesis as the default feature evaluation method unless otherwise stated.

5.2.3 Plotting Classification Results

The proposed approach calculates a variety of results using many datasets with combinations of stylometric, deictic and grammatical features. This section describes a heuristic for visualizing the results of datasets with non-lexical features.

In order to facilitate comprehensibility of results, the proposed visualization heuristic arranges the results in a monotonically increasing row. Hereby, it distinguishes the order of features participating in the classified datasets and assumes that the chosen feature order defines the importance of particular features in classification.

Roughly described, the heuristic defines randomly a particular feature order; composes a list with all feature combinations; assigns each feature combination a number on the basis of the chosen feature order; calculates classification results using the dataset with feature combinations; plots the acquired results. Visualized results are inspected manually, and if the visualization function can not be considered to be monotonically increasing, the feature order is varied. This process repeats until a feature order is found that meets the monotonicity requirement.

A set of combinations of elements is defined in combinatorial mathematics as a sum of un-ordered collections of unique sizes. The number of un-ordered combinations (each of size k) from a set of size n equals the binomial coefficient ([Graham et al., 1992])

$$C_k^n = \binom{n}{k} = \frac{n!}{k!(n-k)!} \tag{18}$$

and the sum of binomial coefficients is

$$2^n = \sum_{k=0}^{n} C_k^n \qquad (19)$$

For instance, a set of combinations of 10 grammatical features is a sum of a subset of size 1 containing 10 elements, a subset of size 2 containing 45 elements, and so on, overall 1,023 feature combinations.

Note that the formula (19) considers combinations of all lengths and also of the zero length ($k=0$). However, $k>0$ and $k=0$ has to be excluded from further consideration. Since combination lengths are always greater than 0, the case $k=0$

$$C_0^n = \binom{n}{0} = 1 \qquad (20)$$

have to be extracted from formula (19) yielding the total amount of combinations χ

$$\chi = \sum_{k=1}^{n} C_k^n = 2^n - 1 \qquad (21)$$

where n is the number of features participating in visualization.

This thesis defines the visualization function f mathematically as

$$f: \{1,..., \chi\} \to \{0..1\} \qquad (22)$$

where function f maps combination numbers in the set $\{1,...,\chi\}$ onto results in the set $\{0..1\}$. Resolved, the visualization function f is

$$f: \{1,..., 2^n-1\} \to \{0..1\} \qquad (23)$$

Particular feature combinations have to be numbered. For numbering, the following heuristic is applied: each combination K containing feature elements $F_m...F_k$ is assigned a number i that can be represented as a binary consisting of n bits where each bit shows the presence (value *1*) or absence (value *0*) of a particular feature in the feature combination K. Hence, the binary number i_2 is calculated as follows:

$$i_2 = b_n... b_1 b_0 \qquad (24)$$

where bit $b_m = 1$ if $F_m \in K$, and 0 otherwise. Note that power 2 plays a significant role in numbering.

The following algorithm plots the visualization function f:

1. Choose features participating in visualization. Compose the list of un-ordered feature combinations l having the size according to the formula (21).

2. Extract a feature combination K from the list l and number it as the integer i according to the formula (24);

3. Compose and classify a dataset with a feature combination K yielding the recall value r. For instance, compose a dataset with grammatical features and classify it using SVM yielding the recall value $r=SVM(K)$;

4. Plot the point $r = f(i)$.

5. If the list l is not empty, extract the next feature combination and go to step 2. Otherwise, continue.

6. Inspect the resulting plot manually and refine the chosen feature order in order to meet the monotonicity requirement. If necessary, go to step 1.

For example, grammatical features are initially ordered as *299 300a 300b 300c 301 302 303a 303b 303c 304-305* in the sequence of narration in section 5.1.3. $1,023=2^{10}-1$ datasets with a particular combination of grammatical features are composed and numbered according to the formula (24). The dataset with one feature {*299*} is numbered as 512 or 1000000000_2, the dataset with one feature {*300a*} is numbered as 256 or 0100000000_2, ..., the dataset with two features {*299, 300a*} is numbered as 768 or 1100000000_2, the dataset with two features {*299, 300b*} is numbered as 640 or 1010000000_2,... The datasets with feature combination *301 302 303a 303c 304-305* is numbered as 0000111011_2 where each *1* represents a feature present in the feature combination (*301* for the first *1*, *302* for the second *1*, and so on). Binary number 0000111011_2 corresponds to $59_{10} = 2^5+2^4+2^3+2^1+2^0$ (Figure 29).

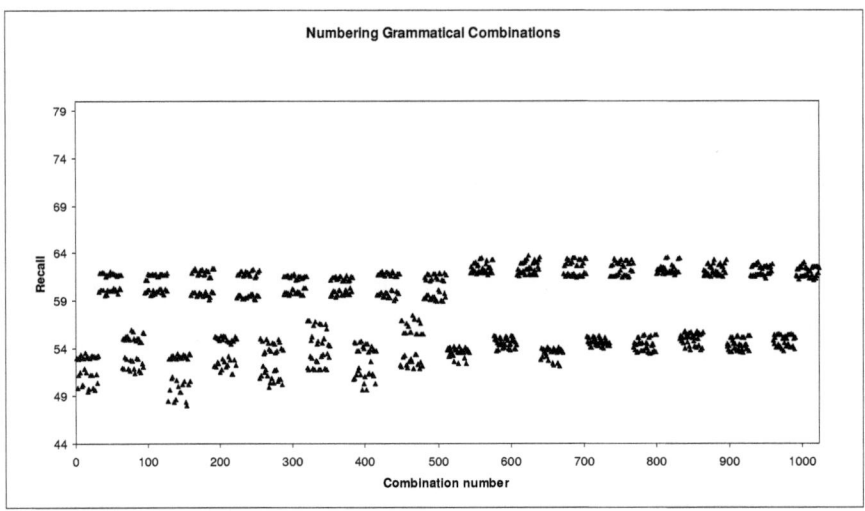

Figure 29: Numbering Grammatical Combinations in PMRC

The *Combination number* axis shows the number i (the number of a feature combination) numbered using the *301 304-305 299 300a 300b 300c 302 303a 303b 303c* feature order. The *Recall* axis presents the recall value of the dataset with the corresponding feature combination (%).

Points in Figure 29 build a periodic, not monotonically increasing function indicating that the feature order chosen for numbering combinations has to be rearranged. The most distinctive period of oscillations is 64 corresponding to the power 6 of 2. Hence, the rightmost feature (*304-305*) and the 6th feature (*301*) have to be exchanged. Combinations are renumbered according to the changed feature order and the classification results are visualized yielding further oscillations, however, of minor intensity. After a similar renumbering of feature combinations, a data series is yielded that can be considered as monotonically increasing (Figure 30).

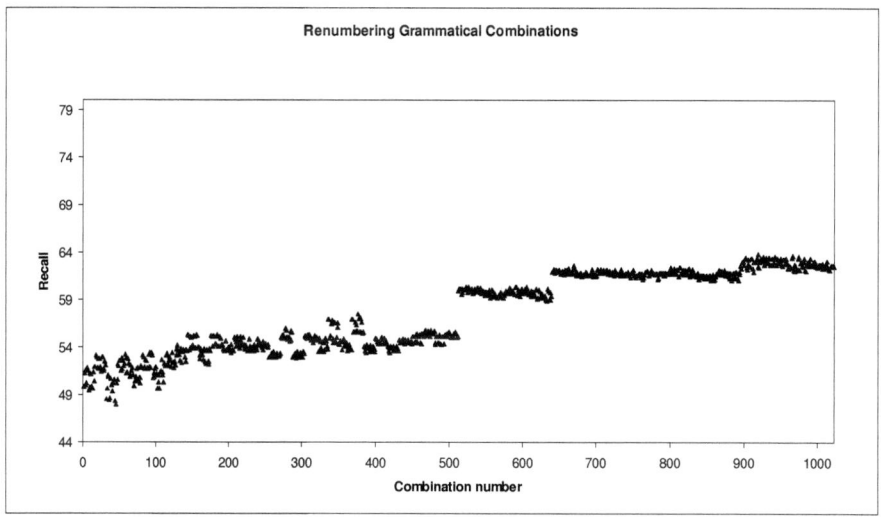

Figure 30: Renumbering Grammatical Combinations in PMRC

Figure 30 shows an almost monotonically increasing data series of classification results in PMRC using the feature order *301 304-305 299 300a 300b 300c 302 303a 303b 303c*.

5.2.4 FEATURE VALUE NORMALIZATION

A typical question of data mining is the issue concerning normalization of feature values: should feature values be normalized or not? For instance, the values of lexical features can be normalized by dividing their counts through the number of words in a sentence or through the number of sentences in a classified text. This thesis examines if normalization of feature values yields better classification results. In other words, the intention is the following: if it is possible to show that classification results *using* normalized feature values are significantly higher than the classification results *without* normalization of feature values then the feature values should be normalized.

To explore this issue, classification results of datasets with normalized features and classification results of datasets with non-normalized features are compared. This thesis examines normalization of values using datasets with deictic features without stopwords. It is done for the following reasons: first, deictic features represent per se very often words and possibly participate in every classified text what implies that normalization can directly influence classification results; second, stopwords are excluded from further consideration since they are included in the set of deictic features; third, the number of combinations of deictic features without stopwords (31) is low what significantly facilitates comparison.

The datasets containing deictic features without stopwords ($31=2^5-1$ files) are composed from combinations of 5 deictic features (demonstratives as determiners, demonstratives as pronouns, time references, place references, forms of the third person). The feature values are evaluated as counts and if necessary normalized through the number of sentences (Figure 31).

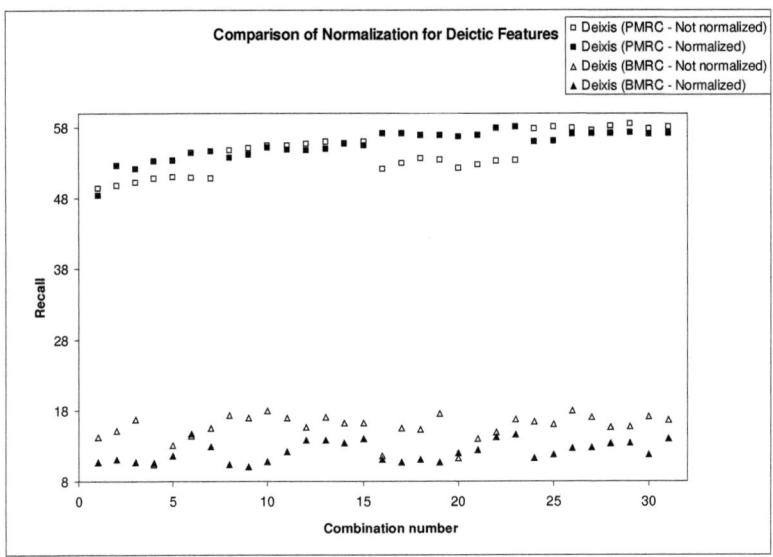

Figure 31: Normalized/non-normalized values of deictic features

The *Combination number* axis shows the number of the deictic combination in the *placereferences formsthirdperson demonstratives pronouns timereferences* feature order. The *Recall* axis presents the corresponding recall value (%). Normalization is yielded through division through the number of sentences in the review text of the corresponding corpora (PMRC, BMRC).

Noteworthy that datasets with the normalized feature values in both corpora can be outperformed by datasets with the non-normalized feature values, and otherwise. Hence, clear answer to the normalization issue is not evident and therefore further experiments in this thesis are performed without normalization of feature values.

5.2.5 OPTIMIZING THE FEATURE SPACE

Previous sections discussed approaches to feature extraction that described methods for composing the feature space. This section explains methods that optimize classification results by reducing the feature space.

The task of feature space optimization can be understood as a task of of selecting/eliminating features that scored best/worst ranks respectively. Hereby, features can be ranked, for instance, using GainRatio, ChiSquared, IG, OneR, ReliefF, SymmetricalUncert, SVMAttributeEval evaluation methods ([Witten & Frank, 2005]). This thesis performed experiments on optimization of feature space as follows: the features were selected/eliminated that yielded the highest/lowest ranking and the datasets containing these features were classified using SVM. However, such optimization did not reveal improvement of classification results. Thus, this thesis performs optimization of the feature space in other manner. It uses "brute force" to find selected/eliminated features without consideration of feature ranks: the proposed optimization approaches select or eliminate features by detecting features which selection/elimination actually improves classification results.

Since classification of datasets using the lexical features yields the best results in all corpora (cf. section 5.5), this thesis examines optimizing the space of lexical features. In the following, two optimizing heuristics are introduced: the forward selection heuristic (FSH) and the backward elimination heuristic (BEH).

5.2.5.1 Forward Selection Heuristic

Lexical features can be evaluated using different methods, for instance, as a frequency vector or as a presence vector. Theoretically in the standard optimization method, the feature evaluation method is chosen prior to optimization: first, optimization begins with a choice of a feature evaluation method; second, a feature from the optimized dataset is selected and evaluated corresponding to the chosen feature evaluation method; the feature is added to the resulting dataset if this addition improves classification results; a next feature is selected and so on. In contrast, the proposed heuristic to forward selection (FSH) chooses a feature evaluation method dynamically whilst optimizing:

1. Choose an optimized dataset o where FSH has to be conducted, for instance, the dataset with the complete set of 2,033 unigrams in the SAL corpus ($n=1$). Create the empty resulting dataset $d=empty$; set the baseline recall value $r_0=0$.

2. Select the first feature $f=f_0$ (e.g. the most frequent unigram) in the optimized dataset o.

3. Calculate recall values r_f, r_p, r_i using dataset d with feature f evaluated according to the frequency method (f), or the presence method (p), or the inversed frequency method (i) respectively.

4. Calculate the maximum recall value $r_{max}=\max(r_f, r_p, r_i)$.

5. If r_{max} increases after adding the feature ($r_{max} > r_0$) update r_0 with the calculated recall value ($r_0 = r_{max}$'); add feature f to d.

6. Select the next feature from the optimized dataset o as feature f and continue with step 3.

7. If f was the last feature, return resulting dataset d.

Note that FSH has low computational costs and thus can be applied to datasets with many features. For example, FSH optimized in a reasonable time the feature space of the dataset with all 2,033 lexical features in SAL ($n=1$).

5.2.5.2 Backward Elimination Heuristic

Feature space optimization can be done using the backward elimination heuristic (BEH) as follows:

1. Choose the optimized dataset o. Classify this dataset using, for example, SVM and calculate the baseline recall value $r_0=SVM(o)$. Set the resulting dataset $d=o$.

2. Construct a priority queue[37] for storing priorities of features/feature pairs. The heuristic for calculating priorities is shown below. Save the maximal priority value in the variable σ_{max}.

---

[37] *Priority queue* is an abstract data type: a collection of elements each associated with a particular priority where elements of the priority queue are extracted in the order of the specified priority. For instance, the priority queue <(el1, pr1), (el2, pr2), (el3, pr3)> contains three element pairs: element *el1* is associated with priority *pr1*, element *el2* is associated with priority *pr2*, element el3 is associated with priority *pr3*. Elements of this priority queue are extracted in the order <el3, el1, el2> if *pr3>pr1>pr2*.

3. Extract a feature or a feature pair from the priority queue having the highest priority σ (the candidate c for elimination) and remove c from the priority queue. Eliminate the candidate c from dataset d and classify the resulting dataset yielding the classification recall value r'.

4. If the classification recall value r' improves after the elimination ($r' > r_0$) update r_0 with the calculated recall value ($r_0 = r'$) and use dataset d without the candidate c in further experiments.

5. If f is the last feature in the priority queue, return resulting dataset d. Otherwise, continue with step 3.

The heuristic for constructing the priority queue corresponding to step 2 of the above algorithm is described as follows:

1. Compose a list with all features and an un-ordered collection of feature pairs from the optimized dataset o.

2. Compose the counts' sequence of a particular feature/feature pair containing the numbers of occurrences of this feature/feature pair in instances of a particular class. For example, the feature *the* occurs, typically for a stopword, occurs in all instances of the dataset BMRC-27: in each group of 25 instances from 4-stars-rating to 1-star-rating, in 30 instances that are annotated with 1/2 star, in 10 instances annotated with 0 stars. Hence, feature *the* yields the counts' sequence <25, 25, 25, 25, 25, 25, 25, 30, 10>; the feature pair *the-until* occurs in 15 instances annotated as 4-stars, 2 instances annotated as 3.5-stars, 4 instances with 3 stars, 2 instances with 2.5 stars, 2 instances with 2 stars, 3 instances with 1.5 stars, 5 instances with 1 star, 5 instances with 0.5 star, 2 instances with 0 stars yielding the counts' sequence <15, 2, 4, 2, 2, 3, 5, 5, 2>.

Note that counts' sequences do not contain zero elements. Empirically revealed that such absence improves optimization results. For instance, the counts' sequence for the feature pair *memorable-release* is <6, 1, 1> corresponding to the number of occurrences of this feature pair in the instances of classes 3.5 stars, 3 stars, 1 stars respectively. The counts (0 values) for the rest classes (4 stars, 2.5 stars, 2 stars, 1.5 stars, 0.5 stars, 0 stars) are not present in the counts' sequence.

3. Calculate probabilities' sequence for each feature/feature pair using the counts' sequences and use the standard deviation $\sigma(f|fp)$ of the resulting probabilities' sequence as the priority value

$$\sigma(f|fp) = \sqrt{\frac{1}{N} \sum_{i=1}^{N} [p(f|fp)_i - \overline{p}(f|fp)]^2} \qquad (25)$$

where N is the number of emotional classes in instances that contain non-zero values of the feature f or feature pair fp; $p(f|fp)_i$ is the probability that instances of the dataset containing the feature f or feature pair fp belong to the class i; $\overline{p}(f|fp)$ is the average value of classes' probabilities.

For instance, the probabilities' sequence for feature *the* is calculated through division of the counts' sequence by 215 — the sum of the counts' sequence — yielding the probabilities' sequence <11.63%, 11.63%, 11.63%, 11.63%, 11.63%, 11.63%, 11.63%, 13.95%, 4.65%>. The probabilities' sequence for the feature pair *the-until* is calculated through division of the distribution sequence by 40 — the sum of the counts' sequence — yielding the probabilities' sequence <37.5%, 5%, 10%, 5%, 5%, 7.5%, 12.5%, 12.5%, 5%>. Hence, the standard deviation σ of the probabilities' sequence of the feature *the* is σ(*the*) = 0.0254, the standard deviation σ of the probabilities' sequence of the feature pair *the-until* is σ(*the-until*) = 0.1039. The probabilities' sequence for the feature pair *memorable-release* is <75%, 12.5%, 12.5%>; the standard deviation σ(*memorable-release*) = 0.3608.

4. Add feature f or feature pair fp to the priority queue using the value σ as priority. Note that since counts' sequences providing the basis for calculation of standard deviations can be equal, the values of calculated standard deviation can be also equal. For instance, since the values of the features *the* and *a* representing the stopwords are greater than 0, they have the same probabilities' sequence and consequently the same priority σ = 0.0254. Hence, the priority queue contains two elements that represent the features *the* and *a* added in the LIFO[38] order.

5. Stop adding features/feature pairs to the priority queue, if σ is less than the empirical $\sigma_{max}/2$. Otherwise, stop adding features/feature pairs if the resulting priority queue contains 2,000 elements.

Note that the constructed priority queue contains a significantly lower number of elements than the number of elements in an unordered collection of the features/feature pairs. For example, BEH can be applied to the dataset BMRC-27 with 561 lexical features. The list of candidates for

---

[38] *LIFO (Last In, First Out)* defines an addition order in a list where elements can only be added or taken off from only one end ([Wikipedia, 2008]).

elimination would contain therefore 561 single feature words and 157,080 unordered feature word pairs. However, according to the condition $\sigma > \sigma_{max}/2$, the number of elimination candidates shrinks to 1,509 and thus the algorithm can be completed in a reasonable time.

Classification of datasets which features/feature pairs are eliminated according to the priority value calculated using formula (25) yields empirically best classification rates. However, there are also other functions that can be used to measure the priority of particular features/feature pairs and, thus, as the basis for the feature elimination. For instance, the probabilistic information entropy measure φ, often used for estimating an information value of particular data, can be used as a priority value. This value is defined in accordance with [Witten & Frank, 2005] as

$$\phi(f|fp) = -\sum_{i=1}^{N} p_i \, log \, p_i \qquad (26)$$

where N is the number of emotional classes, p_i is the probability that instances of the class i containing the feature f or feature pair fp.

Alternatively, features can be eliminated according to their frequency in the studied corpus. For example, the feature pair *to-that* occurs in BMRC 215 times, and the feature *even* occurs in BMRC 154 times. Accordingly, the priority of the feature pair *to-that* can be 215 and the priority of the feature *even* can be 154.

However, performed experiments revealed that the priority according to the information entropy and the frequency formula did not significantly improve classification results and were therefore discarded from further consideration.

Note that BEH has high computational costs and therefore can not be always completed in a reasonable time: in BMRC and CwPR, it was possible to apply BEH to all 49 datasets; in other corpora, for instance, in PMRC such comprehensive study was not feasible. Hence, in PMRC, only one dataset from 49 datasets that yielded acceptably high classification recall value was chosen for optimization using BEH.

5.3 INTERPRETING CLASSIFICATION RESULTS IN EMOTIONAL CORPORA

Typically, the primary aim of classification is to calculate possibly high classification results. Result characterization is provided through data mining measures, for example, through the *recall* measure: the higher is the result, the better is the proposed approach to opinion mining. In the most cases, such standard procedure works perfectly satisfactorily. However, classification results in the emotional domain can be additionally interpreted using special considerations.

First of all, emotional classes can be similar. For instance, a movie review can be annotated by a human using the *zero* label and classified by an automatic approach as a review of the similar *half-star* class. Of course, the difference between the *zero* and *half-star* reviews is significant for a computer but not evident for a human. Is there yet a way to teach a computer-aided approach to interpreting results considering this similarity?

Traditional data mining measures do not consider costs of misclassification of emotional corpora. Thus, even if an approach to emotion recognition misclassifies a *half-star*-review as a *zero-stars*-review, a computer detects this misclassification as a fact that the calculated data mining result (*zero*) is not equal to the expected result (*half-star*). However, the slight difference between the expected and calculated classes, tolerable and evident for a human, is not apparent for a computer. Is there yet a way to teach a computer-aided approach to interpret results using misclassification costs?

Finally, data mining measures do not consider the number of emotional classes when interpreting classification results. For example, an approach to emotion recognition classifies a corpus with weblogs annotated with 2 classes (e.g. positive/negative) and yields the high recall value of 85.95% whereas classification of a corpus with 9 classes (e.g. movie reviews annotated from 0 stars to 9 stars) yields the recall value of only 34.22%. Does it mean the utilized classification approach yields a remarkably good result in the first case (a high recall value of 85.95%) and fails in the second case (a low recall value of 34.22%)? Is it actually fair? No. Correspondingly, is there yet a way to teach a computer-aided approach to interpret results considering the number of classification classes?

In order to answer the questions above, this thesis presents different interpretation measures that can be utilized insofar: the first measure considers similarity between classification classes; the second measure relies on classification success value under consideration of psychological plausibility and the costs of misclassification; the third approach computes a success measure under consideration of the number of analyzed classes in the scrutinized corpus.

5.3.1 CLASSES-SIMILARITY EVALUATION MEASURE

Emotional classes used in emotion recognition can be semantically similar. It means that the difference between emotional classes is not always evident: particular texts can represent one emotional class but also, equally well, a similar class.

In order to interpret classification results more realistically, the semantic similarity between emotional classes can be utilized. Hereby, the following intuition underlies interpretation of classification results: the confusion matrices corresponding to the yielded results can be adjusted corresponding to the similarity between classes. After adjusting, the result matrix can be used for calculating the class-similarity measure in the same manner as calculating traditional data mining measure, for instance, the recall value.

For example, the proposed statistical approach classifies reviews in BMRC. The result below is specified as a confusion matrix corresponding to classification result of the dataset with 5,056 unigrams ($n=3$). Unigrams are evaluated using the presence evaluation method; the utilized classifier is SVM (Table 13).

$$\begin{pmatrix} 0 & 8 & 1 & 1 & 0 & 0 & 0 & 0 & 0 \\ 0 & 20 & 6 & 4 & 0 & 0 & 0 & 0 & 0 \\ 0 & 11 & 4 & 8 & 2 & 0 & 0 & 0 & 0 \\ 0 & 10 & 6 & 7 & 1 & 0 & 1 & 0 & 0 \\ 0 & 5 & 3 & 1 & 7 & 3 & 2 & 4 & 0 \\ 0 & 1 & 1 & 1 & 6 & 8 & 6 & 2 & 0 \\ 0 & 0 & 1 & 3 & 3 & 5 & 8 & 4 & 1 \\ 0 & 0 & 0 & 1 & 2 & 4 & 8 & 7 & 3 \\ 0 & 1 & 0 & 0 & 1 & 0 & 3 & 6 & 14 \end{pmatrix}$$

Table 13: 9-classes confusion matrix

This confusion matrix corresponds to the recall value of 31.85%. Now this thesis proposes an approach to calculating the class-similarity evaluation measure: evidently, adjacent emotional classes are similar, for example, a *half-star* class and the *zero* class. Thus, the 9-classes confusion matrix can be transformed in a 5-classes result matrix by calculating the elements of the 5-classes in the manner that reflect the semantic similarity between emotional classes (Table 14).

$$\begin{vmatrix} c_{11} & c_{21} & c_{31} & c_{41} & c_{51} & c_{61} & c_{71} & c_{81} & c_{91} \\ c_{12} & c_{22} & c_{32} & c_{42} & c_{52} & c_{62} & c_{72} & c_{82} & c_{92} \\ c_{13} & c_{23} & c_{33} & c_{43} & c_{53} & c_{63} & c_{73} & c_{83} & c_{93} \\ c_{14} & c_{24} & c_{34} & c_{44} & c_{54} & c_{64} & c_{74} & c_{84} & c_{94} \\ c_{15} & c_{25} & c_{35} & c_{45} & c_{55} & c_{65} & c_{75} & c_{85} & c_{95} \\ c_{16} & c_{26} & c_{36} & c_{46} & c_{56} & c_{66} & c_{76} & c_{86} & c_{96} \\ c_{17} & c_{27} & c_{37} & c_{47} & c_{57} & c_{67} & c_{77} & c_{87} & c_{97} \\ c_{18} & c_{28} & c_{38} & c_{48} & c_{58} & c_{68} & c_{78} & c_{88} & c_{98} \\ c_{19} & c_{29} & c_{39} & c_{49} & c_{59} & c_{69} & c_{79} & c_{89} & c_{99} \end{vmatrix} \Rightarrow \begin{vmatrix} c_{11}+c_{12}+ & c_{13}+c_{14}+ & c_{15}+c_{16}+ & c_{17}+c_{18}+ & c_{19}+c_{29} \\ c_{21}+c_{22} & c_{23}+c_{24} & c_{25}+c_{26} & c_{27}+c_{28} & \\ c_{31}+c_{32}+ & c_{33}+c_{34} & c_{35}+c_{36}+ & c_{37}+c_{38}+ & c_{39}+ \\ c_{41}+c_{42} & +c_{43}+c_{44} & c_{45}+c_{46} & c_{47}+c_{48} & c_{49} \\ c_{51}+c_{52}+ & c_{53}+c_{54}+ & c_{55}+c_{56}+ & c_{57}+c_{58}+ & c_{59}+ \\ c_{61}+c_{62} & c_{63}+c_{64} & c_{65}+c_{66} & c_{67}+c_{68} & c_{69} \\ c_{71}+c_{72}+ & c_{73}+c_{74}+ & c_{75}+c_{76}+ & c_{77}+c_{78}+ & c_{79}+c_{89} \\ c_{81}+c_{82} & c_{83}+c_{84} & c_{85}+c_{86} & c_{87}+c_{88} & \\ c_{91}+c_{92} & c_{93}+c_{94} & c_{95}+c_{96} & c_{97}+c_{98} & c_{99} \end{vmatrix}$$

Table 14: 9-classes transformation specification analytically

c_{ij} represents the elements of the 9-classes confusion matrix (to the left) that are utilized for the transformation in the 5-elements matrix as defined by the corresponding formulae (to the right).

Graphically, the performed transformation can be shown on the following example:

$$\begin{vmatrix} 0 & 8 & 1 & 1 & 0 & 0 & 0 & 0 & 0 \\ 0 & 20 & 6 & 4 & 0 & 0 & 0 & 0 & 0 \\ 0 & 11 & 4 & 8 & 2 & 0 & 0 & 0 & 0 \\ 0 & 10 & 6 & 7 & 1 & 0 & 1 & 0 & 0 \\ 0 & 5 & 3 & 1 & 7 & 3 & 2 & 4 & 0 \\ 0 & 1 & 1 & 1 & 6 & 8 & 6 & 2 & 0 \\ 0 & 0 & 1 & 3 & 3 & 5 & 8 & 4 & 1 \\ 0 & 0 & 0 & 1 & 2 & 4 & 8 & 7 & 3 \\ 0 & 1 & 0 & 0 & 1 & 0 & 3 & 6 & 14 \end{vmatrix} \Rightarrow \begin{vmatrix} 28 & 12 & 0 & 0 & 0 \\ 21 & 25 & 3 & 1 & 0 \\ 6 & 6 & 24 & 14 & 0 \\ 0 & 5 & 14 & 27 & 4 \\ 1 & 0 & 1 & 9 & 14 \end{vmatrix}$$

Table 15: 9-classes transformation example

The cells to the left having the same border map onto the cells to the right (thick line, middle line, thin line). The result matrix is utilized further for calculating the classes-similarity evaluation measure δ analogous to calculation of the conventional recall value and yields a value of 59.8%.

Similarly to the 9-classes case in BMRC, the classes-similarity evaluation measure can be calculated for 5 classes in SAL. Two pairs of classes have close resemblance: the high negative and the low negative turns (*high_neg-low_neg*); the high positive and low positive affect segments (*high_pos-low_pos*).

A 5-elements confusion matrix for the maximal classification result in SAL is:

$$\begin{vmatrix} 140 & 10 & 21 & 1 & 10 \\ 14 & 83 & 12 & 0 & 3 \\ 27 & 20 & 56 & 10 & 26 \\ 1 & 2 & 9 & 9 & 2 \\ 16 & 8 & 22 & 4 & 130 \end{vmatrix}$$

Table 16: 5-classes confusion matrix

The recall value of 60.21% corresponding to this confusion matrix is yielded using SVM; features are evaluated as a presence vector. According to the similarity consideration, the 5-classes result can be transformed in a 3-classes result matrix by grouping similar classes (Table 17).

$$\begin{vmatrix} c_{11} & c_{12} & c_{13} & c_{14} & c_{15} \\ c_{21} & c_{22} & c_{23} & c_{24} & c_{25} \\ c_{31} & c_{32} & c_{33} & c_{34} & c_{35} \\ c_{41} & c_{42} & c_{43} & c_{44} & c_{45} \\ c_{51} & c_{52} & c_{53} & c_{54} & c_{55} \end{vmatrix} \Rightarrow \begin{vmatrix} c_{11}+c_{12}+c_{21}+c_{22} & c_{13}+c_{23} & c_{14}+c_{15}+c_{24}+c_{25} \\ c_{31}+c_{32} & c_{33} & c_{34}+c_{35} \\ c_{41}+c_{42}+c_{51}+c_{52} & c_{34}+c_{35} & c_{44}+c_{45}+c_{54}+c_{55} \end{vmatrix}$$

Table 17: 5-classes transformation specification analytically

c_{ij} represents the elements of the 5-classes confusion matrix (to the left) that are utilized for the transformation in the 3-elements matrix as defined by the corresponding formulae (to the right). Graphically, the performed transformation can be shown on the following example:

140	10	21	1	10
14	83	12	0	3
27	20	56	10	26
1	2	9	9	2
16	8	22	4	130

=>

247	33	13
47	56	36
27	31	145

Table 18: 5-classes transformation example

The cells to the left having the same border map onto the cells to the right (thick line, middle line, thin line). The yielded result matrix is utilized for calculating the classes-similarity evaluation measure δ analogous to calculation of the conventional recall value and yields a value of 65.34%.

5.3.2 COST-BASED EVALUATION MEASURE

In order to interpret classification results more realistically, emotion recognition can consider costs of misclassification of emotional texts.

In the following, this thesis deduces a mathematical definition of the cost-based evaluation measure χ. First of all, it defines the cost matrix K as

$$K = \left(\kappa_{ij}|_{\kappa_{ij} \leq 1}\right) \tag{27}$$

where $1 \leq i, j \leq N$; N is the number of classes in the analyzed corpus; k_{ij} is a cost of misclassification of the instance of the class i as an instance of the class j.

Cost matrices can be defined either analytically or empirically. The analytical cost matrix K_a is defined within the scope of this thesis as

$$K_a = \left(\kappa_{ij}|_{\kappa_{ij} = \frac{|i-j|}{N}}\right) \tag{28}$$

where $1 \leq i, j \leq N$; N is the number of classes in the analyzed corpus; k_{ij} is a cost of misclassification of the instance of the class i as an instance of the class j.

For instance, the analytical cost matrix K_a^2 defines according to the formula (28) the costs of misclassification for a 2-classes problem (positive/negative) as

$$K_a^2 = \begin{pmatrix} 0 & 0.5 \\ 0.5 & 0 \end{pmatrix} \tag{29}$$

Hence, the cost of classification of an instance of the positive/negative class as an instance of the positive/negative class respectively equals 0 whereas the cost of misclassification of an instance of the positive/negative class as an instance of the negative/positive class respectively equals 0.5.

The analytical cost matrix K_a^5 defines according to the formula (28) the costs of misclassification for a 5-classes problem as

$$K_a^{-5} = \begin{pmatrix} 0 & 0.2 & 0.4 & 0.6 & 0.8 \\ 0.2 & 0 & 0.2 & 0.4 & 0.6 \\ 0.4 & 0.2 & 0 & 0.2 & 0.4 \\ 0.6 & 0.4 & 0.2 & 0 & 0.2 \\ 0.8 & 0.6 & 0.4 & 0.2 & 0 \end{pmatrix} \qquad (30)$$

The analytical cost matrix K_a^{-9} defines according to the formula (28) the costs of misclassification for a 9-classes problem as

$$K_a^{-9} = \begin{pmatrix} 0 & 0.11 & 0.22 & 0.33 & 0.44 & 0.55 & 0.66 & 0.77 & 0.88 \\ 0.11 & 0 & 0.11 & 0.22 & 0.33 & 0.44 & 0.55 & 0.66 & 0.77 \\ 0.22 & 0.11 & 0 & 0.11 & 0.22 & 0.33 & 0.44 & 0.55 & 0.66 \\ 0.33 & 0.22 & 0.11 & 0 & 0.11 & 0.22 & 0.33 & 0.44 & 0.55 \\ 0.44 & 0.33 & 0.22 & 0.11 & 0 & 0.11 & 0.22 & 0.33 & 0.44 \\ 0.55 & 0.44 & 0.33 & 0.22 & 0.11 & 0 & 0.11 & 0.22 & 0.33 \\ 0.66 & 0.55 & 0.44 & 0.33 & 0.22 & 0.11 & 0 & 0.11 & 0.22 \\ 0.77 & 0.66 & 0.55 & 0.44 & 0.33 & 0.22 & 0.11 & 0 & 0.11 \\ 0.88 & 0.77 & 0.66 & 0.55 & 0.44 & 0.33 & 0.22 & 0.11 & 0 \end{pmatrix} \qquad (31)$$

A cost-based evaluation measure χ'_c for instances of class c is defined as

$$\chi'_c = 1 - \frac{K_c}{I_c} \qquad (32)$$

where $K_c = \sum_{i=1}^{N} \kappa_{ic}$ is a sum of misclassification costs of instances of class c; I_c is the number of instances of class c; $K_c \leq I_c$.

If max_{κ_c} is the maximum cost value for an instance of class c from the cost matrix K, we observe that

$$(1 - max_{\kappa_c}) \leq \chi'_c \leq 1 \qquad (33)$$

Now the cost-based evaluation measure χ'_c for class c is normalized to the range [0..1] yielding the normalized cost-based evaluation measure χ_c for class c as follows

$$(1 - max_{\kappa_c}) \leq \chi'_c \leq 1 \Rightarrow$$
$$0 \leq \chi'_c - (1 - max_{\kappa_c}) \leq 1 - (1 - max_{\kappa_c}) \Rightarrow$$
$$0 \leq \chi'_c - (1 - max_{\kappa_c}) \leq max_{\kappa_c} \Rightarrow$$
$$0 \leq 1 - \frac{1-\chi'_c}{max_{\kappa_c}} \leq 1$$
$$0 \leq \chi_c \leq 1 \qquad (34)$$

Hence,

$$\chi_c = 1 - \frac{K_c}{I_c max_{\kappa_c}} \qquad (35)$$

and the overall cost-based evaluation measure averaged over classes, χ, is

$$\chi = \frac{1}{N}\sum_{c=1}^{N}\chi_c \qquad (36)$$

Sometimes, it is difficult or impossible to provide an analytical formula for defining the cost matrix (28). In such cases, the cost-based evaluation measure can be calculated using an empirical cost matrix. For 2 classes, the empirical cost matrix can be defined as

$$K_e^2 = \begin{pmatrix} 0 & 1 \\ 1 & 0 \end{pmatrix} \qquad (37)$$

Evidently, in the case of 2 classes χ is numerically equal to the recall value that can be verified using the formula (89).

The empirical cost matrix for the 5-classes misclassification can be defined as follows:

$$K_e^5 = \begin{pmatrix} 0 & 0.5 & 1 & 1 & 1 \\ 0.5 & 0 & 1 & 1 & 1 \\ 1 & 1 & 0 & 1 & 1 \\ 1 & 1 & 1 & 0 & 0.5 \\ 1 & 1 & 1 & 0.5 & 0 \end{pmatrix} \qquad (38)$$

An empirical cost-matrix for the 9-classes misclassification can be defined as follows:

$$K_e^{'9} = \begin{pmatrix} 0 & 0.11 & 0.22 & 0.44 & 1 & 1 & 1 & 1 & 1 \\ 0.11 & 0 & 0.11 & 0.22 & 1 & 1 & 1 & 1 & 1 \\ 0.22 & 0.11 & 0 & 0.11 & 1 & 1 & 1 & 1 & 1 \\ 0.44 & 0.22 & 0.11 & 0 & 1 & 1 & 1 & 1 & 1 \\ 1 & 1 & 1 & 1 & 0 & 1 & 1 & 1 & 1 \\ 1 & 1 & 1 & 1 & 1 & 0 & 0.11 & 0.22 & 0.44 \\ 1 & 1 & 1 & 1 & 1 & 0.11 & 0 & 0.11 & 0.22 \\ 1 & 1 & 1 & 1 & 1 & 0.22 & 0.11 & 0 & 0.11 \\ 1 & 1 & 1 & 1 & 1 & 0.44 & 0.22 & 0.11 & 0 \end{pmatrix}$$
(39)

5.3.3 Classes-Number Evaluation Measure

The cost-based evaluation measure relies on costs of misclassification but do not consider the number of analyzed classes. However, it can be beneficial to relate the classification result to the number of analyzed classes, for instance, the result of emotion recognition using 2 classes as opposed to the result of emotion recognition using 9 classes.

In order to evaluate results in connection with the number of classes, this thesis defines the classes-number evaluation function $v(x)$ as follows

$$\nu(x) = a - \frac{b}{x} \qquad (40)$$

where a, b are equation parameters influenced by the number of classes; x is the classification result in the range [0..1], e.g. the recall value.

Note that the function (40) is not linear. Performed experiments showed that a linear function of the form $v(x) = ax + b$ can not be utilized for interpreting results since the yielded classes-number evaluation measures can not be considered to be descriptive.

In order to determine the parameters a, b, two constraints are defined. The first constraint is:

$$v(max) = 100\% \qquad (41)$$

where *max* is the maximum possible value of classification, preferably 100%. This equation defines that the classes-number function is equal to 1 if its argument has the maximal value *max*.

The second constraint that should hold is described by the equation:

$$\nu(min)=0 \qquad (42)$$

where *min* is the minimum value of classification result, for example, meaning that the classes-number function should evaluate to 0 if its argument is a result yielded by chance, i.e. *min* = 1/*N* where *N* is the number of analyzed classes.

Combination of the constraints (41) and (42) yields the following derivation

$$\begin{aligned}\nu(min) = 0 &\Rightarrow a = \tfrac{b}{min} \\ \nu(max) = 1 &\Rightarrow a = 1 + \tfrac{b}{max}\end{aligned} \qquad (43)$$

resulting in

$$\begin{aligned} a &= \tfrac{max}{max-min} = \tfrac{N-1}{N} \\ b &= \tfrac{min*max}{max-min} = \tfrac{1}{N-1} \end{aligned} \qquad (44)$$

Hence, substitution of *a, b* in the equation (40) for 2 classes defines a classes-number evaluation function as

$$v(x) = 2 - \tfrac{1}{x}\big|_{N=2} \qquad (45)$$

Substitution of *a, b* in the equation (40) for 5 classes, defines a classes-number evaluation function as

$$v(x) = 1.25 - \tfrac{0.25}{x}\big|_{N=5} \qquad (46)$$

Substitution of *a, b* in the equation (40) for 9 classes, defines a classes-number evaluation function as

$$v(x) = 1.13 - \tfrac{0.13}{x}\big|_{N=9} \qquad (47)$$

Figure 32 shows the classes-number evaluation functions as a plot.

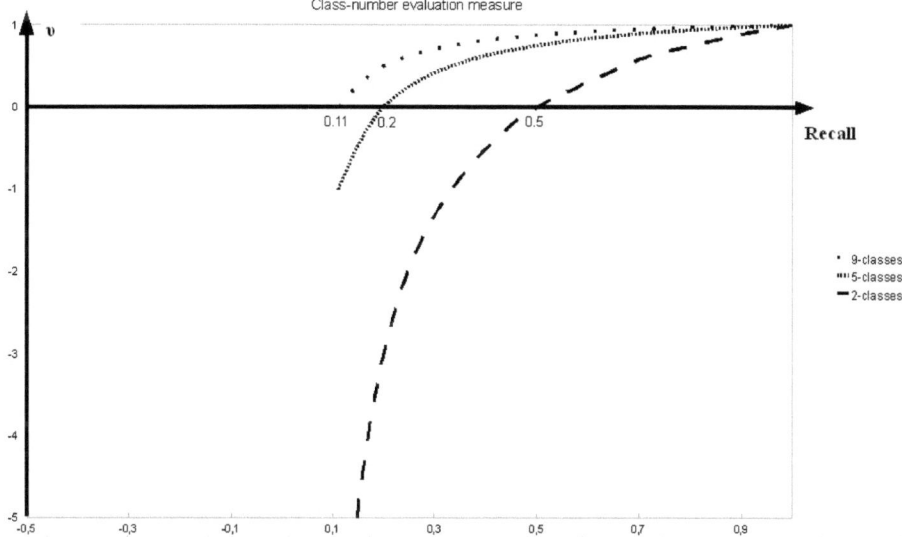

Figure 32: Classes-number evaluation function

The v axis shows the classes-number evaluation measure dependent on the number of classes N ($N=2$, $N=5$, $N=9$); a value of the corresponding recall measure is shown in the *Recall* axis. Note that the values 0.11, 0.2, 0.5 show the minimum values (*min*) representing the choice by chance for corresponding N.

5.4 CLASSIFICATION RESULTS

This section describes classification results yielded by the statistical approach. For tagging and lemmatizing features, the proposed approach uses the probabilistic TreeTagger ([Schmid, 1994]). Since performed experiments did not reveal any significant difference in the recall and precision measures, figures below show only the recall and not the precision measure. The lexical features are evaluated using the presence evaluation method besides datasets with features selected by FSH; the classifier is SVM. The recall value is averaged over classes using the ten-fold classification with stratification.

For better readability, the result diagrams below do not contain data points that can be considered as insignificant, i.e. data points that represent low classification results.

5.4.1 PANG MOVIE REVIEWS CORPUS

As the baseline for assessing opinion mining in PMRC the proposed approach uses the accuracy value of 87.2% from literature.

5.4.1.1 Results Using Lexical Features

Table 19 shows results of opinion mining in PMRC using lexical features.

List	Recall (%)	Lexical features
PMRC list	**85.95**	38,746 ($n=1$)
Lemmatized PMRC list	83.3	19,238 ($n=2$)
BNC list	85.9	91,782 ($n=10$)
Lemmatized BNC list	83.35	27,174 ($n=100$)
DAL list	82.15	8,743 ($n=1$)
Lemmatized DAL list	77.65	5,124 ($n=2$)

Table 19: Maximal results of opinion mining in PMRC using lexical features

The *List* column shows the source of lexical features; the *Recall* column shows the maximal recall value yielded by the dataset with the lexical features; the *Lexical features* column shows the number of lexical features and the parameter n from Table 12 utilized for composing the corresponding dataset. The maximal values are shown in bold.

Figure 33 shows results of opinion mining graphically using six sources of lexical features.

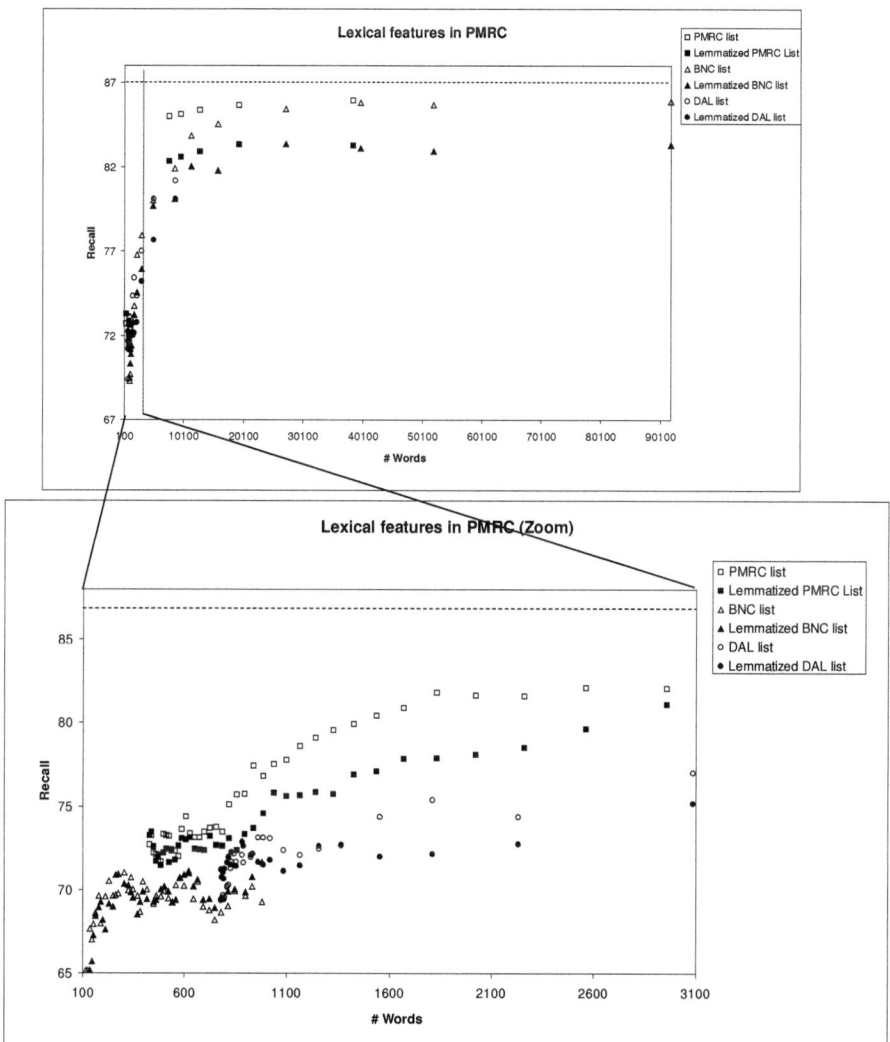

Figure 33: Lexical features in PMRC

The *#Words* axis shows the number of utilized lexical features; the *Recall* axis presents the yielded recall values (%). The dotted horizontal lines correspond to the baseline value of 87.2%.

This thesis performed optimization of the feature space. The results after applying optimization heuristics are shown in the context of classification results of all corpora in Table 29.

5.4.1.2 Results Using Stylometric, Deictic, Grammatical Features

Figure 34 shows results of opinion mining as plot using datasets with stylometric, deictic, grammatical feature combinations.

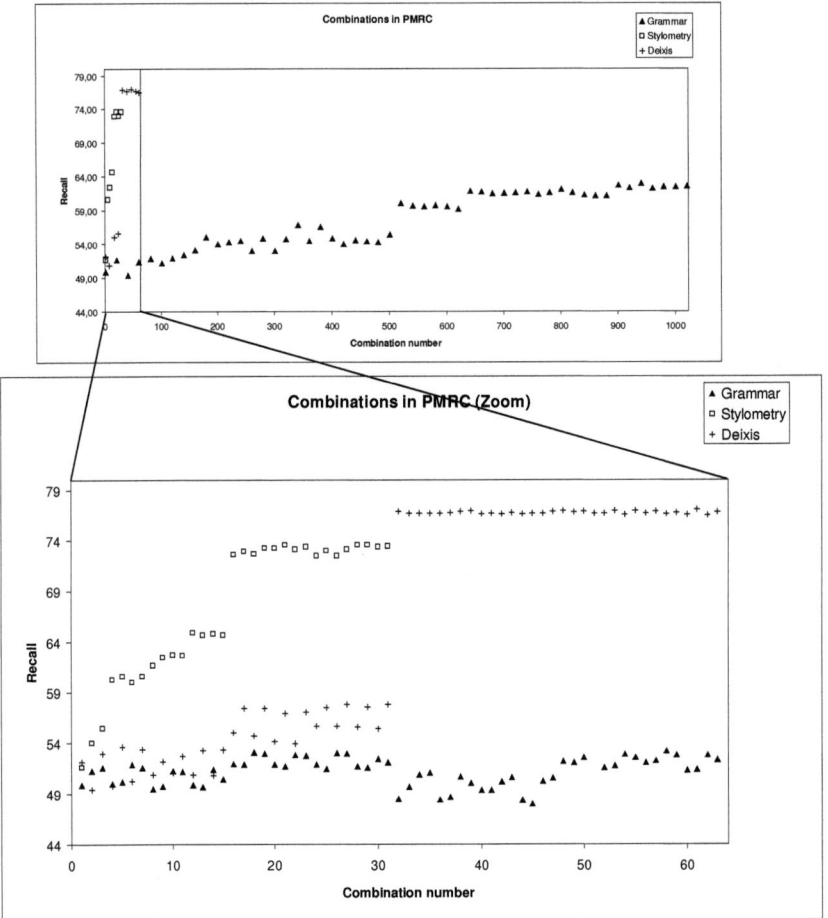

Figure 34: Stylometric, grammatical, deictic features in PMRC

The *Combination number* axis shows the numbers of feature combinations: grammatical feature combinations are numbered using the *301 304-305 299 300a 300b 300c 302 303a 303b 303c* feature order; stylometric feature combinations are numbered using the *digrams letters word_length sdwl sdsl* feature order; deictic feature combinations are numbered using the *stopwords formsthirdperson demonstratives pronouns timereferences placereferences* feature order. The recall value yielded by the dataset with the corresponding feature combination is shown in the *Recall* axis (%). Combination numbers are calculated according to the formula (24). The baseline value of 20% is not shown because of its low value.

Table 20 outlines the results of opinion mining using stylometric, deictic, grammatical features in PMRC.

Feature type	Recall (%)	Features
Stylometric	73.6	digrams; letters; word lengths
Deictic	**77.1**	stopwords; forms third person; demonstratives; pronouns; place references
Grammatical	63.8	299 300 301 303a 303b 303c 304-305

Table 20: Results of opinion mining in PMRC using stylometric, deictic, grammatical features

The *Feature type* column shows the type of features; the *Recall* column shows the maximal recall value yielded by the dataset of the corresponding type; the *Features* column shows the extracted features. The maximal value is shown in bold. Note that all deictic features are present in the maximal deictic feature combination besides the *timereferences* feature.

5.4.2 MULTIMODAL CORPUS WITH SPONTANEOUS DIALOGUES

Emotion recognition in spontaneous dialogues such as dialogues in SAL is a great challenging task due to the properties of dialogue turns: dialogue turns can be short texts (often short sentences or even single words) that do not contain evident signs of emotional meaning, for instance, emotion words. Furthermore, they can contain repetitions and incorrect wordings.

As already mentioned, dialogue turns can be considered as semantically connected. This thesis verifies to what extent the turn history influences results of emotion recognition.

The baseline for opinion mining in SAL is 20% (choice by chance for a 5-classes problem).

5.4.2.1 Results Using Lexical Features

This thesis studies the influence of the history in two stages: in the first stage, the best of 6 sources of lexical features is chosen as a source of lexical features without the history consideration; in the second stage, the chosen source is utilized for composing datasets under consideration of turns' history.

Table 21 shows results of opinion mining in SAL for the first stage (no history).

List	Recall (%)	Lexical features
SAL list	**32.70**	1,019 ($n=2$)
Lemmatized SAL list	31.48	1,019 ($n=2$)
BNC list	30.00	39,697 ($n=50$)
Lemmatized BNC list	32.29	15,781 ($n=250$)
DAL list	31.24	5,124 ($n=2$)
Lemmatized DAL list	31.02	1,259 ($n=8$)

Table 21: Maximal results of emotion recognition in SAL using lexical features (no history)

The *List* column shows the source of lexical features; the *Recall* column shows the maximal recall value yielded by the dataset with lexical features of the corresponding word list (%); the *Lexical features* column shows the number of lexical features and the parameter n from Table 12 utilized for composing the corresponding dataset. The maximal value for all word lists is shown in bold.

Figure 35 shows recall values for the lexical features as a plot.

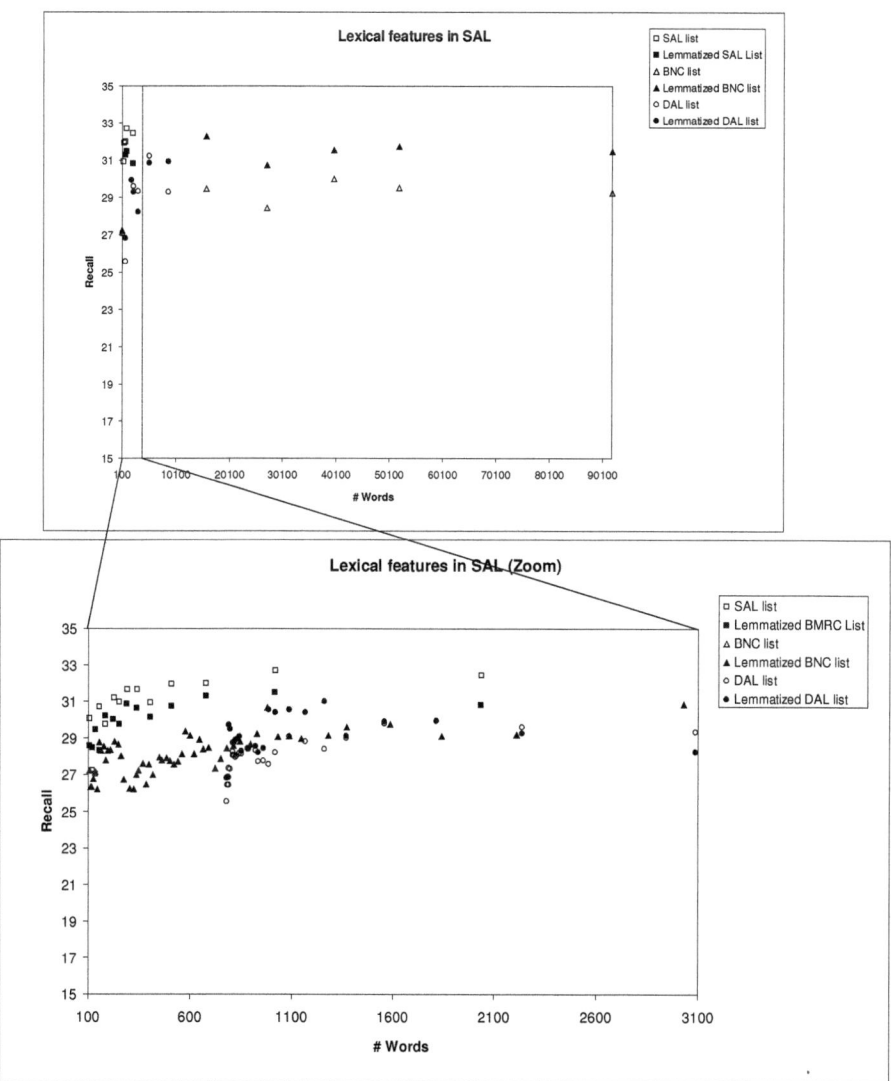

Figure 35: Lexical features in SAL

The *#Words* axis shows the number of utilized lexical features from six word lists, the *Recall* axis presents the calculated recall value (%). The maximal recall result value of 32.70% yields a dataset containing 1,019 unigram features from the SAL frequency list (*n=2*, the half of the frequency list).

Since the highest recall value is calculated using a dataset with the non-lemmatized SAL list, the second stage uses this list as a source of lexical features. Figure 36 shows results of emotion recognition in SAL using the history of dialogue turns.

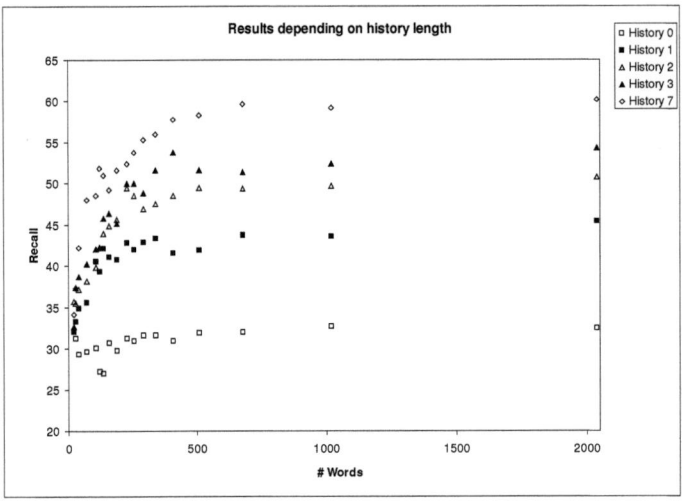

Figure 36: SAL results depending on the history length

The *#Words* axis shows the number of utilized lexical features; the *Recall* axis presents the calculated recall value (%). The baseline value of 20% is invisible because of its low value.

Figure 36 presents results of emotion recognition for the most significant lengths of dialogue history: the data series *History 0* shows classification results without consideration of the dialogue history (using only the text of the turn being classified); the data series *History 1* shows the classification results using the text of the turn being classified in the context of the text of the previous turn in a dialogue, and so on. Note that the yielded results increase monotonically with increase of the length of the history that can be considered as an evidence of the influence of the dialogue history on classification results.

Experiments were performed for history lengths from 0 to 8. However, Figure 36 shows data series of not all history lengths but only the most remarkable. For instance, the data series *History 8* is omitted since its results are lower than the results of the data series for *History 7* for all numbers of lexical features.

Evidently, classification of turns in the context of history 7 yields the best rates (Table 22).

List	Recall (%)	Lexical features
SAL list	**60,21**	2,033 ($n=1$)
Lemmatized SAL list	58.3	2,033 ($n=1$)
BNC list	59.95	91,782 ($n=10$)
Lemmatized BNC list	59.6	91,782 ($n=10$)
DAL list	59.71	8,743 ($n=1$)
Lemmatized DAL list	59.55	2,234 ($n=4$)

Table 22: Maximal results of emotion recognition in SAL using lexical features (history 7)

The *List* column shows the source of lexical features; the *Recall* column shows the maximal recall value yielded by the dataset with lexical features; the *Lexical features* column shows the number of lexical features and the parameter n from Table 12 that was utilized for composing the corresponding dataset.

The maximal recall value of 60.21% yields the dataset containing all lexical features (2,033 features — $n=1$) (shown in bold). The maximal cost-based evaluation measure χ of 0.63 is yielded by the same dataset using the empirical cost matrix $K_e^{'5}$.

5.4.2.2 Results Using Stylometric, Deictic, Grammatical Features

When conducting experiments with stylometric, deictic, grammatical features, this thesis omitted the first stage as in the case of lexical features and started immediately with composition of datasets for the history 7. Table 23 outlines the yielded results of emotion recognition in the context of the history 7.

Feature type	Recall (%)	Features
Stylometric	58.97	standard deviation of word lengths; digrams; word lengths
Deictic	**59.65**	forms third person; stopwords
Grammatical	31.35	299; 300a; 300b; 300c; 301; 303a; 303b; 304-305

Table 23: Results of emotion recognition in SAL using stylometric, deictic, grammatical features

The *Feature type* column shows the type of features; the *Recall* column shows the maximal recall value yielded by the dataset of the corresponding type; the *Features* column shows features utilized in emotion recognition. The maximal value for all feature types is shown in bold.

Figure 37 shows results of emotion recognition graphically using datasets with stylometric, deictic, grammatical feature combinations.

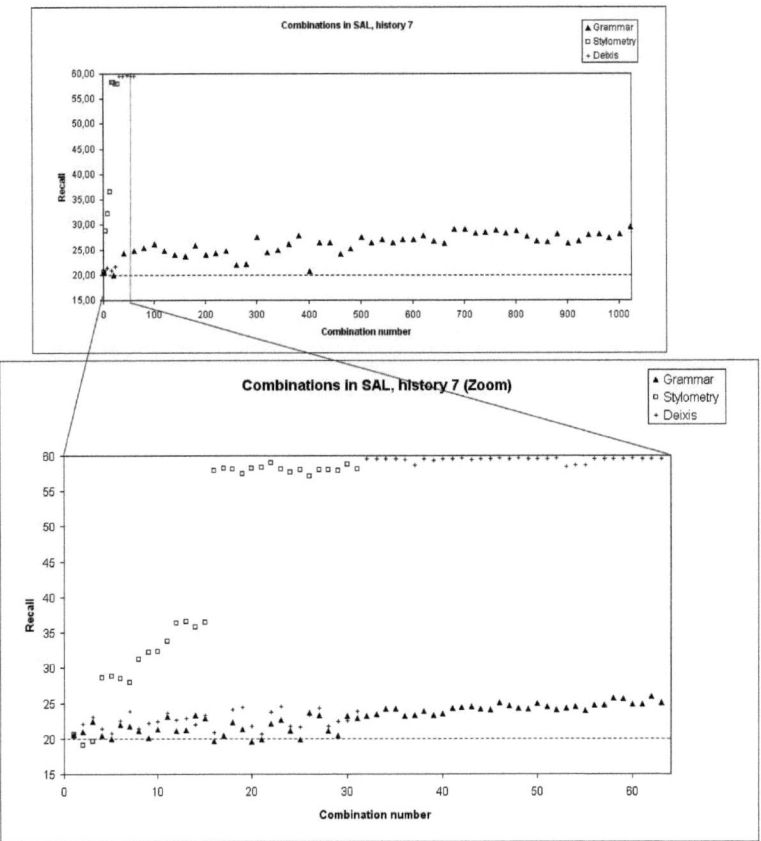

Figure 37: Classification results for history length 7

The *Combination number* axis shows the numbers of a feature combination: grammatical feature combinations are numbered using the *301 304-305 299 300a 300b 300c 302 303a 303b 303c* feature order, stylometric feature combinations are numbered using the *digrams letters word_length sdwl sdsl* feature order, deictic feature combinations are numbered using the *stopwords formsthirdperson demonstratives pronouns timereferences placereferences* feature order. The recall value yielded by the dataset with the corresponding feature combination is shown in the *Recall* axis (%). Combination numbers are calculated according to the formula (24). The dotted horizontal lines in both diagrams correspond to the baseline value of 20%.

5.4.3 Corpus with Product Reviews

The baseline value for classification of reviews in CwPR is 20% as a choice by chance for a 5-classes problem.

5.4.3.1 Results Using Lexical Features

Table 24 shows maximal results of opinion mining in CwPR using lexical features.

List	Recall (%)	Lexical features
CwPR list	51.0	2,813 ($n=5$)
Lemmatized CwPR list	51.33	2,813 ($n=5$)
BNC list	**51.67**	3,029 ($n=2700$)
Lemmatized BNC list	50.00	51,955 ($n=30$)
DAL list	48.67	8,743 ($n=1$)
Lemmatized DAL list	48.00	8,743 ($n=1$)

Table 24: Maximal results of opinion mining in CwPR using lexical features

The *List* column shows the source of lexical features; the *Recall* column shows the maximal recall value yielded by the dataset with lexical features of the corresponding word list (%); the *Lexical features* column shows the number of lexical features and the parameter n from Table 12 utilized for composing the corresponding dataset. The maximal value for all word lists is shown in bold.

Figure 38 shows results of opinion mining in CwPR graphically using datasets with lexical features.

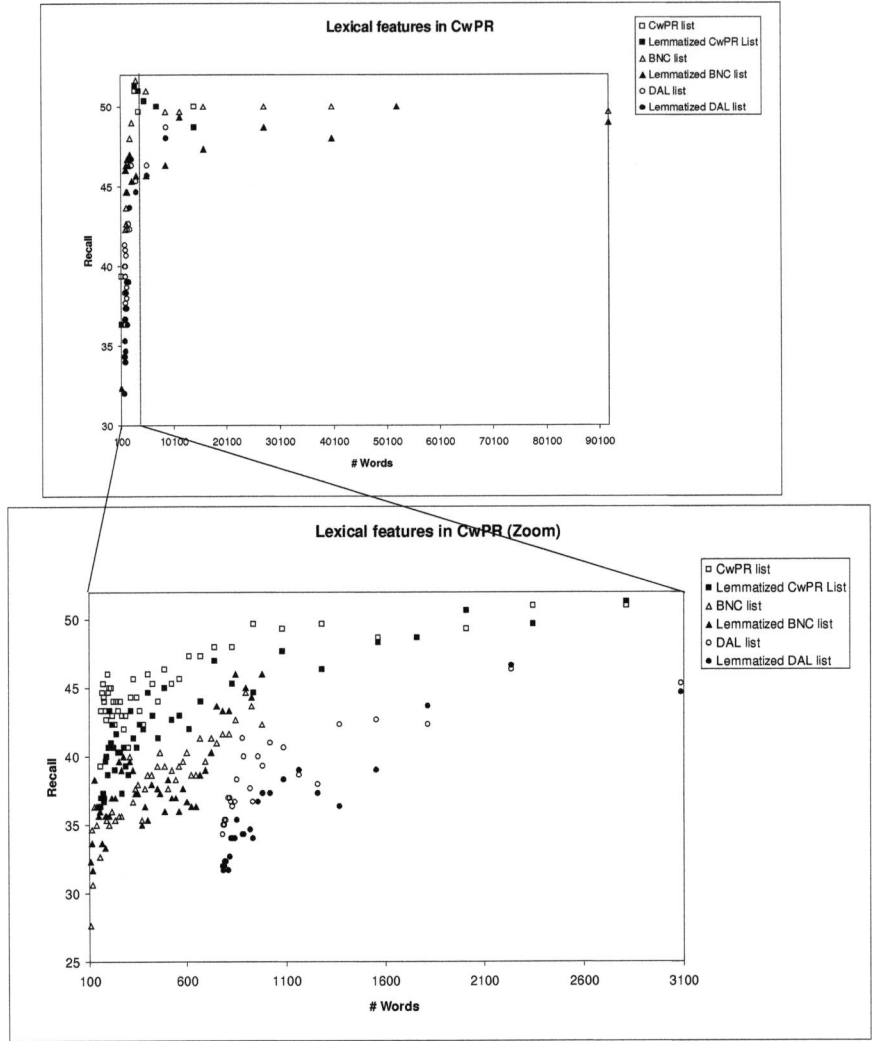

Figure 38: Lexical features in CwPR

The *#Words* axis shows the number of utilized lexical features from six word lists; the *Recall* axis presents the calculated recall value (%). The maximal recall value of 51.89% yields the dataset with 2,344 words from the lemmatized CwPR list (n=6). The baseline value of 20% is invisible because of its low value.

To improve recognitions results, BEH is applied to composed datasets (Figure 39).

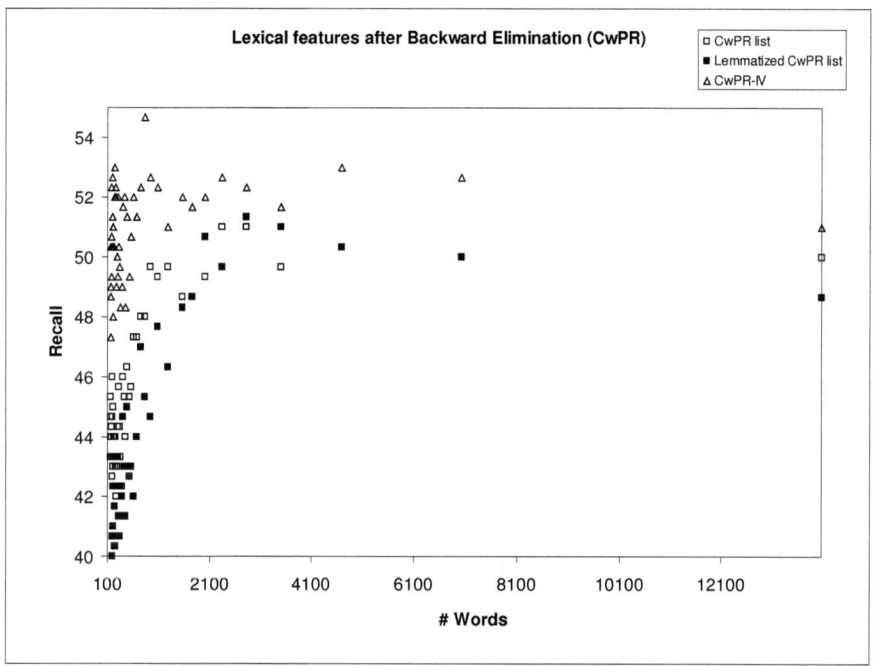

Figure 39: Applying BEH in CwPR

The *CwPR-IV* data series shows recall values after applying BEH. To facilitate comparison with the already yielded results, the plot shows additionally the *CwPR list* data series and the *Lemmatized CwPR list* data series from Figure 38.

The maximal recall value of 54.67% yields the dataset with 803 words ($n=17$) after applying BEH. For the list of eliminated words see Table 29.

5.4.3.2 Results Using Stylometric, Deictic, Grammatical Features

Table 25 outlines the results of opinion mining for datasets with stylometric, deictic, grammatical features in CwPR.

Feature type	Recall (%)	Features
Stylometric	**45.0**	standard deviation sentence length; digrams; letters; word lengths
Deictic	41.0	time references; stopwords
Grammatical	35.67	299; 300b; 300c; 301; 302; 304-305

Table 25: Results of opinion mining in CwPR using stylometric, deictic, grammatical features

The *Feature type* column shows the type of utilized features; the *Recall* column shows the maximal recall value yielded by the dataset with features of the corresponding type (%); the *Features* column describes utilized features. The maximal value for all feature types is shown in bold.

Figure 40 shows results of opinion mining graphically using datasets with stylometric, deictic, grammatical feature combinations.

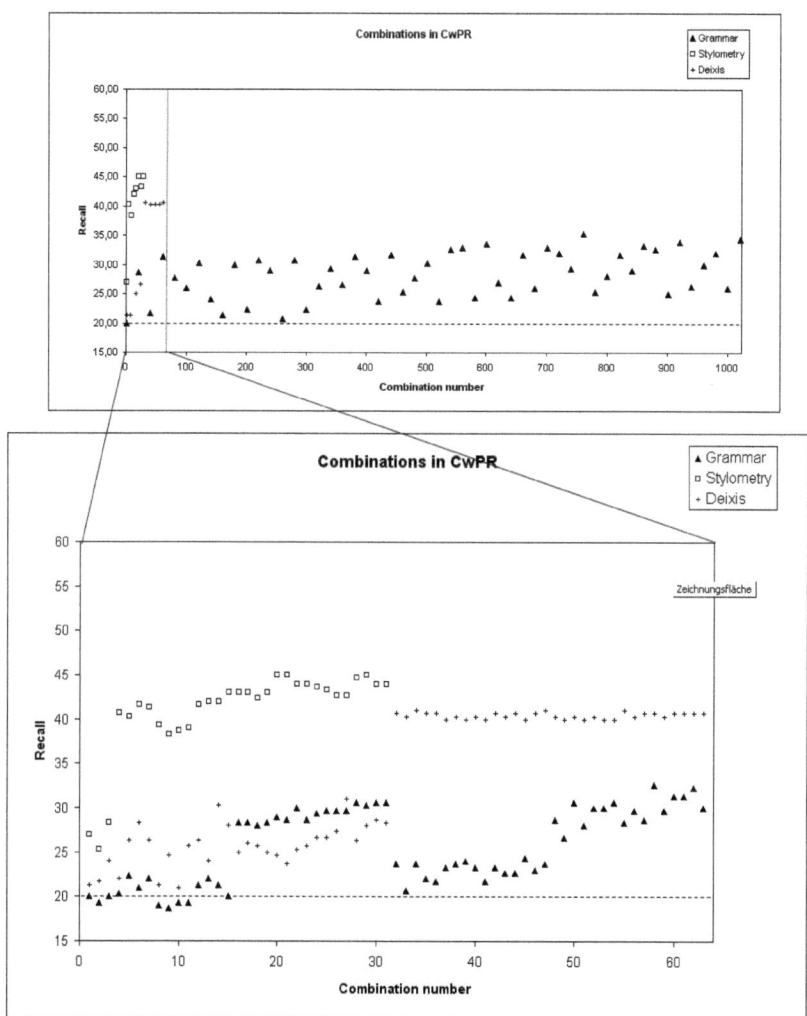

Figure 40: Feature combinations in CwPR

The *Combination number* axis shows grammatical feature combinations numbered using the *301 304-305 299 300a 300b 300c 302 303a 303b 303c* feature order; stylometric feature combinations are numbered using the *digrams letters word_length sdwl sdsl* feature order; deictic feature combinations are numbered using the *stopwords formsthirdperson demonstratives pronouns timereferences placereferences* feature order. The recall value yielded by the dataset with the corresponding feature combination is shown in the *Recall* axis (%). Combination numbers are calculated according to the formula (24).

Note big oscillations of classification rates in the *Grammar* data series indicating a higher importance of the *300c* feature (repetitions) in CwPR than in the other corpora. To get a monotonically increasing data series the feature *301* and the feature *300c* in the feature order are exchanged what yields the feature order <u>*300c*</u> *301 304-305 299 300a 300b 302 303a 303b 303c* (Figure 41).

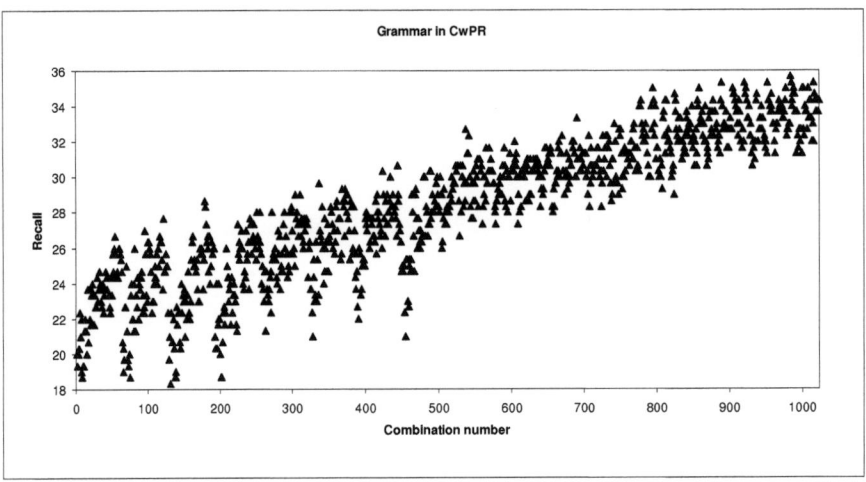

Figure 41: Grammatical combinations in CwPR

Numbering due to the changed feature order yields an almost monotonically increasing data series. Accordingly, the *300c* feature has the highest importance in CwPR that can be explained as follows: repetitions (the *300c* rule) in product reviews are intentional and their use emphasizes special details about the particular product. In this way, lexical drawbacks of product descriptions (incorrect wordings, grammatical mistakes) can be corrected. For instance, a product review that discusses the fastness and the properties of the lens of the camera D70 says *The D70 has a better <u>faster</u> <u>lens</u>, <u>faster</u> EVERYTHING, filters that fit, and wowee, even a <u>lens</u> hood* repeating in one sentence the word *faster* and the word *lens*.

5.4.4 BERARDINELLI MOVIE REVIEW CORPUS

The baseline for opinion mining in BMRC is 11.(1)%, choice by chance for a 9-classes problem.

5.4.4.1 Results Using Lexical Features

Table 26 shows yielded results of opinion mining in BMRC using lexical features.

List	Recall (%)	Lexical features
BMRC list	31.85	5,056 ($n=3$)
Lemmatized BMRC list	**34.22**	7,585 ($n=2$)
BNC list	33.42	39,697 ($n=50$)
Lemmatized BNC list	33.78	91,782 ($n=10$)
DAL list	30.0	2,234 ($n=4$)
Lemmatized DAL list	32.89	5,124 ($n=2$)

Table 26: Maximal results of opinion mining in BMRC using lexical features

The *List* column shows the source of lexical features; the *Recall* column shows the maximal recall value yielded by the dataset with lexical features of the corresponding word list (%); the *Lexical features* column shows the number of lexical features and the parameter n from Table 12 utilized for composing the corresponding dataset. The maximal value for all word lists is shown in bold.

Figure 42 shows the results using datasets with lexical features as a plot.

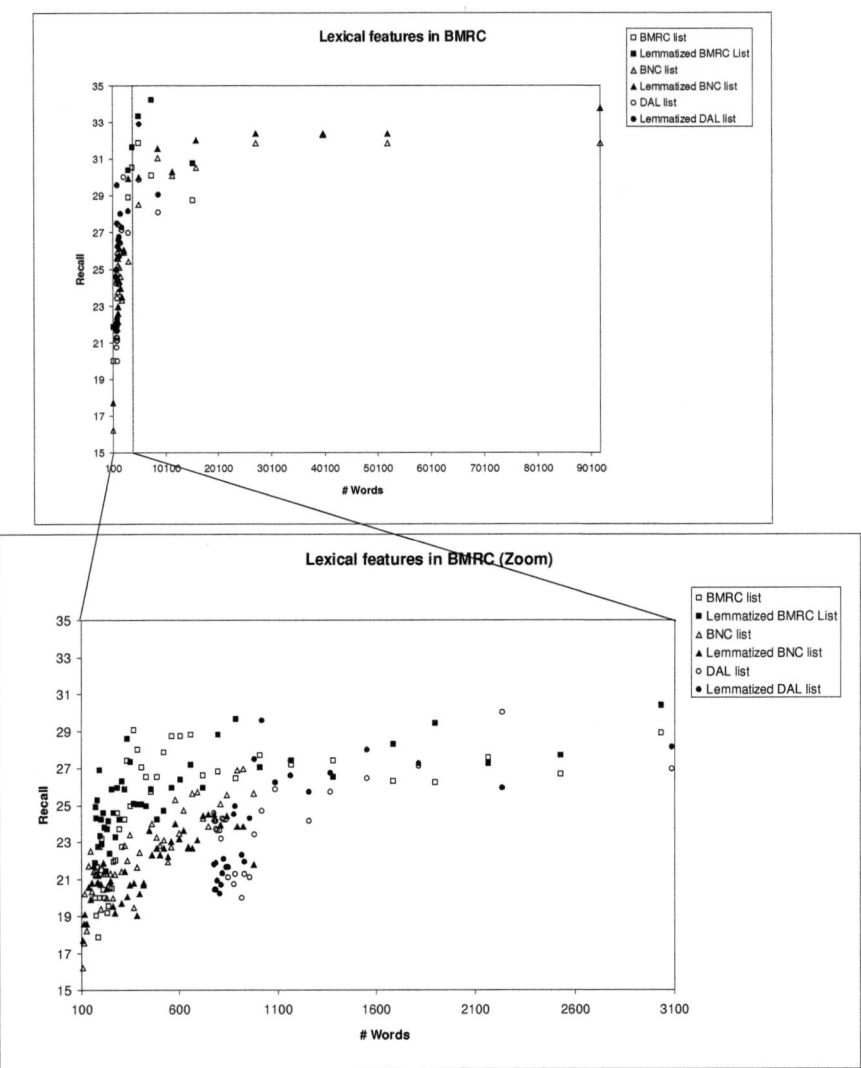

Figure 42: Lexical features in BMRC

The *#Words* axis shows the number of utilized lexical features from six word lists; the *Recall* axis presents the calculated recall value (%). The maximal recall value of 34.22% provides the dataset with 7,585 lemmatized words (the most frequent half of the lemmatized BMRC word list). The baseline value, 11.(1)%, is invisible because of its low value.

The proposed approach calculates the maximal recall value of 34.22%. The 9-classes confusion matrix corresponding to this result can be mapped onto a 5-classes result matrix as shown in Table 14. The classes-similarity evaluation measure δ equals to 59.8%. Note that the maximal classes-similarity evaluation measure δ (62.7%) is yielded by a dataset with 8,603 unigrams from the lemmatized BNC list ($n = 650$). The maximal cost-based evaluation measure χ, 82%, is yielded also by a different dataset with 7,585 unigrams from the non-lemmatized BMRC frequency list ($n=2$).

To improve classification results, BEH is applied to the composed datasets (Figure 43).

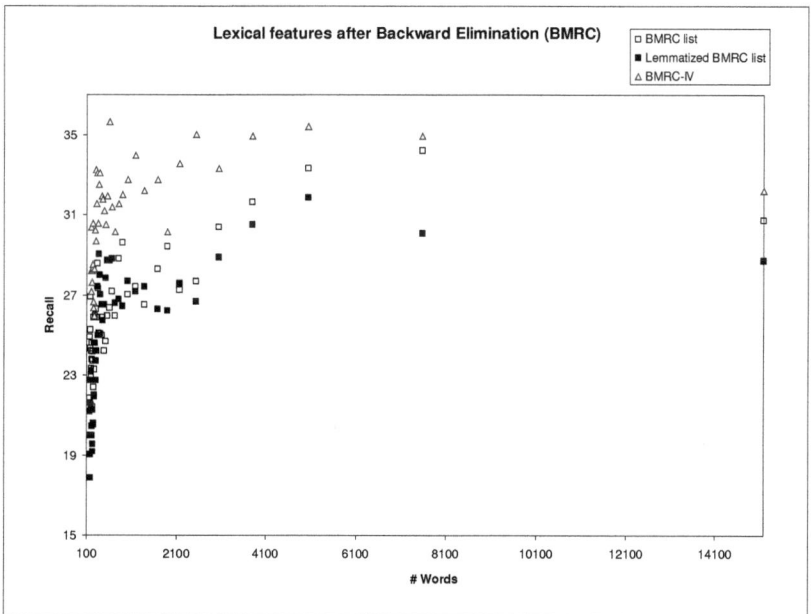

Figure 43: Applying BEH in BMRC

The *BMRC-IV* data series shows recall values yielded using BEH. To facilitate comparison with the already yielded results, the plot shows additionally the *BMRC list* data series and the *Lemmatized BMRC list* data series from Figure 42.

The maximal recall value of 38.67% achieves an optimized dataset with 375 words from the BMRC frequency list ($n=37$). For the list of eliminated words see Table 29.

5.4.4.2 Results Using Stylometric, Deictic, Grammatical Features

Table 27 outlines results of opinion mining in BMRC using datasets with stylometric, deictic, grammatical features.

Feature type	Recall (%)	Features
Stylometric	**28.07**	standard deviation of word lengths; standard deviation of sentence lengths; digrams; letters; word lengths
Deictic	25.11	demonstratives; pronouns; time references; forms third person; stopwords
Grammatical	16.89	300a; 300c; 301; 302; 303a; 304-305

Table 27: Results of opinion mining in BMRC using stylometric, deictic, grammatical features

The *Feature type* column shows the type of utilized features; the *Recall* column shows the maximal recall value yielded by the dataset with features of the corresponding type (%); the *Features* column shows utilized features. The maximal value for all feature types is shown in bold.

Figure 44 shows results of opinion mining using datasets with stylometric, deictic, grammatical feature combinations.

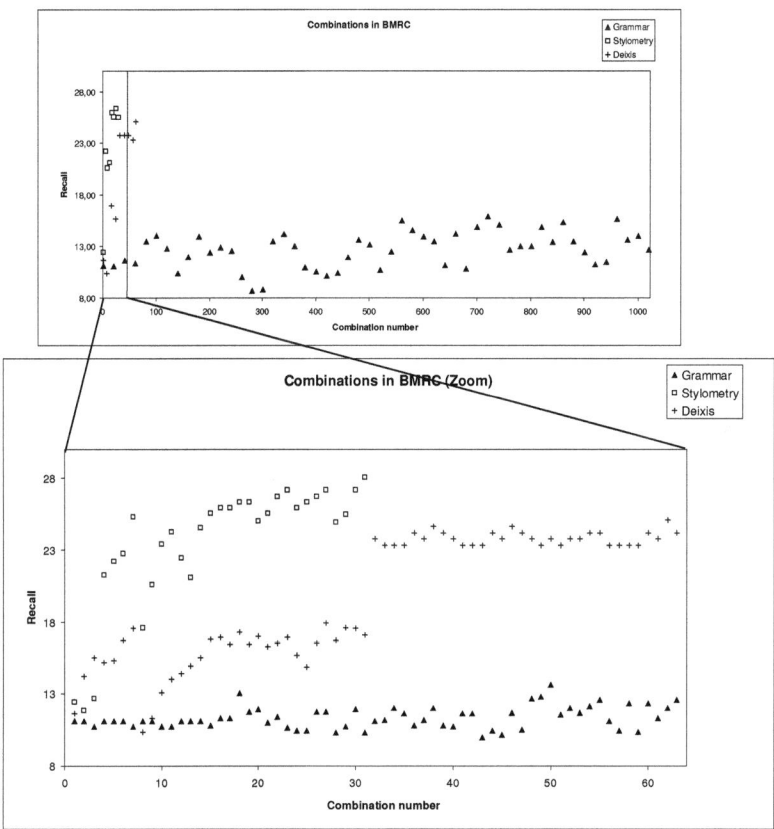

Figure 44: Grammatical, deictic, stylometric features in BMRC

The *Combination number* axis shows the number of feature combinations: grammatical feature combinations are numbered using the *301 304-305 299 300a 300b 300c 302 303a 303b 303c* feature order; stylometric feature combinations are numbered using the *digrams letters word_length sdwl sdsl* feature order; deictic feature combinations are numbered using the *stopwords formsthirdperson demonstratives pronouns timereferences placereferences* feature order. The recall value yielded by the dataset with the corresponding feature combination is shown in the *Recall* axis (%). Combination numbers are calculated according to the formula (24). The baseline value of 11.(1)% is invisible because of its low value.

5.5 DISCUSSION

Table 28 outlines the best results of classification before applying the heuristics to optimizing the feature space and discusses these results in the context of corpora properties in Table 10.

Corpus/ Group	PMRC	SAL	CwPR	BMRC
Baseline	87.2%	20%	20%	11.(1)%
Non-lemmatized word lists	**85.95**	**60.21%**	**51.89%**	31.85%
Lemmatized word lists	83.35%	59.6%	51.33%	**34.22%**
Stylometric Features	73.6%	58.97%	45.0%	28.07%
Deictic features	77.1%	59.65%	41.0%	25.11%
Grammatical Features	63.8%	31.35%	35.67%	16.89%
Classes-similarity evaluation measure δ	—	65.34% (N=5)	—	59.8% (N=9)
Cost-based evaluation measure χ	86% (K_e^2)	63% (K_e^5)	77% (K_a^5)	82% (K_a^9)
Classes-number evaluation measure υ	84% (N=2)	83% (N=5)	77% (N=5)	76% (N=9)

Table 28: Maximal classification results before applying the optimizing heuristics

The names of the analyzed corpora are shown in the uppermost row. The feature group names used for composing classified datasets are presented in the most left column. The maximal recall values of classification are shown in bold. The evaluation measures δ, χ and υ are shown below the double line. The parameter values used for calculating the result interpretation measures are designated in brackets, for instance, the cost matrix K_e^5 used for calculating the cost-based measure δ. Calculation of the classes-number evaluation measure is performed using the corresponding maximal recall value.

Noteworthy that the statistical approach can be considered as language-independent. Certainly, lexical features in the statistical approach by themselves are language-dependent, but after feature evaluation, for instance, as counts of words they become language-independent since the dataset with these features, e.g. lexical features, contains only counts of words or better counts of symbols. The features are evaluated independent of the utilized language.

The results of opinion mining using the proposed features suggest the counter-intuitive possibility of emotional analysis without humanly plausible emotional information. This intuition is also confirmed by findings in [Osherenko & André, 2007]. For example, the BNC frequency list used for extracting lexical features contains stopwords that are not necessary emotional. The same applies to the not emotional frequency lists of other corpora. The only word list that can be considered as emotional is DAL. But even so its datasets do not achieve maximal classification results. Not to mention datasets with stylometric, deictic, grammatical features that score much better results than the choice by chance but are also not emotional.

An attentive reader would wonder if opinion mining is really possible without semantic analysis of participating words and interdependencies between them. For example, is it imaginable that an approach to opinion mining analyzes affect without considering the meaning of emotion words? What is the explanation of such strange state of affairs?

Surprisingly, but the explanation is rather straightforward. Recall that the statistical approach is by definition a mathematical method! It does not require the human plausibilty to work correctly and can therefore rely on shallow means. An explanation of the analysis procedure is necessary only for a human that, for example, tries to influence it but not for a computer.

Furthermore, humanly comprehensible information as information on emotion words does not apply to stylometric or deictic features. For instance, the stylometric features (standard deviation of word lengths or sentence lengths) are not affective. Evidently, the conclusion should be drawn that statistical opinion mining can be conducted without the use of humanly comprehensible affective information, for instance, without emotion words.

The following sections discuss the yielded results more thoroughly focusing on the types of utilized features.

5.5.1 LEXICAL FEATURES

Classification results using lexical features as opposed to classification results with deictic, stylometric, or grammatical features are maximal in all corpora. The classification results show a significant, almost triple enhancement of recall values compared with the choice by chance: in PMRC, the maximal recall value of 85.95% is much higher than the choice-by-chance value of 50%; in SAL, the maximal recall value of 60.21% is much higher than the-choice-by-chance value of 20%; in CwPR, the maximal recall value of 51.66% is much higher than the choice-by-chance value of 20%; in BMRC, the maximal recall value of 34.22% is much higher than the choice-by-chance value of 11.(1)%.

The choice of words (lexical features) can improve classification results (see also Table 29 in the next section). In order to verify this statement, Table 28 contains additionally results of opinion mining after text lemmatization. However, the only corpus which classification rates improve by 2.37% after lemmatization is BMRC (34.22% vs. 31.85%) that is explained by the fact that BMRC as opposed to the other studied corpora is the only corpus that contains grammatically correct texts. Consequently, better classification of datasets with lemmata can be attributed to the better exactness of tagging and lemmatizing yielded by TreeTagger. On the contrary, classification rates in corpora containing grammatically *incorrect* sentences can decrease due to the lower tagging/lemmatization exactness of TreeTagger (in SAL, 60.21% vs. 59.6%; in CwPR, 51.66% vs. 51.33%). The recognition rate without lemmatization is even significantly higher in PMRC (85.95% vs. 83.35%).

Particularly noteworthy is the high recall value of 60.21% in SAL although such high value is almost improbable for short texts as SAL turns: despite the shortness of particular turns, classification rates can be offset by analyzing texts as dialogue history, continuous turns (the *Continuity* property). Hence, short turns can be joined together to long texts what considerably improves classification results: the corpora of the semantic approach in section 4.2 also contain short but not continuous texts and, thus, their classification scores lower classification results.

Although classification results in different corpora differ significantly, for instance, 85.95% in PMRC vs. 34.22% in BMRC, the evaluation measures do not differ in the same scale. For example, the classes-similarity evaluation measure δ is 59.8% in BMRC whereas this value is 65.34% in SAL; the maximal cost-based evaluation measures are 86% in PMRC vs. 63% in SAL; the maximal classes-number evaluation measures are 84% in PMRC vs. 76% in BMRC. This thesis assumes that the measures are similar because they interpret results of the same sensing approach more realistically. Hereby, the similarity of measures can be only considered as evidence of the correctness of the interpretation.

Classification results are encouraging. Beyond question, yielded results are imperfect (not 100% percent) but is it worth to strive for it? Take into consideration the hypothetical case if the 100%-perfection is reached! Probably this intention would do rather a disservice to classification: learning is not general and every emotional corpus extracts different lexical features for its classification. Maybe, there is no need to tighten up on achieving the perfect solution of classification and unhand at some point: it is more beneficial to leave "freedom of choice" and merely provide an intelligent interpretation of already yielded results. Presumably, such "freedom"

5.5.2 OPTIMIZING THE SPACE OF LEXICAL FEATURES

The space of lexical features can be optimized using FSH and BEH (Table 29).

Corpus	Recall	Lexical features
PMRC	85.95%	38,476 words
	83.3%	19,238 lemmatized words
	86.90%	after BEH: 12,825 words – 34 words[39]. Cancelled due to the high computational complexity.
	74%	after the conventional forward selection: 69 words[40].
	79.35%	after FSH: 106 words[41]. Cancelled due to computational intensity.

---

[39] 34 eliminated features: attention away bland *change* comedy considered constantly dull *enjoyable* faces forces group history last later masterpiece minutes must original perfect perhaps period personal side similar society sort stupid such superb turned wasted wonderfully worth

[40] 69 selected features: a already annoyance as attempt bad barb baseball beautiful been body boiler boring bunch can cassandra character direction dogmatic drama eyes fear fine four guys happens have himself hip his interested its jackie kevin known large let live most obvious order other others ponder possibly previous production psycho quickly screenplay ship sometimes spend story supposed talented that the this tom tourist try upon version video went will worst would

[41] 106 selected features: 1977[i], act[f], adorable[i], after[i], also[f], an[i], and[f], angle[i], another[f], assume[f], asteroid[f], back[i], bad[f], beavis[f], big[i], but[f], certainly[i], country[i], crossing[f], daylight[i], develops[f], director[f], discover[i], do[f], draw[f], dune[f], elusive[f], english[f], even[f], experience[f], fa[f], few[f], film[i], focus[i], for[f], gal[f], get[f], good[i], gordy[i], great[i], hammer[f], harder[f], heckerling[i], here[f], hired[f], hour[f], however[f], i[i], interpretation[f], into[i], is[f], island[f], jesus[f], later[i], liu[i], love[i], make[f], male[f], many[i], marital[f], mckellar[f], moment[f], more[f], most[i], mother[i], movies[f], new[f], no[f], none[f], occasions[f], only[f], page[f], parodies[f], performance[i], pitiful[f], pollack[f], real[f], really[f], rita[f], robinson[f], rourke[f], sayles[i], scene[f], school[f], settles[i], sherman[f], society[f], something[f], stereotyped[f], supposed[f], sweet[f], than[i], that[f], the[f], them[f], this[f], time[f], titles[f], to[f], true[f], unfortunately[i], van[f], viking[f], wanted[f], well[f], while[i]

SAL	60.21%	2,033 words
	59.6%	91,782 lemmatized BNC words
	60.93%	after BEH: 2,027 = 2,033 words – 6 words[42]
	61.16%	after the conventional forward selection: 77 words[43]
	65.76%	after FSH: 87 words[44]
CwPR	51.89%	2,344 words
	51.33%	2,813 lemmatized words
	54.67%	after BEH: 803 = 827– 24 words[45]
	62%	after the conventional forward selection: 59 words[46]
	69.68%	after FSH: 72 words[47]

---

[42] 6 eliminated features: *a* be in know laugh *the*

[43] 77 selected features: 01 all annoyed anywhere around at be but circles cope ends er erm feel few forget general get gets go going good ground gum hammocks huh i imagine in insulted intake job just know laugh let like little makes maybe mean might morning neck not obidiah one ones only out people please race rude stops students such sure symbol tackle taking the think to took true tube two usually was well who whole wiser wonder work you

[44] 87 selected features: a[f], absolutely[f], all[f], and[f], annoyed[f], annoying[f], at[f], away[f], be[f], been[i], blah[i], but[f], by[i], candy[f], certain[f], chancellor[f], coordinate[f], creeps[f], done[f], else[f], end[i], er[f], erm[f], excuse[f], expected[f], family[f], finding[f], from[f], furious[f], get[f], has[f], have[i], how[f], i[f], if[i], in[f], instance[f], irritating[f], it[f], just[i], keep[f], know[f], laugh[i], lives[i], lots[f], lottery[f], mind[f], miserable[f], new[f], no[f], not[f], of[f], on[f], or[f], other[f], person[f], petty[f], probably[f], regret[f], requirements[f], running[f], sack[f], said[f], senior[f], service[f], smacking[f], solve[i], spike[i], starting[f], sure[f], take[f], than[i], that[f], the[f], them[f], things[f], think[i], three[i], to[i], uch[f], we[f], what[f], world[i], worthwhile[i], would[i], you[f], yourself[f]

[45] 24 eliminated features: compartment fluid remove build supplied situations pleasing look areas they relatively push recorded purple automatic 30 charge available resolution rear slr feet since reader

[46] 59 selected features: 2448 3 8800 a510 a520 a640 aiaf also area as batteries bikers brainer can card compares digital directly draws dreaded epinions features gains good however hp ii indication is landscape lens optical or out problems red responsive s330 s400 sd700 selection share speed staff supplied surfing texture the this url use versatile vignetting was wheel widescreen xt you zoom

[47] 72 selected features: 35mm[f], 4x6[f], 52[f], 5x[f], a40[i], a630[i], a640[f], a[i], and[i], applies[i], archive[f], are[f], at[i], battery[i], bothersome[f], but[f], camera[i], can[f], co[i], commented[f], counts[f], default[f], digital[i], down[f], dynamic[f], elements[f], feels[f], for[f], grain[f], groundskeepers[f], handheld[f], has[f], importance[i], in[f], is[i], it[i], ive[f], lumix[i], machines[f], models[i], my[f], not[f], of[i], operation[f], option[f], or[f], ounce[f], pentaprism[i], photographic[i], pics[f], point[f], popular[f], preview[f], producing[i], put[f], render[f], resetting[f], rests[f], slr[f], system[f], telephoto[f], that[f], the[f], thing[f], tought[f], use[f], v570[f], very[f], viewpoints[i], washing[f], with[f], works[f]

BMRC	31.85%	5,056 words
	34.22%	7,585 lemmatized words
	38.67%	after BEH: 375 = 410 words – 35 features[48]
	41.92%	after BEH using the frequency feature evaluation: 621 = 651 words - 40 words[49]
	45.04	after the conventional forward selection: 53 words[50]
	56.81%	after FSH: 70 words[51]

Table 29: Optimizing the space of lexical features

The name of the studied corpus is shown in the *Corpus* column, the yielded recall value is shown in the *Recall* column; the number of utilized lexical features is shown in the *Lexical features* column. The lists of selected features are shown according to the pattern *<unigram> [<evaluation method>]* where the feature *<unigram>* is evaluated using the evaluation method *<evaluation method>*, using the frequency method (*f*), or using the presence method (*p*), or using the inversion method (*i*). For instance, the pattern *the[f]* represents the selected unigram *the* evaluated as frequency vector (*f*). In contrast, the pattern *think[i]* defines the unigram *think* evaluated as inversed frequency vector (*i*). Note that no selected features are evaluated as a presence vector.

Noteworthy that the optimization heuristics improve classification results in all corpora besides PMRC (both FSH, as well as BEH). Most remarkable is the improvement of the classification result in BMRC using FSH from 31.85% (not lemmatized unigrams) to 56.81%; using BEH from 31.85% to 38.67%. In all corpora except PMRC, FSH yields better results than BEH and also better results than the conventional forward selection. Note that the datasets after FSH contain at most 106 words although the initial datasets contained thousands of features. In PMRC, classification results decrease after FSH (from 85.95% to 79.35%) and increase after BEH (from 85.95% to 86.90%).

---

[48] 35 eliminated features: alien best close come could david drama else especially get given group having *horror* human involved kane men my nearly perfect played recent same several supposed takes title turn until used video war whether young

[49] 40 eliminated features: act adam against appears bad called could day did effort else got images known left line live *memorable* moment mother music none numerous opens oscar power represents same set supporting sure talent top until version viewer want war william worse

[50] 53 selected features: all although american amityville antz class clockwork cruz dracula editing elvis end film first football gras have hiding his hours house i inner interested its jesse just knock like military moments more most mother movie night past picture pretty sequel several splendor star the thornton time too underused we weapon wes while worst

[51] 70 selected features: 1963[f], 80[i], 8[f], about[f], all[f], amusing[f], and[f], as[i], at[f], awful[f], be[f], bed[i], breast[f], but[f], camp[f], chases[f], city[f], clyde[i], deep[f], dizzy[f], dr[i], element[f], fatal[i], freddie[f], freddy[f], from[f], gender[i], heartbreaking[i], his[i], hole[f], is[i], it[f], jim[i], john[f], jon[i], jonny[f], jordi[i], jump[f], karl[f], least[f], lester[i], machine[i], merry[i], monster[f], most[f], mrs[i], nine[i], noir[f], nonexistent[i], of[f], olds[f], pupil[i], rescued[f], restored[f], schrader[f], shore[i], silent[i],

This thesis performed brief analysis of selected/eliminated features. This study revealed no semantic characterization of optimizied unigrams: the words are not always emotional, for instance, *a* or *change*, but also not always neutral, for example, *horror* or *memorable*. Furthermore, the word features represent not necessarily positive or negative as *enjoyable* or *horror*. Consideration of the frequency of selected/eliminated unigrams also did not provide evident cognitions on optimized features.

5.5.3 COMPARISON WITH OTHER FEATURE GROUPS

Results of opinion mining using lexical features are maximal. However, the difference is not significant when compared with the second best result using other feature types: in PMRC, the difference is 8.85%=85.95%–77.1%; in CwPR; the difference is 6.89%=51.89%–45.0%; in BMRC, the difference is 6.15%=34.22%–28.07%. This has a not evident advantage: in the case of opinion mining using non-lexical features, classification relies on the features that are known in advance and are applicable for every classified corpus. In contrast, features from corpus frequency lists are known first after traversing the corresponding corpus.

Moreover, since the difference is not significant, the classification advantage of lexical features can be made up by the choice of features of other feature types (stylometric, deictic, grammatical).

Low results of opinion mining using grammatical features can be attributed to the low descriptive power of these features in general (63.8% in PMRC, 31.35% in SAL, 35.67% in CwPR, 16.89% in BMRC). Thus, these features can not carry the main weight in opinion mining. Nevertheless, the yielded values exceed the choice by chance. Hence, opinion mining can be done using non-grammatical feature groups whereas grammatical features can play a supporting role.

5.6 FURTHER RESEARCH

This chapter discussed classification of emotional corpora and introduced approaches to interpretation of their results.

Classification results impoved significantly after applying the heuristics to optimizing feature space. In order to reveal reasons thereof and identify features that should be selected/eliminated

slapstick[f], standoff[f], than[f], that[i], the[f], this[i], time[f], to[i], unforgettable[f], victor[f], which[i], with[f], worst[f]

analytically, feature extraction should be elaborated exactly. For example, the conventional attribute evaluation methods as IG can be reconsidered for ranking features or methods for feature selection in [Oberlander & Nowson, 2006] can be utilized. Hereby, in addition to the trivial methods of feature evaluation that were discussed in section 5.1.1.3, feature evaluation can be performed using other mathematical functions such as logarithm or exponential functions.

There is an assumption that the length of the classified text influences the result of classification: the longer this text is, the better is its classsification. If this assumption is true, improvement of classification can be achieved by manipulating the text to be classified by enlarging it, for example, the text to classify can be composed as the sum of its parts: a sum of the text plus its two thirds plus its last third.

Application of FSH and BSH showed that selecting/eliminating features corresponding to seldom unigrams almost never contribute to improvement of classification — words that occur rarely in classified texts enlarge the number of features but are useless for improving classification results. It can be preferable to group seldom features in order to enhance classification. For example, it can be superior to extract features representing communities of seldom words.

Opinion mining using datasets containing low number of features such as non-lexical features calculate worthy results. Hence, it can be used in applications where the processing speed and not the processing exactness carry the main weight, for example, in robotics applications or in dialogue systems.

Results of FSH and BSH attest that there is a room for further classification improvements. Since FSH as well as BEH are modality-independent they can be applied to optimizing feature space in multimodal fusion and hereby improve fusion results (cf. chapter 8).

6   SEMANTIC AFFECT SENSING

The previous chapter explored emotion recognition as a data mining problem using statistical methods. The proposed approach made use of such information as word counts or numbers of deictic words. This shallow information determined the analysis of emotional texts. No matter what shallow information was chosen to analyze texts in the statistical approach, the analysis procedure had the same shortcoming: it was incomprehensible and unexplainable for a human since the statistical approach did not consider the semantic content of the text being analyzed and the meaning of particular words.

In the following, this thesis discusses the semantic approach to affect sensing that fills the incomprehensibility gap. In contrast to the statistical method, this approach considers the emotional meaning of words that participate in the analyzed text and takes into account grammatical interdependencies between them.

6.1   GENERAL CONSIDERATIONS

6.1.1   PRIME EXAMPLES

To get an idea of humanly plausible affect sensing, this section discusses prime examples that originate the sought approach to semantic affect sensing.

How should the sought approach analyze the emotional meaning of the text *I'm not very happy*? and calculate a negative meaning? Hereby, the approach should detect the emotion word *happy*, the negation *not*, the intensifier *very*. Then it should calculate the negative meaning of the text considering the positive meaning of the word *happy* that is intensified by the word *very* and negated by the word *not*.

Alternatively, the sought approach should be able to distinguish emotional meanings of the text *It is a great film!* and the text *There is a great amount of this stuff here*! Hereby, it should calculate the *positive* emotional meaning of the first text and the *neutral* emotional meaning of the second text. For this purpose, the sought approach should identify significant domain notions, for instance, the notions *film*, *regisseur*, or *acting* in the movie review domain and infer the positive meaning of the example from the combination of the emotion word *great* and the notion *film*. In contrast, the sought approach should detect in the text *There is a great amount of this stuff here.* the emotion word *great* applied to the non-notion word *amount* and yield the neutral meaning of the text.

Moreover, the sought approach should be able to analyze the text *Alexander is very happy if everybody else is sad!* that contains both the positive word *happy* and the negative word *sad*. What is the expected emotional meaning of the text? *positive*, *negative*, or *neutral*? The sought approach should answer this question. It can assume that the calculated emotional meaning is conveyed by the first found emotional phrase, or the calculated emotional meaning is conveyed by the last found emotional phrase; or the calculated emotional meaning is derived from emotional meanings of all found emotional phrases.

6.1.2 RESTRICTIONS

Texts can be very different. To reduce possible complexity, the following restrictions are imposed on the analyzed texts:

1. Analyzed texts are assumed to be grammatically correct sentences. Hence, the analysis result of a grammatically improper text such as *I applies with different means.* is unreliable;

2. The text context is not considered in the semantic approach. For instance, the proposed approach does not take into account the *negative* emotional meaning of the context *I lost my book.* when calculating the *positive* emotional meaning of the text *It is a good book!*. Otherwise, the emotional meaning could be *negative*;

3. Anaphora resolution is not taken into account. For instance, this thesis does not study the resolution of the pronoun *it* in the text *I will remember it!* that refers to the text *a marvelous meeting*. Hence, the proposed semantic approach acquires the *neutral* emotional meaning of the text instead of the *positive* emotional meaning by resolving the emotional meaning of the pronoun *it*.

6.2 INFORMATION SOURCES

This section discusses information sources that are used in the proposed semantic approach. For detailed information on linguistic foundations see Appendix A.

6.2.1 Sources of Affect Information

This section discusses sources of affect information in the proposed semantic approach. Hereafter symbol → can be read as *implies*.

6.2.1.1 Emotion Words from Affect Dictionaries

Emotion words in affect dictionaries can be used as the basis for semantic affect sensing. In this thesis, emotion words are annotated using a 3-segment annotation scheme (*low_neg* for annotating words with low evaluation and low arousal, *low_pos* for annotating words with high evaluation and low arousal, *neutral* for annotating words with evaluation and arousal around zero). In contrast, emotional texts are analysed using a 5-segment scheme (*low_neg* for sensing affect with low evaluation and low arousal, *high_neg* for sensing affect with low evaluation and high arousal, *low_pos* for sensing affect with high evaluation and low arousal, *high_pos* for sensing affect with high evaluation and high arousal, *neutral* for sensing affect with evaluation and arousal around zero).

Why does this thesis annotate words using a 3-segment scheme but analyzes texts using a 5-segment scheme? The reason for this difference is anticipatory: the 5-segment scheme allows the increase of affect intensities if words are annotated using the 3-segment scheme. Consider the following example! What is the emotional meaning of the text *happy* vs. the text *very happy*? Intuitively, the positive emotional meaning of the word *happy* is lower than the positive emotional meaning of the phrase *very happy*. However, intensification of emotional meaning is not possible: the emotional meaning of the word *happy* cannot increase and remains positive whatever intensifier is used in this phrase. In contrast, using the proposed 5-segment scheme an emotional meaning of a text can change, for instance, increase from low positive to high positive by using intensifiers.

Consequently, this thesis defines an emotion word as follows:

<*emotion word*>
→ <*3-segment-emotion-word*> (48)

For example, the emotion word *happy* is interpreted as a low positive word:

happy
→ *low_pos* (49)

A classified text is analyzed following the scheme:

<text>
→ <5-segment-emotional-meaning>   (50)

For example, analysis of the text *I am very happy*.:

I am very happy
→ *high_pos*   (51)

yields the emotional meaning *high_pos*.

6.2.1.2 Movie Glossary

The proposed approach distinguishes emotional meanings of important notions of a specific domain. In this thesis, semantically significant items are termed *concepts*. In the movie review domain, concepts are notions found in the glossary of the movie domain, for instance, the concept *actor* in the freely available glossary from [IMDB, 2008] or movie titles such as *Independence day*.

In this thesis, concepts are considered to convey neutral emotional meaning or, in other words, concepts have no influence on the calculated emotional meaning of a text. For instance, the sentence *Actually, one of the biggest problems with Happy Gilmore is that it pretends to have a plot* expresses negative affect. Its emotional meaning is conveyed by the word *problems*. However, this sentence can be erroneously considered by an analysis approach as positive because it contains the positive emotion word *happy* in the movie title *Happy Gilmore*. To resolve such ambiguity, the text *Happy Gilsmore* is considered as concept in the proposed approach that has a neutral emotional meaning.

6.2.2 SOURCES OF GRAMMATICAL INFORMATION

6.2.2.1 Affect Analysis in the Linguistic Literature

As already mentioned in section 2.1.2, [Leech & Svartvik, 2003] discuss grammatical means of expressing affect in a text from the point of view of linguistics. In this thesis, these means were already discussed in connection with the statistical approach in section 5.1.3. In this section, these means are discussed once more: in the case of semantic affect sensing, they are interpreted as intensifiers of emotional meaning:

- Interjections (299), for example, *Oh, what a beautiful present!*;

Interjection *Oh* states that the analyzed sentence conveys an emotion but this emotion is not expressed by the interjection itself. Actually, the adjective *beautiful* discloses a (positive) emotional meaning of the text and the interjection *Oh* only intensifies this meaning. This conclusion can be proven on a similar example by substituting the positive adjective *beautiful* with the negative adjective *disgusting* what yields the sentence <u>*Oh*</u>, *what a disgusting present!*. Now the modified example expresses the high negative affect, but the interjection itself did not cause this change. Instead, remarkable change of the emotional meaning of the sentence was caused by substitution of the adjective although the grammatical structure of the original positive sentence containing the interjection retained.

Hence, words tagged as interjections are interpreted in the semantic analysis as intensifiers of emotional meaning:

<interjection>
→ *<intensifier>* (52)

- Exclamations (300a), for example, *What a wonderful time we've had!*;

Exclamations like interjections are considered in the proposed approach as intensifiers of the experienced emotion that do not by themselves convey a particular emotion.

Word pairs tagged as a question word at the beginning of the text and an exclamation mark *!* at its end can be considered als intensifiers of emotional meaning:

<question word>... *<exclamation mark>*
→ *<intensifier>* (53)

- Emphatic *so* and *such* (300b), for example, *I'm <u>so</u> afraid they'll get lost!*;

According to linguistic theory, the words *so* and *such* are interpreted as intensifiers. Similarly, the word *so* is interpreted in the proposed approach as:

so
→ *<intensifier>* (54)

- Repetitions (300c), for example, *This house is <u>far, far</u> too expensive!*

Repetitions of word pairs can be interpreted in the proposed approach as intensifiers:

if <word1>==<word2> and <POS-word1> == < POS-word2>
→ *<intensifier>*   (55)

- Intensifying adverbs and modifiers (301), for example, *We are <u>utterly</u> powerless.*;

    Particular adverbs and modifiers can be considered as intensifiers, for instance, the adverb *utterly*:

    utterly
    → *<intensifier-utterly>*   (56)

- Emphasis *ever, on earth, in heaven's name* (302), for example, in the sentence *How <u>ever</u> did they escape?*;

    The word *ever*, or the phrase *on earth*, or the phrase *in heaven's earth* can be interpreted in the proposed approach as an intensifier; furthermore, a word pattern containing a "what-question"[52] followed by an intensifier and an emotional item (emotion word or emotional phrase) is interpreted as an emotional phrase:

    <wh-question> <intensifier> <emotional item>
    → *<emotional phrase>*   (57)

- Intensifying a negative sentence (303a), for instance, in the sentence *She didn't speak to us <u>at all</u>* the phrase *at all* can be considered in the proposed approach as an intensifier assuming that this phrase would appear in a negated sentence:

    at all
    → *<intensifier-at-all>*   (58)

- A negative noun phrase beginning with *not a* (303b), for instance, the phrase *not a* in the sentence *We arrived <u>not a</u> moment too soon!* appears in the noun phrase *not a moment*;

---

[52] *What-question* is a question why, when, where, what, how.

\<noun-phrase-not-a\>
→ \<intensifier-not-a\> (59)

- Fronted negation (303c), for instance, the word *never* in the sentence <u>Never</u> *have I seen such a crowd of people* can be considered in the proposed approach as an intensifier;

\<fronted negation\>
→ \<intensifier-fronted-negation\> (60)

- Exclamatory and rhetorical questions (304, 305), for instance, *Hasn't she grown!* or *What difference does it make?*.

Similarly to section 5.1.3, exclamatory and rhetorical questions can be identified in the proposed approach using the syntax of the analyzed text: semantic identification of exclamatory and rhetorical questions is not necessary since there is an assumption that any question mark in studied texts is rhetorical and any exclamation mark denotes an exclamation.

6.2.2.2 Grammatical Information from Empirical Examples

The grammatical information in the previous section is not exhaustive and concerns not every text which affect has to be analysed. For the purpose of revealing additional grammatical information, this thesis investigates in detail 25 empirical examples and reveals a great importance of emotion words, intensifiers and negations in semantic analysis. For instance, this thesis explored the example *I am not very happy* and acquired grammatical information on interdependencies between negations (*not*), intensifiers (*very*), and emotion words (*happy*).

Also, this thesis considered 10 scenario-dependent empirical examples as sources of grammatical information, for instance, this thesis scrutinized the text *Not every film is so good!* containing negations (word *not*), concepts (word *film*), intensifiers (word *so*), emotion words (word *good*) and revealed significant interdependencies between them.

6.2.3 DIFFERENTIATED LINKING CLAUSES AND PHRASES

This thesis assumes that it is possible to analyze emotional meaning of a sentence using the emotional meanings of its parts. Hereby, affect sensing can rely on differentiated analysis that calculates the emotional meaning of the analyzed text by linking together the emotional meanings of constituent parts. Hereby, emotional meanings of the parts can be not only positive or negative meanings but also high/low positive or high/low negative meanings.

Thus, the proposed approach scrutinizes the emotional meaning of the text not only as a whole, but additionally by splitting it in smaller units and analyzing their emotional meanings independently. Afterwards it infers emotional meaning of the original text from the emotional meanings of the constituent units.

Hence, the proposed approach maintains means for splitting text and linking clauses and phrases. For instance, the sentence *Alexander is sad if everybody else is happy.* is split in clauses; emotional meaning of the clauses is analyzed yielding the subsentence combination *<negative superordinate clause> <positive subordinate clause>* that empirically implies the *negative* emotional meaning of the original text. Alternatively, if the proposed approach analyzes the example *Alexander is very sad if everybody else is happy.* it splits it in clauses getting the subsentence combination *<high negative superordinate clause> <low positive subordinate clause>* that empirically implies the *high negative* emotional meaning of the original text.

6.3 IMPLEMENTATION OF SEMANTIC AFFECT SENSING

In the following, the implemented system to semantic analysis is described thoroughly.

6.3.1 SYSTEM ARCHITECTURE

The proposed system uses means of two parsers for performing semantic affect sensing: means of the SPIN parser and the means of the Stanford parser.

Hereafter the string *<Verb>* denotes the POS tags of verbs *VB, VBD, VBP, VBG, VBN, VBZ*; the string *<Noun>* denotes the POS tags of nouns *NN, NNS, NNP, NNPS*; the string *<Preposition>* denotes the POS tags of prepositions (*IN*). All tags are extracted from the Penn Treebank tagset.

6.3.1.1 SPIN Parser

The SPIN parser ([Engel, 2006]) is a semantic parser for spoken dialogue systems, a rule-based framework, that detects predefined patterns of words and creates instances of user-defined classes (hereafter referred to as SPIN rules). A SPIN rule can match words in texts order-independently.

For instance, the SPIN rule

definitely
→ *Intensifier(orth:definitely)* (61)

finds the word *definitely* in the text *Is he definitely happy?* and instantiates the class *Intensifier* with the attribute *orth* that has the value *definitely*.

The SPIN parser has many advantages but also a significant drawback: it is unable to perform dynamic tagging. The example below aims at showing consequences of the tagging drawback.

The sought approach should classify two texts: the text *I like this game* expressing the positive emotional meaning and the text *I am like my father* expressing the neutral emotional meaning. Hereby, the SPIN rule can match the word *like* as follows

like
→ *EmotionalItem(semCat:low_pos)* (62)

SPIN rule (62) always matches the word *like* whatever function it has in the original text (e.g. verb or preposition) and instantiates the class *EmotionalItem* with an attribute *semCat* evaluated as *low_pos*. However, in the first example the word *like* is a verb conveying a *positive* emotion and the resulting affective meaning of the original text is positive; in the second text, the word *like* is a preposition conveying *neutral* affect meaning and the resulting affective meaning of the original text is neutral.

More precise SPIN rules should consider the POS tagging of the word *like*:

[like <Verb>]
→ *EmotionalItem(semCat:low_pos, orth: like)* (63)

[like <Preposition>]
→ *EmotionalItem(semCat:neutral, orth: like)* (64)

Note that the SPIN rule (63) matches only the verb *like* and instantiates the class *EmotionalItem* having the attribute *semCat* evaluated as *low_pos*. In contrast, the SPIN rule (64) matches only the preposition *like* and instantiates the class *EmotionalItem* having the attribute *semCat* evaluated as *neutral*.

6.3.1.2 Stanford Parser

To overcome the aforementioned tagging drawback, the proposed system uses in addition to the SPIN parser the probabilistic Stanford parser ([Klein & Manning, 2003]). The Stanford parser is an order-dependent parser capable of dynamic word tagging. Note that it is also able to lemmatize words and to detect sentence parts as clauses and phrases what will be utilized in the proposed system.

But first let us explore the last example with two texts and how the Stanford parser can contribute to the correct affect sensing. Below is the parsing tree of the sentence *I like this game.* calculated by the Stanford parser:

(ROOT
    (S
        (NP (PRP I))
            (VP (VBP like)
                (NP (DT this) (NN game)))
        (. .))) (65)

The *ROOT* node marks the root of the parsing tree that contains the sentence *S* node with the noun phrase *NP* (a personal pronoun *I*) and the verb phrase with the head *like* containing the noun phrase *this game*. Note that the word *like* is tagged correctly as a verb (the *VBP* tag).

Now compare the parsing tree (65) with the parsing tree for the sentence *I am like my father:*

(ROOT
    (S
        (NP (PRP I))
            (VP (VBP am)
                (PP (IN like)
                    (NP (PRP$ my) (NN father))))
        (. .))) (66)

The *ROOT* node marks the root of the parsing tree and contains the sentence *S* node with the noun phrase *NP* (a personal pronoun *I*) and with the verb phrase (*am like my father*). Now in contrast to the parsing tree (65), the calculated parsing tree *(66)* has a remarkable difference: the verb phrase contains the preposition phrase *like my father*. Consequently, the word *like* is tagged correctly as a preposition (the *IN* tag).

6.3.2 Constructing SPIN Rules

The SPIN engine plays a significant role in the proposed system and maintains corresponding SPIN rules. SPIN rules are composed in the step of the system development using affect information in section 6.2. The implemented system maintains SPIN rules on the basis of affect information (section 6.3.2.1.1) and notions from the movie glossary (section 6.3.2.1.2); grammatical SPIN rules both from empirical examples (section 6.3.2.2.1) and from literature (section 6.3.2.2.2); grammatical SPIN rules for linking clauses and phrases (section 6.3.2.3).

6.3.2.1 SPIN Rules from Affect Information

6.3.2.1.1 Word-spotting SPIN Rules

The proposed semantic system maintains rules for the Levin verbs, emotion words from WordNet-Affect, GI, EQI (hereafter referred to as word-spotting SPIN rules).

Several affect dictionaries can contain the same emotion word that is annotated ambiguously. For instance, the word *admire* is present both in GI as a positive word and as a negative word in WordNet-Affect which emotional meaning is calculated on the basis of scores in DAL. To resolve this ambiguity, this thesis defines the order of dictionaries of emotion words for constructing the word-spotting SPIN rules: first, Levin verbs then the positive and negative GI dictionaries, then WordNet-Affect, and finally EQI. The dictionary order is defined empirically under consideration of two criteria (the size of the corresponding dictionary and the utilized compilation method): smaller rather than bigger; manually compiled rather than automatically compiled.

Word-spotting SPIN rules for the Levin verbs are composed manually yielding for empirically positive verbs the SPIN rules of the form

[<positive verb> <Verb>]
$\rightarrow$ *EmotionalItem(semCat:low_pos, orth: <positive verb>)* (67)

or yielding for empirically negative verbs the word-spotting SPIN rules of the form

[<negative verb> <Verb>]
$\rightarrow$ *EmotionalItem(semCat:low_neg, orth: <negative verb>)* (68)

Positive and negative words in GI except 17 ambiguous words are utilized for building word-spotting SPIN rules (cf. the list of the ambiguous words in section 3.1.1). Hence, 1,635 words from the *Positiv* category in GI build the basis for the word-spotting SPIN rules of the form

[<positive word> <POS>]
→ *EmotionalItem(semCat:low_pos, orth: <positive word>)* (69)

2,005 negative words from the *Negativ* category in GI form the basis for the word-spotting SPIN rules of the form

[<negative word> <POS>]
→ *EmotionalItem(semCat:low_neg, orth: <negative word>)* (70)

798 words from WordNet-Affect (280 nouns, 273 adjectives, 122 verbs, 123 adverbs) form a basis for the corresponding word-spotting SPIN rules. Noteworthy that composition of the word-spotting SPIN rules for emotion words from WordNet-Affect differs significantly from composition of the word-spotting SPIN rules for Levin verbs or emotion words in GI: emotion words from WordNet-Affect do not have an annotated emotional meaning and this meaning has to be extracted elsewhere, for example, from DAL. Hence, word-spotting SPIN rules for emotion words from WordNet-Affect have the form

[<word> <POS>]
→ *EmotionalItem(semCat:<semCat>, orth: <word>, ee:<ee>, aa: <aa>, ii: <ii>)* (71)

where the word *<word>* and its POS *<POS>* are defined in WordNet-Affect; emotional category *<semCat>* is calculated on the basis of values of the evaluation *<ee>*, the activation *<aa>*, the imagery *<ii>* dimensions extracted from DAL (Figure 45).

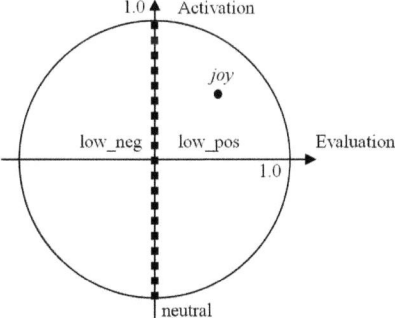

Figure 45: Affect segmentation for emotion words

Figure 45 shows the 3-segment E/A space (*low_pos*, *low_neg*, *neutral*) used for calculating the semantic category of words from WordNet-Affect and for composing the corresponding word-spotting SPIN rules. The dotted line lying on the *Activation* axis illustrates the *neutral* affect segment.

For instance, the proposed approach reads the word *joy* from WordNet-Affect, extracts its POS and values for its emotional dimensions from DAL (*evaluation*=0.89, *activation*=0.31, *imagery*=–0.4) and compiles a word-spotting SPIN rule:

[joy <Noun>]
→ *EmotionalItem(semCat:low_pos, orth: joy, ee: 0.89, aa: 0.31, ii: –0.4)* (72)

Word-spotting rules for words from WordNet-Affect were revised manually since they can not be considered as trustworthy due to unreliable values of the DAL dimensions (cf. Table 1). For instance, the automatically created word-spotting SPIN rule for the verb *admire* is

[admire <Verb>]
→ *EmotionalItem(semCat: low_neg, orth: admire, evaluation:–0.1, activation: –0.4, imagery: 0.8)* (73)

where the negative affect *low_neg* in the automatical rule is calculated on the basis of the DAL scores and was manually changed in the positive affect *low_pos*.

Not every word from WordNet-Affect is present in DAL. For 503 words, it was possible to calculate an emotional segment using their scores in DAL. Words in WordNet-Affect that were not found in DAL are stored in the proposed system for reference purposes without emotional annotation as a comment in the form

#<word>
#→ EmotionalItem(semCat:<semCat>, orth: <word>) (74)

The emotional semantic category *<semCat>* has to be annotated in future.

Finally, words from EQI are used for constructing word-spotting SPIN rules. However, since they are defined in EQI without emotional meaning the constructed SPIN rules are stored as comments of the form (74).

Overall, 4,177 word-spotting SPIN rules are compiled that do not need manual adjustment: SPIN rules for 34 Levin verbs, SPIN rules for 3,640 GI words (1,635 positive and 2,005 negative), SPIN rules for 503 words from WordNet-Affect with semantic category calculated on the basis of DAL. Considering words from the EQI dictionary the overall number grows to 6,298 word-spotting SPIN rules but 2,121 word-spotting rules have to be adjusted manually since they do not have an emotional annotation. Nevertheless, words without emotional annotation from WordNet-Affect and EQI should be considered further since they complete the set of emotion words and their emotional category should be annotated in future.

6.3.2.1.2 SPIN Rules from Movie Glossary

Movie titles are transformed in the corresponding SPIN rules without defining the emotional meaning. For instance, the SPIN rule

[21 CD Gram NNS]
$\rightarrow$ *Concept(orth:"21 Grams")* (75)

transforms text *21 CD Gram NNS* in the instance of class *Concept* (*21 Grams*). SPIN rules from the movie glossary were composed for 13 movie titles and 15 notions of the movie domain.

6.3.2.2 Grammatical SPIN Rules

This section describes the composition of SPIN rules on the basis of information from grammatical sources in section 6.2.2 (hereafter referred to as grammatical SPIN rules).

6.3.2.2.1 Grammatical SPIN Rules from Literature

Grammatical SPIN rules for expressing affect are composed from examples in [Leech & Svartvik, 2003] (cf. preliminaries in section 6.2.2.1). For instance, the text *Oh, what a wonderful day!* is processed by the rule representing the means 299:

[Word() UH] EmotionalItem(semCat:high_pos)
$\rightarrow$ *EmotionalPhrase(semCat:high_pos)* (76)

A complete list of 18 SPIN rules from literature is shown in Table 35.

6.3.2.2.2 Grammatical SPIN Rules from Empirical Examples

To implement SPIN rules from the empirical examples, 74 intensifiers from [Quirk & Greenbaum, 1988] as well as negations, e.g. *not*, *never*, *any*, *almost* were collected. Table 36 shows a complete list of SPIN rules containing 20 grammatical SPIN rules that are composed from the empirical examples.

Grammatical SPIN rules can be composed on the basis of scenario-dependent examples (hereafter referred to as scenario-dependent SPIN rules), for example, on the basis of the example *Not every film is so good!* A complete list of scenario-dependent 20 SPIN rules and corresponding examples is shown in Table 37.

6.3.2.3 SPIN Rules for Linking Clauses and Phrases

The emotional meaning of a complex sentence is deduced from the emotional meanings of clauses by performing linking. Super-/subordinate clauses in a complex sentence are identified by the Stanford parser. The super-/subordinate clauses are represented by classes *Superordinate* or *Subordinate* respectively.

For instance, SPIN rules for linking heterogeneous clauses (super/subordinate) have the form

$$Superordinate(emotCat:<meaning>) \; Subordinate(emotCat <meaning>)$$
$$\rightarrow Result(emotCat: <meaning>) \qquad (77)$$

where the *Superordinate* instance represents a superordinate clause; a *Subordinate* instance represents a subordinate clause; *Result* is an instance of the result class representing the emotional meaning of the original text where the attribute *emotCat* has the value *meaning*.

For example, the SPIN rule according to the form (77) can be

$$Superordinate(emotCat:neutral) \; Subordinate(emotCat:high\_neg)$$
$$\rightarrow Result(emotCat: high\_neg)) \qquad (78)$$

Hence, if the proposed approach processes the text *I think he is very upset.*, it instantiates the class *Superordinate* (superordinate clause *I think*) and the class *Subordinate* (subordinate clause *he is very upset*) and applies the rule (78) that links a neutral superordinate clause and a high negative subordinate clause yielding a high negative result *high_neg*. Similarly, emotional meaning of a clause can be deduced from emotional meanings of constituent phrases.

SPIN rules for linking homogeneous clauses (e.g. superordinate) have the form

$$Superordinate(emotCat:<meaning>) \; Superordinate(emotCat <meaning>)$$
$$\rightarrow Result(emotCat: <meaning>) \qquad (79)$$

For instance, the proposed approach analyzes the text *Alexander is very sad and everybody is happy.* using the rule:

Superordinate(emotCat:high_neg) Superordinate(emotCat:low_pos)
$\rightarrow$ *Result(emotCat: high_neg))* (80)

and calculates the meaning *high_neg*.

A complete list of 19 SPIN rules for linking phrases can be found in Table 39. A complete list of 97 SPIN rules for linking clauses can be found in Table 40.

6.3.3 ALGORITHM

This section discusses the algorithm for semantic affect sensing.

Emotional meaning of a sentence is analyzed in two stages: in the first stage (division), the system splits the analyzed text in parts of different granularity (leaves the text unchanged, splits the text in phrases or clauses) and analyzes the emotional meaning of each extracted part using the chosen word-spotting strategy (first phrase, last phrase, average vote); in the second stage (consolidation), the system calculates the emotional meaning of the original text by deducing it from emotional meanings of the extracted parts. The choice of the granularity of extracted parts is a matter of study (cf. results in section 6.3.5).

The proposed algorithm for semantic affect sensing can be described as follows:

1. The approach creates a parsing tree for the analyzed text using the Stanford parser, extracts super/subordinate clauses in the analyzed text. Hereby, the nodes that are marked in the parsing tree with a *S* or *FRAG* tag are interpreted as superordinate clauses, the nodes that are marked with a *SBAR*, *SBARQ* tag as subordinate clauses;

2. To perform processing under consideration of POS tags, the approach constructs a text containing lemmatized words of the analyzed text and adds their POS tags (referred to hereafter as the lemmatized text).

3. Depending on the chosen granularity of analysis:

    a. *Whole text*: The approach detects emotion words in the lemmatized text and creates instances of the corresponding words using the word-spotting SPIN rules. It classifies emotional meaning of the lemmatized text according to the chosen word-spotting strategy.

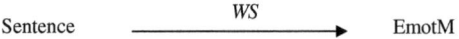

Figure 46: Affect recognition using the whole text

The *WS* arrow denotes the application of the word-spotting SPIN rules; *EmotM* represents an emotional meaning of the lemmatized text.

b. *Subsentences.* The approach calculates the emotional meaning of the lemmatized text on the basis of emotional meanings of its clauses. Thus, it detects clauses, classifies their emotional meaning by applying the word-spotting SPIN rules according to the chosen word-spotting strategy, constructs an auxiliary text reflecting the emotional structure of the lemmatized text using the emotional meanings of clauses (subsentence combination), and classifies its emotional meaning by linking clauses (Figure 47).

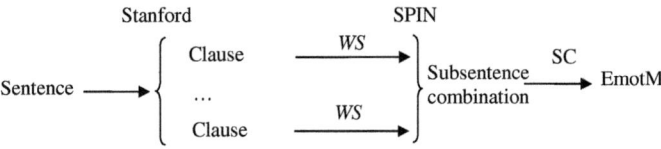

Figure 47: Affect recognition using clauses

The *WS* arrow denotes application of the word-spotting SPIN rules according to the chosen word-spotting strategy, the *SC* arrow means application of SPIN rules for linking clauses using the subsentence combination, *EmotM* represents the emotional meaning of the lemmatized text. Figure 47 contains the names of the parsers (SPIN, Stanford) utilized for the corresponding processing.

c. *Phrases.* The approach performs analysis of emotional meanings of texts not using subsentence combinations, but using other auxiliary texts: phrase combinations. Phrase combinations reflect similarly to subsentence combinations the emotional meaning of phrases.

The approach detects super-/subordinate clauses, then phrases contained in the detected clauses, classifies the emotional meaning of phrases according to the chosen word-spotting strategy by applying the word-spotting SPIN rules, constructs a phrase combination representing the emotional structure of the corresponding clause, classifies emotional meaning of a clause by linking phrases, compiles a subsentence combination, and calculates the emotional meaning of the lemmatized text by linking clauses (Figure 48).

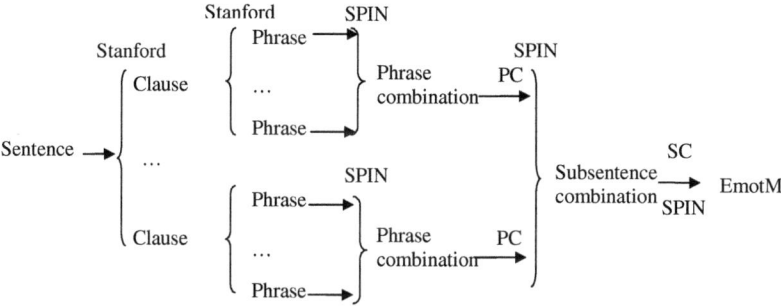

Figure 48: Affect recognition using phrases

The *WS* arrow denotes the application of the word-spotting SPIN rules according to the chosen word-spotting strategy, the *SC* arrow denotes application of SPIN rules for linking clauses, the *PC* arrow corresponds to the application of SPIN rules for linking phrases, *EmotM* is the emotional meaning of the lemmatized text. Figure 48 shows the names of parsers (SPIN, Stanford) that perform the corresponding processing.

d. *Majority.* The approach calculates the majority of affect votes yielded by the granularities above (*Whole text*, *Subsentences*, *Phrases*). If the majority vote can not be calculated, i.e. classification results are all different, the result of classification equals the result of the *subsentences* granularity since the *subsentences* granularity yields a high classification rate (see classification results in section 6.3.5).

6.3.4 PROCESSING EXAMPLE

In the following, the affect sensing algorithm in section 6.3.3 is explored on the example of affect sensing in the emotional sentence *Finally, I was so angry that I could burst with rage* using the first phrase word-spotting strategy:

1. The approach uses the Stanford parser for composing a parsing tree

   (ROOT
      (S
         (ADVP (RB Finally))
         (NP (PRP I))
         (VP (VBD was)
            (ADJP (RB so) (JJ angry))
            (SBAR (IN that)
               (S
                  (NP (PRP I))
                  (VP (MD could)
                  (VP (VB burst)
                     (PP (IN with)
                     (NP (NN rage))))))))
   (. .)))

   The approach extracts 2 clauses: the superordinate clause *Finally, I was so angry* marked with the *S* tag and the subordinate clause *I could burst with rage* marked with an *SBAR* tag.

2. The approach compiles the lemmatized text as *Finally RB , , I PRP so RB angry JJ be VBD I PRP could MD burst VB with IN rage NN*. In the following, the POS tags are omitted for better readability.

3. Depending on the chosen granularity of analysis:

   a. *Whole text*: The approach applies word-spotting SPIN rules to the lemmatized text *Finally, I was so angry...* and classifies its emotional meaning by applying the first phrase word-spotting strategy. Since the SPIN parser interprets the word *angry* as the first emotional phrase with a low negative meaning (*low_neg*), this meaning is interpreted as the emotional meaning of the whole text.

   b. *Subsentences*. The approach detects the superordinate clause *Finally, I was so angry* and the subordinate clause *I could burst with rage*. It constructs the subsentence combination *superord_high_neg subord_low_neg* where *superord_high_neg* represents the high negative meaning of the superordinate clause and *subord_low_neg* represents the low negative meaning of the subordinate clause. Finally, the approach classifies the lemmatized text as high negative (*high_neg*) by linking clauses.

   c. *Phrases*. The approach detects the superordinate clause *Finally, I was so angry* and the subordinate clause *I could burst with rage*. In the superordinate clause, it extracts 4 phrases:

the adverb phrase (*finally*), the noun phrase (*I*), the verb phrase (*was*), the adjective phrase (*so angry*); in the subordinate clause, the approach extracts 3 phrases: the noun phrase (*I*), the verb phrase (*could burst with*), the noun phrase (*rage*) phrases. The approach constructs the phrase combination *phrase_null phrase_null phrase_null phrase_high_neg* for the superordinate clause where *phrase_null* corresponds to a neutral meaning, *phrase_high_neg* corresponds to the high negative meaning of a phrase (phrase *so angry* is classified as *high_neg*); the phrase combination for the subordinate clause is a string *phrase_null phrase_null phrase_low_neg*. After linking phrase combinations, the approach constructs a subsentence combination *superord_high_neg subord_low_neg* and classifies it as *high_neg* by linking clauses.

d. *Majority.* The approach calculates the majority vote on the basis of votes yielded by the granularities above. Hence, it utilizes the value *low_neg* (the *Whole text* granularity), the value *high_neg* (the *Subsentences* granularity), the value *high_neg* (the *Phrases* granularity) and calculates the majority vote *high_neg*.

6.3.5 IMPLEMENTATION DETAILS

6.3.5.1 Analyzing Rule Performance and Gathering Statistics

The performance of the utilized grammatical SPIN rules is analyzed in comparison of counts of application of sophisticated grammar SPIN rules and counts of application of the simple grammar SPIN rule, the word-spotting SPIN rule of the form (referred to hereafter as the one-grammar rule):

EmotionalItem(semCat:<meaning>)
$\rightarrow$ *EmotionalPhrase(semCat:<meaning>)* (81)

The rule (81) matches an instance of the class *EmotionalItem* with the attribute *semCat* having the value *<meaning>* and transfers this value to an instance of the class *EmotionalPhrase*.

Statistics is gathered by the means of the programming language (Java) that counts applications of applied SPIN rules.

The performance of the utilized SPIN rules and the gathered statistics are discussed in section 6.4.

6.3.5.2 Implementation of the Strategies of the Word-Spotting

An emotional text can contain several emotional phrases. For instance, the sentence *I am happy and sad* contains 2 emotional phrases corresponding to the emotion word *happy* (considered to express a positive meaning) and the emotion word *sad* (considered to express a negative meaning). To analyze the emotional meaning of this sentence, the proposed approach implements 3 strategies of word-spotting corresponding to the order of the detected emotional phrases: the first phrase word-spotting strategy, the last word word-spotting strategy, the average vote word-spotting strategy.

According to the first phrase word-spotting strategy, the emotional meaning of the text is conveyed by the emotional meaning of the first emotional phrase (the word *happy* defines the *positive* meaning of the text). According to the last phrase word-spotting strategy, the emotional meaning of the text is conveyed by the emotional meaning of the last emotional phrase (the emotion word *sad* defines the *negative* meaning of the text). According to the average vote word-spotting strategy, the emotional meaning of the text is conveyed by the majority of emotional meanings; accordingly, the above example has the *neutral* emotional meaning (*happy* vs. *sad*).

The first phrase word-spotting strategy and the last phrase word-spotting strategy are implemented in the proposed computer system using the means of the system programming language (Java). In contrast, the average vote word-spotting strategy is implemented using a special SPIN rule that confronts negative emotional items with positive emotional items:

$$<negative\text{-}emotional\text{-}item> <positive\text{-}emotional\text{-}item>$$
$$\rightarrow <placeholder> \quad (82)$$

The rule (82) balances low/high negative emotional items and low/high positive emotional items instantiating a placeholder class that does not have the emotional meaning. Thereby, this rule eliminates the balanced pairs of emotional items in the SPIN parsing. Note that the order of emotional items in the rule (82) — *<negative-emotional-item> <positive-emotional-item>* — is insignificant since processing is done by the SPIN parser order-independently.

6.3.5.3 Choosing SPIN rules

In general, the SPIN engine parses an input text and applies the matching SPIN rules. Hereby, the engine produces several possible parsing solutions if the text can be matched by several SPIN rules. An approach to affect sensing has to choose the best parsing solution.

In this thesis, the best parsing solution is chosen using the following considerations: first, the best parsing solution contains the least instances of user-defined classes; second, one of instantiated classes is an instance of the class *EmotionalPhrase* that holds the emotional meaning of the analyzed text.

For example, the approach analyzes the sentence *I am so happy*. Below are 4 possible variants of parsing produced by the SPIN engine (POS tags are omitted for better readability):

1. *Intensifier(orth: so) EmotionalPhrase(semCat: high_pos)*
2. *Intensifier(orth: so) happy*
3. *EmotionalPhrase(semCat: high_pos)*
4. *Intensifier(orth: so) happy*

Using the heuristic above, the approach chooses the result, *high_pos*, from the variant 3 because it contains only one instantiated class that is an instance of the class *EmotionalPhrase*. Other parsing variants cannot be used: the variant 1 contains an instance of class *EmotionalPhrase* but in total 2 instances; the variant 2 contains no instances of the class *EmotionalPhrase* class at all; the variant 4 contains no instance of the class *EmotionalPhrase*.

6.3.6 RESULTS

The proposed approach calculates results as solutions of a 3-classes problem or as a 5-classes problem. Table 30 shows the results of semantic affect sensing as a 3-classes problem (classes *pos*, *neg*, *unclassifiable* in FWF, classes *positive*, *negative*, *neutral* in BMRC-S). Note that the analysis of affect as a 3-classes problem is performed by using a set of 5-classes SPIN rules: the results of 5-classes analysis are mapped onto 3 classes (in FWF, high/low positive classes onto the *pos* class, high/low negative classes onto the *neg* class, neutral onto *unclassifiable*; in BMRC-S, high/low positive classes onto the *positive* class, high/low negative classes onto the *negative* class, neutral onto the *neutral* class).

Corpus	Baseln.	Gran.	Strategy	R_a	$R_{a\text{-}g}$	max R_a	max $R_{a\text{-}g}$	P_a	$P_{a\text{-}g}$
FWF	37.20	Majority	First phrase	47.20	45.02	-	-	44.09	42.76
			Last phrase	**47.64**	46.24	-	-	44.26	43.45
			Average vote	45.92	45.66	-	-	43.14	43.05
		Whole Text	First phrase	45.41	**47.30**	53.44	51.71	42.90	43.90
			Last phrase	47.45	46.70	53.87	50.90	44.05	43.57
			Average vote	42.79	44.36	52.05	50.43	41.15	42.18
		Subsent.	First phrase	47.20	45.22	53.44	51.71	44.08	42.88
			Last phrase	47.24	45.84	53.87	50.90	44.03	43.22
			Average vote	46.04	45.66	52.05	50.43	43.22	43.05
		Phrase	First phrase	44.79	43.71	53.44	51.71	42.90	42.13
			Last phrase	45.21	44.54	53.87	50.90	43.13	42.65
			Average vote	44.22	44.16	52.05	50.43	42.41	42.40
BMRC-S	52.34	Majority	First phrase	54.18	52.21	-	-	51.39	49.52
			Last phrase	53.33	53.15	-	-	50.45	50.38
			Average vote	52.11	51.88	-	-	48.72	48.21
		Whole Text	First phrase	49.34	**52.63**	62.17	60.29	46.37	49.98
			Last phrase	48.76	51.18	61.69	59.31	45.71	48.69
			Average vote	44.43	49.24	63.26	59.67	45.64	46.68
		Subsent.	First phrase	54.24	52.29	62.17	60.29	51.46	49.59
			Last phrase	53.72	53.06	61.69	59.31	50.86	50.23
			Average vote	52.86	52.14	63.26	59.67	49.34	48.41
		Phrase	First phrase	**54.65**	53.69	62.17	60.29	50.56	49.49
			Last phrase	54.60	**54.49**	61.69	59.31	50.50	50.36
			Average vote	54.44	53.29	63.26	59.67	50.01	48.86

Table 30: Semantic affect sensing for 3 classes

The *Corpus* column presents the tested corpus (FWF or BMRC-S); the *Baseln.* column is the baseline value averaged over classes calculated using the statistical approach in chapter 5 without optimizing the feature space; the *Gran.* column represents the granularity of the text division (either whole text, subsentences, phrases, or the majority vote); the *Strategy* column shows the utilized word-spotting strategy (first phrase, last phrase, average vote).

Results of affect sensing are calculated using 2 sets of SPIN rules that differ in the set of utilized grammatical SPIN rules: the first set contains all word-spotting SPIN rules and all grammatical SPIN rules; the second set consists of all word-spotting SPIN rules and the one-grammar rule-set corresponding to formula (81). Hence, columns with index *a* are values yielded using the first set of SPIN rules, columns with index *a-g* represent values using the second set of SPIN rules. The R_a column and the $R_{a\text{-}g}$ column show recall values averaged over classes, the P_a column and the $P_{a\text{-}g}$ column are the precision values averaged over classes. The *max* R_a column and the *max* $R_{a\text{-}g}$ column contain the maximal recall values averaged over classes for the case if one of the granularity yields correct results. The rows containing three maximal recall values are marked bold (maximal value for word-spotting, maximal value for all SPIN rules in the R_a column and the maximal value for one-grammar-rule set in the $R_{a\text{-}g}$ column). The results corresponding to the pure word-spotting are shown in rows *Whole text*. Note that other values such as, for instance, values in rows *Phrase* can not be considered as the results of the pure word-spotting since they are yielded by linking clauses and phrases.

Table 31 shows results of semantic affect sensing as solution of a 5-classes problem (*low_pos, high_pos, low_neg, high_neg, neutral* in BMRC-S).

Corpus	Baseln.	Gran.	Strategy	R_a	$R_{a\text{-}g}$	max R_a	max $R_{a\text{-}g}$	P_a	$P_{a\text{-}g}$
BMRC-S	30.81	Majority	First phrase	32.14	29.98	-	-	33.61	22.63
			Last phrase	31.49	30.72	-	-	32.96	23.08
			Average vote	30.75	29.84	-	-	32.12	21.64
		Whole Text	First phrase	28.77	**30.31**	38.73	35.23	27.37	22.58
			Last phrase	29.08	29.62	38.91	34.43	28.45	22.42
			Average vote	25.49	28.01	38.49	34.58	26.50	19.86
		Subsent.	First phrase	31.98	30.00	38.73	35.23	33.13	22.65
			Last phrase	31.54	30.70	38.91	34.43	32.49	23.04
			Average vote	31.17	30.04	38.49	34.58	31.93	21.79
		Phrase	First phrase	32.62	31.20	38.73	35.23	33.40	22.57
			Last phrase	**32.79**	**31.61**	38.91	34.43	33.52	22.87
			Average vote	32.78	30.81	38.49	34.58	34.42	21.94

Table 31: Semantic affect sensing for 5-classes

The descriptions of columns are the same as the descriptions of columns in Table 30.

6.4 DISCUSSION

The proposed approach to semantic affect sensing analyzes affect in short texts and calculates encouraging results that are considerably higher than choice by chance for different number of classes. In the 3-classes affect sensing in FWF: 33.33% vs. 47.64%; in BMRC-S, 33.33% vs. 54.65%. In the 5-classes affect sensing in BMRC-S: 20% vs. 32.79%.

Table 30 shows that the proposed semantic approach significantly improves classification rates as opposed to the statistical approach. For instance, in FWF, the *Majority, Last phrase* classification rate is 47.64% that is much higher than the statistical baseline value of 37.20%. Similarly, in BMRC-S the *Phrase, First phrase* classification rate of 54.65% is higher than the statistical baseline value of 52.34%).

Classification rates using the first grammar set are not significantly higher than classification rates using the second one-grammar-rule set: in FWF, the *Majority, Last phrase* value of 47.64% vs. the *Whole text, First phrase* value of 47.30%; in BMRC-S, the *Phrase, First phrase* value of 54.65% vs. the *Whole text, First phrase* value of 52.63%. This means that sophisticated grammar SPIN rules were used not in every application of semantic affect sensing.

In addition, the average vote word-spotting strategy does not generally provide enhancement of classification results: in FWF, the *Majority, Last phrase* value of 47.64% vs. the *Majority, Average vote* value of 45.66% in contrast to the *Phrase, First phrase* value of 54.65% vs. the *Phrase, Average vote* value of 54.44%.

To assess the utilized SPIN rules, statistics of their use were collected. This statistics illustrate what rules were chosen by the SPIN engine for affect sensing in a classified text (cf. Table 38). Noteworthy are the last two, the most frequently used rules: the rule *EmotionalItem(semCat:$T) Concept() → EmotionalPhrase(semCat:$T)* used 172 times in FWF and 428 times in BMRC-S, and the rule *EmotionalItem(semCat:$T) → EmotionalPhrase(semCat:$T)* used 173 times in FWF and 203 times in BMRC-S. This means that sophisticated grammatical rules did not fired.

Note that Table 38 shows the SPIN rules and the frequency of their use, but does not assess the correctness of the rule application. For instance, if a rule matches a text, this matching can be considered as valid in the following case: not only the application result has to be correct but also the applied rule was dedicated to apply. Otherwise, a rule can fire and yield a correct result value occasionally. Such study, however, would go outside the scope of this thesis since it requires an emotional corpus annotated with special means of lexical affect sensing like tags defining the desirable method of affect sensing.

6.5 FURTHER RESEARCH

Evidently, the result of the semantic approach significantly depends on emotion words. However, existing dictionaries, e.g. GI or WordNet-Affect, are not exhaustive and contain not every emotion word or phrase that has an emotional meaning. For instance, the example *That's a fat lot of good!* expresses the negative meaning since it contains an idiom *a fat lot of good*. However, the proposed semantic approach would only detect the positive word *good* because it is present in the system dictionary and oversee the negative idiom *a fat lot of good*. To overcome this shortcoming, the system should maintain processing rules not only for particular emotion words, but also for emotional phrases (emotional idioms). Dictionaries of emotional phrases/idioms can be found in [Cambridge, 2006a] and [Cambridge, 2006b]. Emotion words denoted as taboo words and swearwords are contained in [Swan, 2005].

Words can acquire an emotional meaning through the context of their use. For instance, the text *It was a good book!* expresses the positive affect since it contains the word *good*. However, if the book referred to is lost the text can be understood as negative. In order to resolve such issues, semantic affect sensing should consider contextual peculiarities.

Further research can elaborate on an algorithm for calculating an integral meaning deduced from the emotional meanings of particular granularities and thus make the sophisticated grammatical processing worth implementing. Moreover, since classification rates of such hypothetical algorithm are influenced by the *max* R_a and the *max* R_{a-g} variables that are significantly lower than 100%, future research should assess the algorithm using these values.

Recalling the problem of dedicated application of grammatical rules, semantic affect sensing should be conducted additionally on corpora that are labeled using the desirable rule application.

The proposed method to affect sensing analyzed affect of 3 classes or 5 classes. However, it can be generalized for affect sensing using other number of classes by adjusting corresponding rules for linking. For instance, a semantic approach to affect sensing can define phrase patterns that interpret the semantics of four emotional classes instead of five classes as in this thesis.

The proposed semantic approach relies on rules for linking phrases and clauses. Possible extension of rules that analyze clauses or phrases can provide conjunctions between analyzed clauses. For example, the structure of the analyzed text can be reflected more exactly by considering it in the subsentence/phrase combination: the text *Alexander is very sad even if everybody is happy.* would be represented by the subsentence combination *<high negative superordinate clause> even if <low positive subordinate clause>* that considers the subordinator *even if*.

Further research can implement a computer system that relies on the proposed semantic approach. Although it is difficult to give general recommendations on the choice of a granularity and a word-spotting strategy, some suggestions can be still made: combination *Majority, First phrase* yields a high classification rate as a 3-classes problem in FWF (47.20%) and a high classification rate as a 3-classes problem in BMRC-S (54.18%). This combination also produces a high classification rate of 32.14% in the 5-classes affect sensing in BMRC-S.

7 HYBRID EMOTION RECOGNITION

Chapter 5 described a statistical, fully automatic approach to opinion mining that categorized affect in texts using data mining techniques. However, the approach was difficult to comprehend for a human since it used only shallow information on classified texts. Chapter 6 introduced a semantic approach to affect sensing that is humanly plausible. However, it was inflexible and tailored to a particular corpus.

This chapter explores if it is possible to achieve a synergetic effect by combining strengths of both kinds of approach and at the same time by minimizing their weaknesses. In other words, the intention is to implement an approach to emotion recognition that classifies affect fully automatically and does not need hand-crafted work still remaining plausible for a human.

7.1 ANALYSIS OF LONG TEXTS

This section shows a hybrid approach to emotion recognition in long texts, e.g. movie reviews.

7.1.1 Feature Extraction and Evaluation

The main idea of the proposed hybrid approach is to split long texts in sentences; analyze each sentence separately by the proposed semantic approach; compose data mining datasets by evaluating features using yielded the values and scrutinize composed datasets using SVM.

Performed experiments use BMRC data. The approach extracts 8,932 sentences from 215 reviews and analyzes them using the semantic approach in chapter 6. Hence, the sentence:

Even the execrable Leprechaun wasn't this guilty (83)

is evaluated by the semantic approach yielding a 3-classes meaning

[majority: neg, whole_text: neg, phrases:neg, subsentences:neg] (84)

This meaning can be utilized for extraction of 4 features corresponding to particular granularities (referred hereafter to as granularity features).

The analyzed datasets are composed as follows:

1. A review is split in sentences using text syntax. Hence, symbols ".", "?", "!" are considered as sentence delimiters.

2. The algorithm calculates the maximal number of sentences in reviews, σ_{max} (in BMRC, σ_{max}=128 sentences). Some sentences can be dropped in order to compile different datasets.

3. The composed datasets contain 4×σ_{max} features (in BMRC, σ_{max}=512). The initial value of features is *neutral*.

4. Emotional meaning of each sentence is analyzed by the semantic approach in chapter 6 using the average vote word-spotting strategy.

5. For each sentence, a group of 4 granularity features is extracted in the order of granularities: majority, whole text, phrases, subsentences. The features are evaluated as 3-classes: *pos, neutral, neg*. For instance, 4 granularity features for the sentence (83) are evaluated as *neg, neg, neg, neg* as in (84).

In order to improve classification, the proposed approach drops $\sigma = \frac{n-1}{n}$ part of sentences (n is the number of the composed dataset) at the end of a review while composing analyzed datasets. This means that corresponding values of granularity features are not modified by the values of the semantic approach. For instance, no feature values of the first dataset (n=1) are modified by semantic values; the first 256 feature values of the second dataset (n=2) are modified by the values of granularity features from the semantic approach, and so on. The proposed approach composed 10 datasets each with 512 features where only 4 values are modified by the values of granularity features from the semantic approach.

7.1.2 RESULTS

The maximal recall value of 21.33% yields the forth dataset (n=4). It means that the first 96 sentences or 384 values of granularity features are considered for recognition.

7.1.3 DISCUSSION

The yielded recognition rates are significantly higher in BMRC than the choice by chance, 21.33% vs. 11.(1)%. Moreover, this result is higher than the grammatical result (16.89%) and is comparable with the recognition rates of the stylometric datasets (28.07%) and deictic datasets (25.11%).

7.2 ANALYSIS OF SHORT TEXTS

This section shows a hybrid approach to emotion recognition in short texts. The hybrid analysis of short texts can be performed using two methods: in the first method, the statistical approach is chosen as leading and the semantic approach supplies additional features; in the second method, affect sensing is performed using a rule-based approach that utilizes results of the semantic approach and the statistical approach.

Affect sensing using the hybrid approach is studied on 759 sentences from FWF. The approach utilizes 49 datasets from the statistical approach with s/n unigram features where $s=2,532$ is the number of unigrams in FWF; n is the chosen number of the dataset. The features are evaluated using the presence method; the utilized classifier is SVM; results are averaged over classes.

7.2.1 STATISTICAL APPROACH AS LEADING

This section discusses the hybrid approach to lexical affect sensing in short texts where the statistical approach can be considered as the main approach and the semantic approach is supplementary.

7.2.1.1 Feature Extraction and Evaluation

The statistical approach in chapter 5 is extended by additional features extracted from the semantic approach. Hence, in addition to the most frequent unigrams from the statistical approach, features resulting from the semantic approach are extracted (referred to hereafter as semantic features):

1. Four features corresponding to a granularity in the semantic approach: the *majority* feature, the *whole text* feature, the *subsentences* feature, the *phrases* feature. These features are evaluated as *value* based on the values from the semantic approach (*semantic_approach_result*) using three methods:

    a. The 01 method evaluates a semantic feature to 1 if the result of the semantic approach is either *neg* or *pos*, and evaluates to 0, otherwise, as follows.

    value = 1 if *semantic_approach_result*==*neg* or *semantic_approach_result*==*pos*;
    else *value* = 0 if *semantic_approach_result*==*null*
      or *semantic_approach_result*==*unclassifiable*;

b. The 012 method evaluates a semantic feature as follows

   value = 0 if *semantic_approach_result==neg*;
   value = 1 if *semantic_approach_result==unclassifiable*
      or *semantic_approach_result==neutral*
      or *value* = 1 if *semantic_approach_result==null*;
   value = 2 if *semantic_approach_result==pos*

c. The 0123 method evaluates a semantic feature as follows:

   value = 0 if *semantic_approach_result==neg*;
   value = 1 if *semantic_approach_result==unclassifiable*
      or *semantic_approach_result==neutral*;
   value = 2 if *semantic_approach_result==null*;
   value = 3 if *semantic_approach_result==pos*

2. 6 semantic features defined as binary relations between granularities (*majority-whole text, majority-subsentences, majority-phrases, whole text-subsentences, whole text-phrases, subsentences-phrases*) are evaluated using the binary comparison as follows:

   a. The *majority-whole text* feature evaluates to 1 if the *majority* vote is equal to the result of the *whole text* granularity, and 0 otherwise;

   b. The *majority-subsentences* feature evaluates to 1 if the *majority* vote is equal to the result of the *subsentences'* granularity, and 0 otherwise;

   c. The *majority-phrases* feature evaluates to 1 if the *majority* vote is equal to the result of the *phrases'* granularity, and 0 otherwise;

   d. The *whole text-subsentences* feature evaluates to 1 if the *whole text* result is equal to the result of the *subsentences'* granularity, and 0 otherwise;

   e. The *whole text-phrases* feature evaluates to 1 if the *whole text* result is equal to the result of the *subsentences'* granularity, and 0 otherwise;

   f. The *subsentences-phrases* feature evaluates to 1 if the *subsentences* result is equal to the result of the *subsentences'* granularity, and 0 otherwise.

7.2.1.2 Evaluation Example of Semantic Features

Evaluation of the semantic features is illustrated using the following example: the semantic approach yields the *null* result for the *whole text* granularity, the *neg* result for the *subsentences* granularity, the *pos* result for the *phrases* granularity. Accordingly, the *majority* granularity is equal to *null* because there is no majority vote.

1. The granularity features are evaluated as follows:

   a. The 01 method evaluates the *subsentences* and *phrases* granularity features to 1 because the *subsentences* granularity is *neg*, the *phrases* granularity is *pos*. The *whole text* granularity feature is evaluated as 0. The *majority* granularity feature is equal to 0 (there is no majority). Value vector for the granularity features is <0, 0, 1, 1> in the order of *majority, whole text, subsentences, phrases*.

   b. The 012 method evaluates the *subsentences* and *majority* granularity features to 0, the *whole text* granularity to 1, the *phrases* granularity to 2. Value vector for the granularity features is <0, 1, 0, 2> in the same order as above.

   c. The 0123 method evaluates the *subsentences* and *majority* granularity features to 0, the *whole text* granularity feature to 1, the *phrases* granularity feature to 3. Value vector for the granularity features is <0, 1, 0, 3> in the same order as above.

2. The binary relation features are evaluated as:

   a. The *majority-whole text* feature is evaluated as 1 since the *majority* and the *whole text* features are equal (*null* vs. *null*);

   b. The *majority-subsentences* feature is evaluated as 0 since the *majority* and *subsentences* features are not equal (*null* vs. *neg*);

   c. The *majority-phrases* feature is evaluated as 0 since the *majority* and the *phrases* features are not equal (*null* vs. *pos*);

   d. The *whole text-subsentences* feature is evaluated as 0 since the *whole text* and *subsentences* features are not equal (*null* vs. *neg*);

e. The *whole text-phrases* feature is evaluated as 0 since the *whole text* and *phrases* features are not equal (*null* vs. *pos*);

f. The *subsentences-phrases* feature is evaluated as 0 since the *subsentences* and *phrases* features are not equal (*neg* vs. *pos*);

7.2.1.3 Results

Table 32 shows the best classification recall values of the hybrid approach.

Optimization	Statistical source	Semantic source	Recall
—	1,266 words	All grammatical SPIN rules, the last phrase word-spotting strategy, method 01	41.93
—	2,532 words	All grammatical SPIN rules, the average vote word-spotting strategy, method 01	41.67
—	1,266 words	One-grammar rule, the average vote word-spotting strategy, method 01	41.50
simple merge	2,532 words	all semantic features	41.60
BEH	466 words	All grammatical SPIN rules, the first phrase word-spotting strategy, method 01	**44.99**[53]
BEH	361 words	No semantic features	44.49[54]
after conventional forward selection	2,532 words	all semantic features	41.70[55]
FSH	2,532 words	all semantic features	41.63[56]

Table 32: Results of hybrid affect sensing

The *Optimization* column shows the optimization method of the corresponding dataset, the *Statistical source* column shows the number of lexical features (unigrams) that are contained in the classified dataset, the *Semantic source* column shows utilized semantic features and their evaluation method, the *Recall* column shows the corresponding recall value. The last rows show the results of affect sensing using BEH and FSH. The *simple merge* row contains the affect sensing result using

---

[53] 42 eliminated features: a after and as away behind bus could day do fall fell first for head ice in it let looking next night not now of *phrases* please stairs stared stood *subsentences* the their then there they those through under *utterance* went you

[54] 22 eliminated features: a an and are away behind breath could day fell for him just of so some than there they through two was

[55] 27 selected features: addict bar burning castle course drank fire forever girl holds once oxygen same smoke soya start store than the took train turn want watched wet world would

[56] 32 selected features: 5[f], behind[f], blew[f], burning[f], car[i], closed[f], course[f], drank[f], drink[i], drinks[f], drunken[f], eat[f], fire[f], fit[f], flask[f], girl[f], girls[f], himself[f], never[f], old[f], our[f], start[i], stone[i], store[f], the[f], those[f], train[f], whizzed[f], world[f], would[i], wrong[f], yesterday[f]

the pure merging of feature sets. The maximal value after heuristics to feature space optimization is shown in bold.

7.2.1.4 Discussion

Affect sensing results increase when semantic features are added to the statistical affect sensing (the best value of 37.20% in the statistical approach vs. the best value of 41.93% in the hybrid approach), but are still lower than the values of the pure semantic approach (the best value of 41.93% in the hybrid approach vs. the best value of 47.64% in the semantic approach).

The result of hybrid affect sensing after BEH is 44.99%. However, this result is lower than the best result of the pure semantic affect sensing although additional 466 features from the statistical approach were extracted (44.99% vs. 47.64%).

The features eliminated by BEH are all granularity features (*utterance, subsentences, phrases*) besides the *majority* feature. Moreover, the best result of the pure statistical approach after BEH (44.49%) is only 0.5% lower than the result of the hybrid approach after BEH (44.99%).

Furthermore, according to FSH optimization of feature space yields results that are quite different from results after optimization according to FSH in the long text corpora (except PMRC): the recognition rates do not improve not only compared with the pure semantic approach (41.63% vs. 47.64%), but are even unexpectedly worse than the results after BEH (41.63% vs. 44.99%).

7.2.2 SEMANTIC APPROACH AS LEADING

So far, the hybrid approach to affect sensing used the statistical means and utilized a particular data mining algorithm to perform affect recognition (SVM). However, it is also possible to take another, rule-based way to affect sensing and perform affect sensing by utilizing the classification results of the semantic approach and the result of the statistical approach.

This section discusses the hybrid approach to lexical affect sensing that relies on the empirical rules that make use of both the results of semantic affect sensing and the result of statistical affect sensing.

7.2.2.1 Empirical Rules

This section describes empirical rules for hybrid affect sensing. When composing classification rules, this thesis considered C4.5. However, performed experiments did not reveal applicability of C4.5 for rules composition and therefore it is not considered further in this thesis.

Instead, own rules are compiled. The rules utilize 3 results of the semantic approach (result of the *whole text* granularity, result of the *subsentences'* granularity, result of the *phrases'* granularity) and a result of the statistical approach, in total, 4 values (Figure 49).

> *if statistical==unclassifiable and whole_text==unclassifiable and phrases==unclassifiable and subsentences==unclassifiable:*
>> *calculatedRating=unclassifiable*
>
> *elif whole_text==unclassifiable and phrases==unclassifiable and subsentences==unclassifiable:*
>> *calculatedRating=unclassifiable*
>
> *elif no majority with statistical value:*
>> *calculatedRating=semanticmajority*
>
> *else:*
>> *calculatedRating=majority*

Figure 49: Rules in hybrid affect sensing

Variable *statistical* denotes the classification result of statistical affect sensing; variables *whole_text*, *phrases*, *subsentences* are the results calculated by different granularities in the semantic approach; variable *semanticmajority* denotes the majority vote on the basis of the values of the *whole_text*, *phrases*, *subsentences* variables; variable *majority* denotes the majority vote on the basis of the *statistical*, *whole_text*, *phrases*, *subsentences* variables. The value *unclassifiable* refers to neutral annotations in FWF. The variable *calculatedRating* holds the final result of classification.

Note that the proposed rules assume for simplicity that a value of *majority* or *semanticMajority* can be always calculated or otherwise, a value of *calculatedRating* is undefined.

7.2.2.2 Results

The hybrid approach yields the maximal recall value of 48.05% using the rules in Figure 49 where the results of the semantic approach are calculated using all grammatical SPIN rules and the *Last phrase* strategy. Noteworthy that the result of the statistical part in the hybrid approach can be calculated using different number of statistical features: either using 101 words ($n=25$), or using 87 words ($n=29$), or using 76 words ($n=33$), or using 72 words ($n=35$), or using 68 words ($n=37$), or using 64 ($n=39$), or using 61 words ($n=41$), or using 58 words ($n=43$), or using 56 words ($n=45$), or using 53 words ($n=47$), or using 51 words ($n=49$), or using 49 words ($n=51$) where n is the number of the statistical dataset.

7.2.2.3 Discussion

The hybrid approach improves results of affect sensing to 48.05% as opposed to the maximal result of statistical approach of 47.64%.

This improvement is very small (less than 0.5%), but yet possible. It is especially important considering that this result was yielded using simple rules in Figure 49. Since the results of statistical approach or the semantic approach separately yield lower values, it makes sense to examine the hybrid approach more carefully.

The applied rules can be considered as an extension of the majority calculation. In fact, the proposed rules calculate the majority of emotional votes using both the result of statistical affect sensing and the results of different granularities in the semantic approach (*whole text, phrases, subsentences*).

7.3 FURTHER RESEARCH

Although the proposed hybrid approach to analyzing long texts yields recognition rates lower than recognition rates in statistical approach using lexical features, 21.33% vs. 34.22%, this approach shouldn't be underestimated. Similar to the [Pang et al., 2002] approach, the proposed approach can utilize the structure of reviews as follows: in the proposed approach, this was done by dropping some sentences, but further experiments can additionally consider emotional meaning of sentences at the beginning of a review or at its end or in middle. Moreover, since the hybrid approach uses meanings of particular sentences in the semantic approach, the recognition result could improve if the semantic approach improves.

The results of the proposed approach (48.05%) increase compared with results of the semantic approach (47.64%). Hence, it is beneficial to study this approach in future, for instance, develop other rules than those in Figure 49.

Moreover, the findings in the hybrid approach can be utilized in the multimodal fusion since the experimental setting and data have strong resemblance (cf. next chapter).

8 AFFECT SENSING USING MULTIMODAL FUSION

Until now, this thesis discussed approaches to opinion mining/affect sensing utilizing information of only one (lexical) modality. However, the lexical modality is not the single modality that can be used in emotion recognition. For instance, affect analysis can be performed using acoustic information, e.g. the raise or the drop of human voice.

This thesis examines a method of combining data of different modalities called multimodal fusion, an extension of more general data fusion. An introduction to data fusion is shown in Appendix E. Existing approaches to multimodal fusion are discussed in section 8.1. Section 8.2 describes experimental setting in multimodal fusion. Section 8.3 shows results of decision-level fusion. Section 8.4 presents results of feature-level fusion. The fusion results are discussed in section 8.5. Further research is investigated in section 8.6.

8.1 EXISTING APPROACHES

Various approaches examine multimodal fusion. [Kim & André, 2006] study affect sensing using fusion of physiological and acoustic data. The approach uses 77 features from the physiological modality, e.g. mean value, standard deviation, and ratio of max/min of physiological signals such as skin conductivity. Also, the approach utilizes 61 features from the acoustic modality, e.g. mean, absolute extremum, root mean square, standard deviation of energy. The approach implements feature-level fusion, decision-level fusion and hybrid fusion. In feature-level fusion, the approach merges features of two modalities. In decision-level fusion, the output of uni-modal classifiers is combined using a probabilistic approach. Hybrid fusion utilizes the output of the feature-level fusion as an additional input to the decision-level fusion. For classification the approach uses the LDA classifier and yields the best accuracy of 55% using the feature-level fusion.

[Busso et al., 2004] study multimodal fusion using the facial expression modality and the acoustic modality at the feature level and the decision level. The examined corpus includes 258 emotional sentences annotated with 4 emotions. As acoustic features, they use features based on the mean, standard deviation, range, maximum, minimum and medians of pitch and energy. As facial features, the approach uses a 10-dimensional feature vector representing positions of 3D face markers. In feature-level fusion, the approach merges features from both modalities; in decision-level fusion, the approach utilizes either the best 10 features selected using forward selection or uses posterior probabilities and weights modalities. By fusing the facial and acoustic modalities the approach achieves an improvement of accuracy rates while the performance of the two fusion approaches is similar.

[Schuller et al., 2005] study multimodal fusion using the acoustic and the lexical modality. Experiments are performed on 1,144 phrases from seven American movie scripts consisting of 7.0 words in average using the feature-level fusion. Phrases are annotated by 2 annotators. The number of emotional classes is not specified. The number of acoustic features is 276; the lexical features are lemmatized unigrams without 93 stopwords. For classification, the approach utilizes SVM, NB, C4.5, and the ensemble classifier using C4.5 and reveals best classification results using SVM. Correspondingly, the approach yields the classification rate of 90.30% using the dataset containing only acoustic features. In contrast, the approach yields the value of 65.07% using the dataset with only linguistic features. In summary, the fusion yields classification enhancement by absolute value of 3.51%.

Truong and Raaijmakers describe an approach to automatic recognition of spontaneous emotions that relies on the acoustic and the lexical modalities ([Truong & Raaijmakers, 2008]). It uses acoustic features (mean, standard deviation, max-min, the averaged slope of pitch and intensity) and lexical features (N-grams and the speech rate[57]). The approach analyses positive/negative emotions and presents both uni-modal results and results of fusion at the feature level obtaining slight improvement after fusion.

In summary, the fusion of multiple modalities led to an increase of recognition results. However, this thesis extends previous approaches in several respects. First of all, previous work focused mainly on calculating higher classification results without investigating thoroughly the influence of separate modalities. Then, the previous approaches analyzed only a limited number of linguistic features, i.e. lexical, while this thesis studies fusion using acoustic, lexical stylometric, and deictic features. Furthermore, the study in this thesis considers the context of turns in classification. This thesis provides a clear visualization of fusion results by means of a tree representation and explores how changes of classification rates of one modality influence the overall recognition results.

---

[57] *Speech rate* is usually considered as a prosodic feature but since its calculation is based on lexical feature, i.e. number of words per seconds, in this particular case it is assumed to be a lexical feature.

8.2 EXPERIMENTAL SETTING

Multimodal fusion is examined using SAL. Fusion utilizes data of two modalities, the acoustic modality and the linguistic modality with datasets with three already known feature streams: datasets with lexical features, datasets with stylometric features, datasets with deictic features. The acoustic modality interprets a turn as an audio file containing the sound of the turn whereas a turn is interpreted in the lexical stream as its text, e.g. *I'm very happy*. The stylometric stream interprets a turn as, e.g. the lengths of text words, and in the deictic stream a text is interpreted using its deictic properties. Hypothetically possible is the fourth, grammatical stream represented by datasets with grammatical features. However, this stream is discarded in this thesis due to the low classification result and presumably low influence on fusion results (cf. classification result in section 5.3).

In order to reduce computational costs, performed experiments consist of two stages: in the first stage, datasets containing features of a particular modality are composed and classified; in the second stage, only 10 datasets that yielded the highest classification rates are utilized in further experiments.

In the acoustic modality, 2 datasets are utilized for classification — a dataset for dialogue history 0 (without history) and a dataset for dialogue history 7 (current turn in the context of 7 previous turns). The datasets contain 1,316 features based on logarithmised pitch, signal energy, MFCCs; the short-term frequency spectrum, and the harmonics-to-noise ratio that are processed using the EmoVoice software ([Vogt et al., 2008a]).

In the lexical stream, 29 datasets are compiled containing unigrams from the SAL frequency list in the same manner as compilation of datasets in the statistical approach. Consequently, a lexical dataset extracts s/n unigrams where s is the length of the frequency list in words and n is the dataset number (from 1 to 9 in increment 1 and from 11 to 49 in increment 2). The frequency list of SAL (variable s) consists of *2,033* words.

In the stylometric stream, 31 datasets are composed. A dataset contains at most 730 features that are combination of letters, word lengths, digrams, standard deviation of the sequence with word lengths, and sentence lengths in words.

A deictic stream compiles 63 datasets each containing at most 530 features: demonstratives as determiners, demonstratives as pronouns as well as time references, place references, forms of the third person, and 526 stopwords from WEKA (cf. section 5.1.2).

The lexical and deictic features are evaluated in the performed experiments as a *frequency* vector. The acoustic and stylometric features are evaluated corresponding to their names. The classifier is SVM from the WEKA toolkit that uses 10-fold cross-validation; results are averaged over classes.

8.3 RESULTS OF DECISION-LEVEL FUSION

Fusion at the decision level relies on the majority vote from separate datasets. If no majority can be established, the dataset with the lowest recall value in uni-modal recognition is gradually left out, until either majority voting is possible or only one dataset remains (Figure 50).

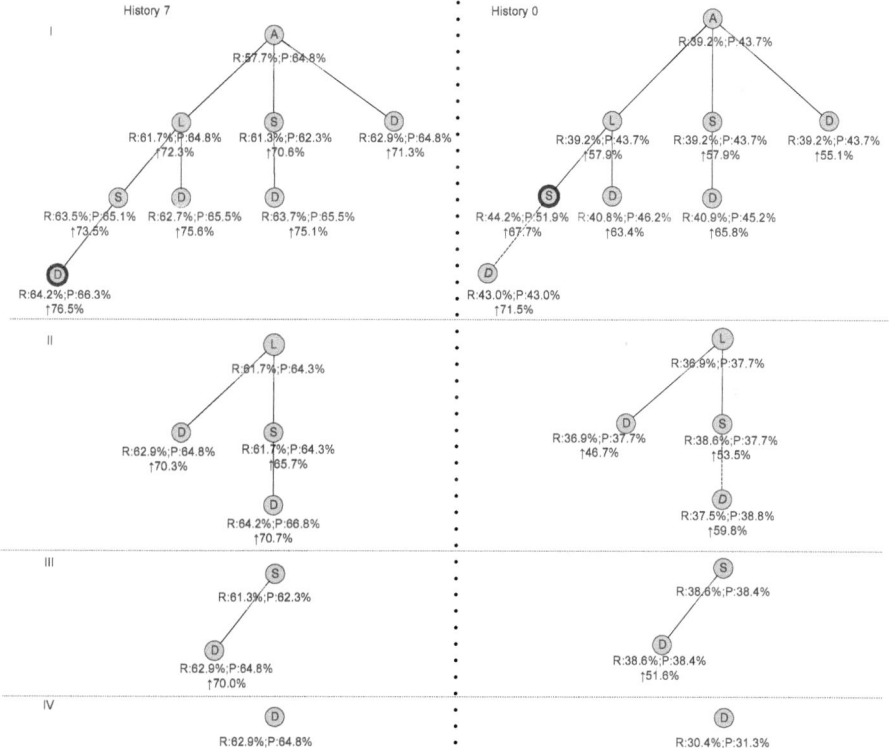

Figure 50: Decision-level fusion

Results of decision-level fusion are shown as trees. Each path in these trees represents a dataset with the feature groups contained in this dataset. Each abstract I, II, III, IV contains result trees for different combinations of datasets starting with a different root modality. The trees to the left show fusion results using the current turn in the context of the turns of history 7. The trees to the right show fusion results without history consideration. For instance, the A-L-S-D path in the abstract I corresponds to a dataset with the acoustic (A), lexical (L), stylometric (S), and deictic features (D); whereas the S-D path in the abstract III represents a dataset with stylometric and deictic features.

Classification results are shown using 2 rows: the first row denotes the class-wise recall (R) and precision values (P) yielded by the corresponding dataset. The second row is shown as $\hat{r}$<*maximal multimodality value*> where <*maximal multimodality value*> is the value that could be obtained in the case of perfect fusion when at least one of the participating datasets would classify a particular instance correctly and the multimodal classification would rely on this dataset. Nodes that represent datasets with maximal recall values are shown in bold circles. Arcs that indicate decreasing recall values are dashed; the names of the corresponding nodes are italicized.

For instance, dataset A yields the recall value of 57.7% for history length 7 and 39.2% for history length 0. Dataset A-L calculates the recall value of 61.7% for history length 7 and 39.2% for history length 0. Dataset A-L-S yields the recall value of 63.5% for history length 7 and 44.2% for history length 0. Dataset A-L-S-D yields the recall value of 64.2% for history length 7 and the recall value of 43.0% for the history length 0.

Dataset A-L calculates the maximal multimodality value of 72.3% for history length 7 and 57.9% for history length 0. Dataset A-L-S calculates the maximal multimodality value of 73.5% for history length 7 and 67.7% for history length 0. Dataset A-L-S-D calculates the maximal multimodality value of 76.5% for history length 7 and 71.5% for the history length 0.

In order to study how overall classification results are influenced by classification rates of one dataset, the acoustic features are discretized. Discretization is a data mining method of feature evaluation that maps values in particular intervals onto interval names. For instance, the value of feature *pitch_mean* can be mapped as follows: values in interval (–∞, 108.5) are interpreted as the name *Interval1*, values in interval (108.5, 165.2) are interpreted as the name *Interval2*, values in interval (165.2, 221.5) are interpreted as the name *Interval3*, values in interval (221.5, -∞) are interpreted as the name *Interval4*. Hence, the sequence (120.9, 105.1, 187.3, 275.1) is interpreted as the sequence (*Interval2, Interval1, Interal3, Interval4*).

The discretization of acoustic datasets is performed using the Fayyad and Irani's discretization filter in the WEKA toolkit ([Fayyad & Irani, 1992]).

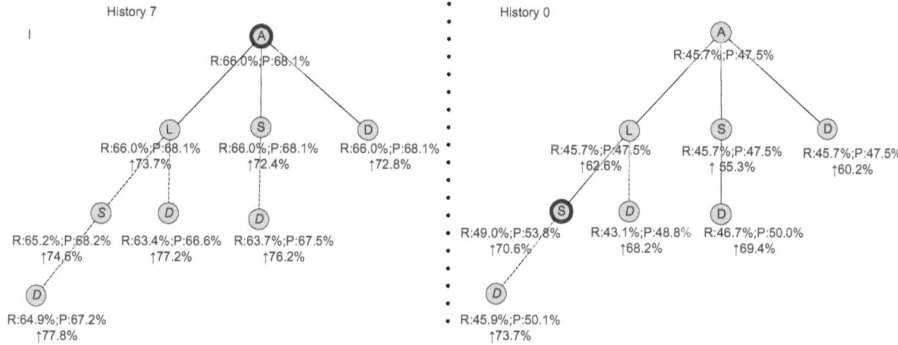

Figure 51. Decision-level fusion after discretization

Results after discretization are represented as trees similar to Figure 50.

8.4 RESULTS OF FEATURE-LEVEL FUSION

In the feature-level fusion, the examined data and the examination method are similar to that in the decision-level fusion. The feature-level fusion is performed by merging feature sets of participating datasets into a single dataset (Figure 52).

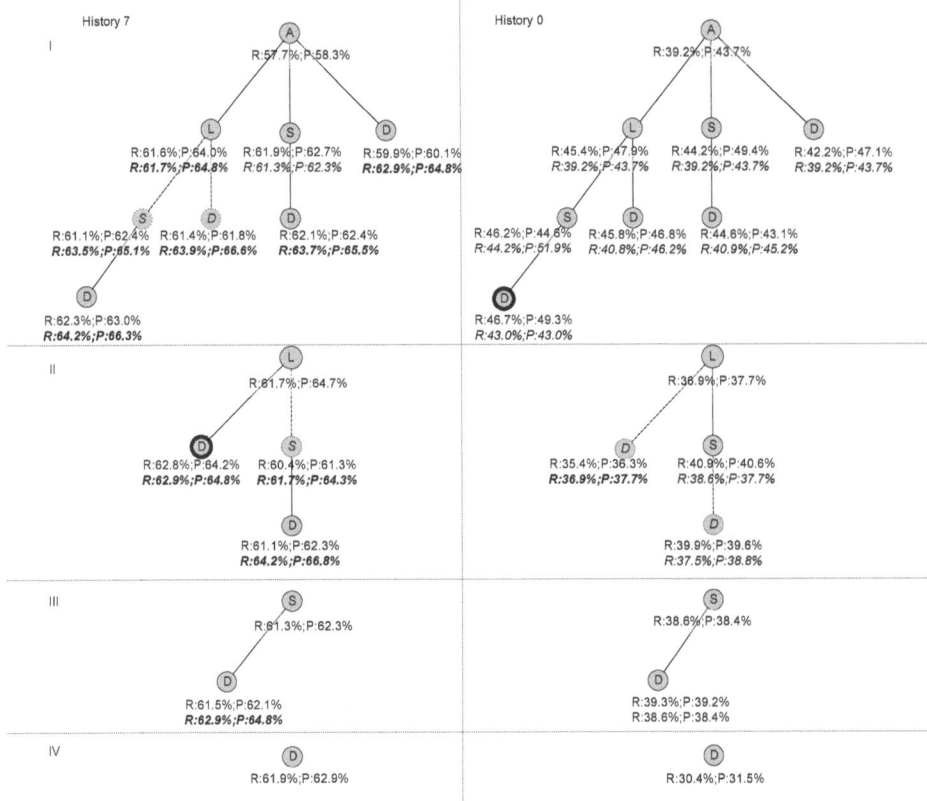

Figure 52: Feature-level fusion

Results are represented as trees similar to Figure 50. However, the results' representation has a slight difference. The first row represents the recall value (R) and the precision value (P). The second row in italics shows the results (R, P) of the decision-level fusion once more in order to facilitate comparison of two fusion types. If the recall value in the feature-level fusion is greater than that in the decision-level fusion the second row is shown in bold.

In the performed experiments, the feature space of the composed datasets for history 7 was optimized using the conventional forward selection and FSH (Table 33).

Optimization	Lexical features	Prosodic features	Recall
—	2,033 words	—	60.21%
after optimizing using the conventional forward selection	2,033 words	—	61.16%
after optimizing using FSH	2,033 words	—	65.76%
—	—	1316 prosodic features	51.71%
merging	2,033 words	1316 prosodic features	56.19%
after optimizing using the conventional forward selection	2,033 words	1316 prosodic features	52.95%[58]
after optimizing using FSH	2,033 words	1316 prosodic features	51.48%[59]

Table 33: Optimizing maximal results in feature-level fusion for history 7

The *Optimization* column describes the optimization method of the corresponding dataset; the initial set of utilized lexical features is shown in the *Lexical features* column; the initial set of utilized prosodic features is shown in the *Prosodic features* column; the yielded recall value is shown in the *Recall* column. The lists of selected features after FSH are provided according to the pattern <*unigram*> [<*evaluation method*>] where the feature <*unigram*> is evaluated using the

---

[58] 90 selected features: i you of it do but erm laugh get on no so nice or yeah them time spike as oh been poppy we happy obadiah life some other lot from doing should holiday else end nothing lots thank before after she anything true mood sit money sleep night ever bloody difficult along engage stop large cheerful pay leave play plane died crunch 0 tight mfcc1d_maxs_mean mfcc1d_maxs_var mfcc2d_maxs_median mfcc9d_maxs_var mfcc9d_maxs_3-1quart mfcc9d_mins_1quart mfcc11d_maxs_max-min mfcc11d_maxs_1quart mfcc11d_mins_mean mfcc12d_mean mfcc12d_maxs_1quart mfcc3dd_maxs_mean mfcc6dd_mean mfcc7dd_mins_1quart mfcc8dd_3quart mfcc9dd_max-min mfcc9dd_var mfcc10dd_maxs_1quart mfcc10dd_mins_mean mfcc11dd_maxs_median mfcc11dd_mins_min energy_maxs_mean energy_maxs_magni_max energy_mins_mean energy_mins_magni_3-1quart energy_delta_mins_var

[59] 95 selected features: a[i], absolute[i], alright[i], and[f], are[f], as[f], box[i], databases[f], erm[f], get[f], go[i], i[f], imagine[i], know[i], laugh[f], lazy[f], like[f], lip[f], mfcc1_median[i], mfcc12_1quart[f], mfcc12dd_mean[i], mfcc1_max[f], mfcc1_maxs_max-min[i], mfcc1_maxs_max[f], mfcc1_maxs_min[f], mfcc1_maxs_var[f], mfcc1_median[f], mfcc1_mins_3quart[i], mfcc1_mins_median[f], mfcc1d_median[i], mfcc1d_mins_3quart[i], mfcc2_max[i], mfcc2_maxs_max-min[f], mfcc2_mean[i], mfcc2_mins_max[f], mfcc2d_max[f], mfcc2d_maxs_1quart[f], mfcc2d_maxs_max-min[f], mfcc2dd_max-min[f], mfcc2dd_max[i], mfcc3_3quart[f], mfcc3_maxs_mean[i], mfcc3_mean[f], mfcc3_mins_mean[f], mfcc3d_maxs_1quart[i], mfcc4_mean[f], mfcc4_median[i], mfcc4d_max-min[f], mfcc4d_max[f], mfcc4d_var[f], mfcc5d_1quart[f], mfcc5d_3-1quart[f], mfcc5d_maxs_3quart[f], mfcc5d_maxs_mean[f], mfcc5d_maxs_var[i], mfcc5d_mean[f], mfcc5d_median[f], mfcc5d_mins_3quart[i], mfcc5d_mins_max[i], mfcc5d_var[f], mfcc5dd_median[i], mfcc6d_mean[f], mfcc9_mean[f], mfcc9_mins_3quart[i], mfcc_mean[f], mfcc_median[f], mfccdd_median[i], mfccdd_mins_3-1quart[i], miss[f], nice[f], oh[f], pitch_mins_magni_3quart[f], pitch_mins_steep_max-min[i], pitch_mins_steep_var[i], poppy[f], rationale[f], real[f], relationships[f], rubbish[f], same[f], session[f], sigh[f], so[f], stress[f], sun[f], them[f], they[f], think[i], three[i], very[i], we[i], would[f], yeah[f], you[i], young[f]

evaluation method <evaluation method> (the frequency method - *f*, or the presence method - *p*, or the inversion method -*i*).

In order to study how overall classification results are influenced by classification rates of one modality, the acoustic features are discretized (Figure 53).

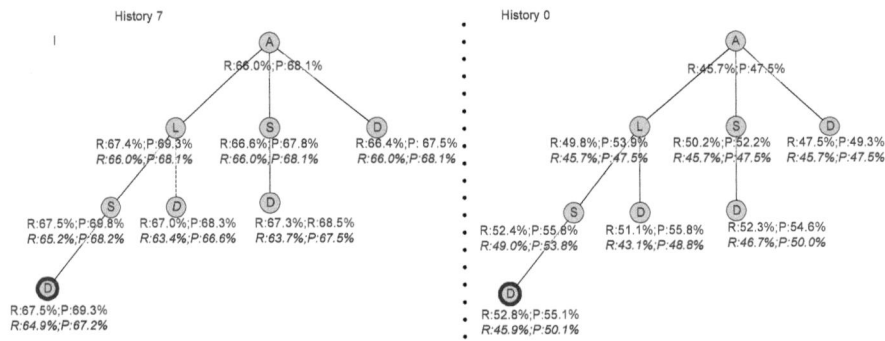

Figure 53. Feature-level fusion after discretization

Results are represented as trees similar to Figure 52.

8.5 DISCUSSION

This section discusses results of multimodal fusion.

The maximal multimodality value can be considered as expectation of the maximal recall value that can be achieved using the participating datasets or as an anticipated upper bound of recognition (the coverage). Moreover, the maximal multimodality value can be assumed to provide a metrics for anticipating fusion result: the higher is this value, the higher overall classification result can be expected. Note that the maximal modality value resembles the max value in the semantic approach (cf. section 6.3.5) since it can be also utilized for assessing the sensing approach.

Correspondingly, this thesis assumes that the classification rates in decision-level fusion would significantly enhance if the proposed maximal multimodality value would go to 100%. The maximal recall value of 64.2% in the decision-level fusion (the A-L-S-D feature tree) is about 1.4% higher in contrast to 62.8% in the feature-level fusion (the L-D feature tree). Moreover, the recall value of 64.2% is only about 12% lower than the maximal multimodality value of 76.5%.

The difference between the calculated recall value and the maximal multimodality value in the decision-level fusion can be utilized for assessing the utilized algorithm for the decision-level fusion. The smaller this value is, the better is the utilized algorithm for the decision-level fusion. For instance, the difference is equal to 12.3% for the A-L-S-D path in the left tree (64.2% vs. 76.5%) whereas the difference is equal in the A-L-S-D path to 28.5% in the right tree (43.0% vs. 71.5%).

Evidently, consideration of the context of a turn allows substantial improvement of sensing rates. For instance, the results improve significantly, e.g. in the dataset L in the abstract I from 36.94% to 61.7% when turns are analyzed using the context. However, the results do not remarkably depend on the number of utilized features. For instance, the increase of the number of features from the dataset A-L in the abstract II to the dataset A-L-S for the history length 7 does not lead to improvement of classification results (61.6% vs. 61.1%). Possibly, there is "feature overfitting" so that further improvement of classification is only possible when specific features are thrown away.

What is the best fusion method: decision-level fusion or feature-level fusion? The answer is not evident and this thesis can not claim that fusion at the feature level or at the decision level is more beneficial. On the one hand, a high number of rows shown in bold in Figure 52 means that decision-level fusion was more advantageous than feature-level fusion before discretization but, on the other hand, decision-level fusion is worse than feature-level fusion after discretization according to Figure 53.

Nevertheless, the decision-level fusion based on the majority vote is very attractive since it can be simply implemented and is humanly comprehensible. The better the sensing results of a particular modality are, the better is the final result of the decision-level fusion. Hard to overlook is also the general advantage of the decision-level fusion over the feature-level fusion — if a particular modality fails to classify data correctly due to missing means (appropriate features) a classification result of another modality can be used instead. The decision-level fusion is independent from the algorithm of affect sensing, for example, SVM, an can hereby rely on rules that can be composed using commonsense. Moreover, the decision-level fusion allows for measuring anticipated result of fusion using the maximal multimodality value. This anticipation is not evident in the feature-level fusion. Moreover, the feature-level fusion scored better results than the decision-level fusion (64.2% vs. 67.5%).

The discretization of acoustic values remarkably improves classification rates. After discretization, acoustic datasets score better than linguistic datasets. In contrast, without discretization, linguistic datasets score better than acoustic features if context is considered. Noteworthy that discretization of acoustic values in the A dataset without history brings about improvement of recognition from 6.5%= 45.7%–39.2% to the almost same improvement for A-L-S-D without history 6.1%=52.8%–46.7% whereas the improvement speed in the A dataset with history 7 stagnates from 8.3%=66.0%–57.7% to only 4.7%=67.5%–62.8% (the half).

The recognition results do not generally improve by fusing linguistic and acoustic features. Only if no context was considered feature-level fusion led to better results than the analysis of the single information streams. However, when considering the context, the recognition rates obtained for the single information streams outperformed the fusion result.

8.6 FURTHER RESEARCH

Future work can elaborate on other rules of semantic analysis in the decision-level fusion than those in section 6.3.3.

Further research can enhance results of the multimodal fusion by improving the classification results of separate modalities or by adding new modalities, for example, the visual modality ([Schröder, 2008]). Different modalities participating in the multimodal fusion can be weighted thus improving results of multimodal fusion. Moreover, optimization methods can be applied to the fused datasets.

9 CONCLUSION

This thesis discussed approaches to emotion recognition from texts and showed corresponding classification results using data of different emotional corpora. This dissertation concludes with the most significant contributions of this thesis and presents opportunities for further research.

9.1 CONTRIBUTIONS

This section presents theoretical contributions of this thesis that address theoretical shortcomings of existing approaches to emotion recognition and compares the proposed approaches. Furthermore, this section discusses experimental contributions that describe results of performed experiments, application-related contributions that define issues for application development, practical contributions of this thesis that led to development of concrete computer systems and implementation of the proposed approaches to emotion recognition. The contributions in this section are described only at high level since more detailed low-level contributions were already discussed in connection with the corresponding approaches in section 5.5 (statistical approach), section 6.4 (semantic approach), sections 7.1.3, 7.2.1.4, 7.2.2.3 (hybrid approach), section 8.5 (affect sensing using fusion). An overview of achievements resulting in regard of this thesis can be found in Appendix F.

9.1.1 COMPARISON OF THE PROPOSED APPROACHES

In the following, this thesis presents the most important findings resulting from the comparison of the corresponding approaches (statistical, semantic, hybrid using fusion):

1. *Statistical-semantic:* This thesis found out that recognition rates for short texts yielded by semantic approaches are higher than corresponding recognition rates yielded by statistical methods.

2. *Statistical-hybrid:* This thesis showed different ways of using the statistical approach as leading in the hybrid emotion recognition. Although the obtained results are not as high as expected, the influence of the statistical approach in hybrid emotion recognition should not be underestimated.

3. *Statistical-fusion*: This thesis showed approaches to multimodal fusion that utilize the statistical approach to opinion mining as leading in order to facilitate fusion both at the decision level and at the feature level.

4. *Semantic-hybrid:* This thesis showed the use of the semantic affect sensing as leading where the approach utilizes rules based on final results of the statistical approach in the hybrid emotion recognition.

5. *Hybrid-fusion:* This thesis showed that the multimodal fusion and the hybrid approach are similar in that they both make use of heterogeneous sources of information in order to improve results of emotion recognition.

9.1.2 THEORETICAL CONTRIBUTIONS

The following theoretical achievements of this thesis are worth noting (with regard to the shortcomings of the existing approaches in section 3.5):

1. *Generality*: The proposed statistical approach can be considered as general since it can be utilized for emotion recognition in any corpus. This thesis discussed in section 5.4 classification rates of corpora whose texts were distinguished regarding such properties as the length, verbal intensity of emotional expression, grammatical correctness, consistency, continuity, and the author of the emotional text/its annotator (cf. shortcoming 1).

2. *Consideration of grammatical findings in statistical opinion mining:* Grammatical features in statistical opinion mining were introduced as well as the method of their extraction and evaluation. Hence, this thesis showed how statistical approach can benefit from grammatical comprehensibility (cf. shortcoming 3).

3. *Consideration of the authorship attribution:* The thesis utilized means from authorship attribution to opinion mining (cf. shortcoming 5).

4. *Results interpretation:* Various measures to interpret the obtained classification results were introduced considering the costs of misclassification, similarity between emotional classes, and the number of classification classes: issues that take into special consideration the peculiarities of the emotional domain (cf. shortcoming 6).

5. *Differentiated semantic approach and its evaluation:* This thesis described in chapter 6 a method for semantic affect sensing that performed the differentiated analysis of short texts whose affect can be distinguished using any number of emotional classes, e.g. four classes. The approach answered such questions as what linguistic elements of short texts are worthy of notice; how utilized rules that carry out differentiated affect sensing look like (cf. shortcoming 8).

6. *Hybrid approach:* A hybrid approach that combines the statistical approach and the semantic approach was discussed in chapter 7. Although the thesis could not demonstrate any significant improvement in recognition results, an approach was introduced that may benefit from the flexibility of the statistical approach and the comprehensibility of the semantic approach (cf. shortcoming 9).

9.1.3 EXPERIMENTAL CONTRIBUTIONS

This thesis presented the following experimental contributions (with regard to the shortcomings of the existing approaches in section 3.5):

1. *Obtained results:* This thesis showed recognition rates of various approaches obtained for different corpora. Recognition rates of statistical opinion mining were shown in section 5.4. Results of semantic affect sensing were presented in section 6.3.6. Sections 7.1.2, 7.2.1.3, 7.2.2.2 showed results of the hybrid emotion recognition. Sections 8.3 and 8.4 showed results of multimodal fusion (cf. shortcoming 1).

2. *Thorough examination of data-mining issues in opinion mining:* This thesis elaborated in section 5.2 on the core data-mining issues of the statistical processing and provided a comparison of classification results for different classifiers, different evaluation methods, and normalized/non-normalized feature values. Furthermore, this thesis performed opinion mining in different corpora and showed in section 5.4 classification rates using datasets with different types of extracted features (lexical, stylometric, deictic, grammatical). In section 5.2.5, two heuristics to optimizing the feature space derived from traditional optimization methods were introduced. The obtained results show that classification rates can be significantly improved by them (cf. shortcoming 2).

3. *Composition of many datasets for comprehensive study of the proposed statistical approach:* A comprehensive study of opinion mining was presented in section 5.1.4 using datasets with lexical, deictic, stylometric, and grammatical features (cf. shortcoming 4).

4. *Plotting results:* This thesis introduced in section 5.2.3 a method for visualizing results in order to facilitate further experiments (cf. shortcoming 7);

5. *Multimodal fusion:* Fusion at the decision level and the feature level was studied in chapter 8. It introduced the maximal multimodality value that can be used for assessing experiments at the decision level and that shows the necessity of adding new modalities. This thesis hypothesized that classification results can be improved if some features are thrown away in order to avoid "feature overfitting" (cf. shortcoming 10).

This thesis described in the semantic approach the results of affect sensing for the proposed 3-classes or 5-classes affect sensing. In order to assess the use of the rules in the semantic approach, it collected corresponding statistics containing frequencies of rules' invocation (cf. Table 38).

9.1.4 APPLICATION-RELATED CONTRIBUTIONS

This thesis took into special consideration the applicability of the proposed approaches to implementing real applications. For this reason, it discussed results of statistical opinion mining using feature lists of different types (lexical, deictic, stylometric, grammatical) in order to facilitate not only exact but also quick emotion recognition. This thesis described different annotation methods of the corpus with spontaneous dialogues in section 5.4.2 in order to construct annotation that is humanly plausible and can be utilized for building believable applications. In section 5.3, different measures to interpreting classification results were introduced considering the similarity and the number of emotional classes, as well as the costs of misclassification. These measures can be utilized for developing realistic applications.

This thesis introduced in chapter 6 a semantic approach to affect sensing that relies on differentiated linking of clauses. Applications can generalize the introduced approach to other number of classes, for example, to four classes in order to consider requirements of some special scenario of affect sensing.

9.1.5   PRACTICAL CONTRIBUTIONS

This thesis introduced the statistical approach (cf. chapter 5) and the semantic approach to affect sensing (cf. chapter 6). These approaches were implemented as standalone/Webinterface/Webservice applications in the EmoText package (cf. section F.3). The semantic approach is applied in the EU projects listed in section F.4. Furthermore, the semantic approach was demonstrated at ACII 2009 (cf. section F.3).

9.2   ANSWERS TO THE RESEARCH QUESTIONS

This thesis answered the research questions in section 1.4:

1. How do the approaches in this thesis address the challenges of emotion recognition?

The thesis described a statistical approach to affect sensing in chapter 5 that addressed the challenges of opinion mining by using shallow information on texts, such as counts of occurring words. There was no need to compose exhaustive lists of emotion words. In contrast, the proposed semantic approach to affect sensing in chapter 6 simplified the problem by processing parts of texts separately, i.e. splitting them in parts and analyzing their emotional meaning independently; the emotional meaning of the original text was inferred from the yielded emotional meanings of the parts. The hybrid approach in chapter 7 considered a solution of the complexity problem by combining the results of the statistical approach and the semantic approach.

2. Are the approaches to emotion recognition in this thesis general enough to analyze a variety of emotional texts?

The thesis introduced a statistical approach to opinion mining that can be considered to be general and can be used for analysis of any corpus: a variety of corpora were examined and the obtained results were presented (section 5.4). In contrast, the proposed semantic approach (chapter 6) relied on grammatical rules based on interdependencies between words; therefore it is not general since it requires specific adjustments that are dependent on the analyzed corpus. Consequently, the hybrid approach (chapter 7) is also not general since it relies on the semantic approach.

3. **The number of existing approaches to emotion recognition is huge. How can the approaches in this thesis contribute to overcoming problems of emotion recognition?**

   Although the number of existing approaches to lexical affect sensing is significant, there are still many problems to be resolved. This thesis showed the shortcomings of existing approaches in section 3.5 and described how the proposed approaches can resolve some problems arising insofar.

4. **What information and what means should be used in emotion recognition for the analysis of emotional texts?**

   This thesis showed a statistical approach to affect sensing in chapter 5 that relied on lexical, deictic, stylometric, and shallow grammatical information. Moreover, it elaborated on questions of statistical affect sensing in section 5.2. Different measures for interpreting classification results were introduced in section 5.3. The semantic approach to affect sensing (chapter 6) utilized such information as emotion words, or grammatical information about intensifiers and negations. It used rules that rely on this information to infer emotional meaning of the analyzed text. The hybrid approach (chapter 7) made use of both approaches and, hence, their information and means.

5. **Can the means of approaches in this thesis be utilized for analysis of texts independent of their language?**

   This thesis described a statistical approach in chapter 5 that can be considered language-independent. In contrast, the semantic approach to affect sensing (chapter 6) is based on emotion words and on the grammar of a particular language and can not be considered to be language-independent. Consequently, the hybrid approach (chapter 7) is also not language-independent.

6. **This thesis investigates in detail emotion recognition using data of the lexical modality (lexical affect sensing). Can data of other modalities be utilized for affect sensing in order to enhance obtained results?**

   Yes. This thesis described a multimodal approach to affect sensing using the fusion of two modalities (linguistic/acoustic). It explored decision-level fusion and feature-level fusion and discussed trees with fusion results.

9.3 OUTLOOK

The obtained results of emotion recognition are encouraging. Nevertheless, there is still room for further enhancements:

1. Future work in statistical opinion mining was described thoroughly in section 5.6. Accordingly, statistical opinion mining can improve classification rates, for example, by considering genre of the analyzed text

2. Section 6.5 described next steps in semantic affect sensing. Consequently, semantic affect sensing can rely on rules other than in Table 35–Table 40. These rules can consider emotional meanings of texts that result from context pecularities;

3. Possible extensions of the hybrid approach were discussed in section 7.3. Thus, the hybrid approach can rely on algorithm other than in Figure 49;

4. Section 8.6 presented possible ways of improving the multimodal fusion. In future, multimodal fusion can add new modalities in order to improve results of affect sensing. Or further research can study multimodal fusion in connection with findings in the hybrid approach — both approaches utilize heterogeneous data from many sources and can be considered to be supplementary.

Other amplifications of this thesis can also be used for further research:

1. *Application development*: Further research could address the findings of this thesis to the development of affective applications such as applications specified in chapter 1.1 that perform recognition, modelling, and simulation of emotions. For instance, an affective application can be a multi-agent system that considers interaction dynamics between participating agents and maintains the BDI agents on the basis of JADEX ([Jadex, 2009]).

2. *Believable models of personality*: further research can utilize the findings of this thesis for building believable models of human personality. For instance, such models can be based on HMMs for affective behaviour implemented in technical companions ([Companions, 2009]). First findings of building believable HMMs relying on perceived emotional data were already discussed in [Osherenko, 2008].

Future work in the field of lexical emotion recognition is manifold and multilateral. It is a challenging task that is difficult to perform. Hence, if you want to try yourself just keep in mind: "Aspire to the way, align with virtue, abide by benevolence, and immerse yourself in the arts".

APPENDIX A: THEORETICAL FOUNDATIONS OF LINGUISTICS

This appendix discusses theoretical foundations from the linguistic theory that can be utilized for lexical affect sensing.

A.1 GRAMMATICAL STRUCTURE

In linguistic theory, a text is a composite structure consisting of complex and simple sentences ([Quirk & Greenbaum, 1988]). Complex sentences contain superordinate/subordinate clauses; simple sentences are superordinate clauses that, in their turn, consist of phrases (Figure 54).

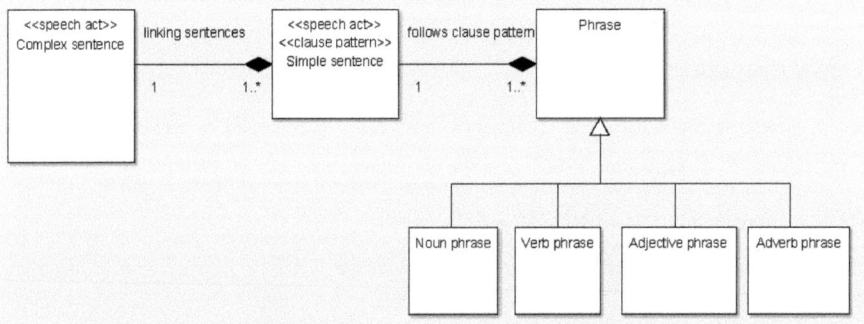

Figure 54: Grammatical sentence structure

Figure 54 describes the most significant elements of a complex sentence. Structurally, a complex sentence consists of clauses joined together using a particular linking method; simple sentences comprise of phrases, for instance, noun phrases, verb phrases, adjective phrases, adverb phrases. Semantically, a complex sentence or a simple sentence can express a speech act ([Searle, 1969]).

Atomic elements of sentences are words. Words comprise phrases:

1. A noun phrase, e.g. *a weak government*;
2. A verb phrase, e.g. *may have succeeded*;
3. An adjective phrase, e.g. *far more enjoyable*;
4. An adverb phrase, e.g. *too impatiently*.

Clauses and phrases can be linked together using different conjunctions ([Quirk & Greenbaum, 1988], [Greenbaum, 1996]):

1. Coordinators that link grammatical units of equal status, e.g. particle *but* in the sentence *I'm very proud but shy.*;

2. Subordinators that grammatically link asymmetrical units: simple subordinators (e.g. *as, because*), compound subordinators (e.g. *in that, so that, now [that], supposing [that], as far as, sooner than, as though*), correlative subordinators (e.g. *if...then, as...so*), for instance, *As far as I know he is not engaged.*;

3. Wh-words, e.g. *where, what, why* in the sentence *I wonder why he left.*

A.2 SENTENCE PATTERNS

Simple sentences follow a particular grammatical form that is represented by a grammatical clause pattern. [Quirk & Greenbaum, 1988] describe 7 grammatical clause patterns in the English language:

1. Subject-Verb pattern (SV), for instance, *The child laughed*;

2. Subject-Verb-Adverbial pattern (SVA), for instance, *Mary is in house*;

3. Subject-Verb-Compliment pattern (SVC), for instance, *Mary is a nurse*;

4. Subject-Verb-Object pattern (SVO), for instance, *Somebody caught the ball*;

5. Subject-Verb-Object-Adverbial pattern (SVOA), for instance, *I put the plate on the table*;

6. Subject-Verb-Object-Compliment pattern (SVOC), for instance, *We have proved him a fool*;

7. Subject-Verb-Object-Object pattern (SVOO), for instance, *She gives me expensive presents.*

The patterns above comprise of clauses distinguished by their function. The English language has 8 function clauses: Subject (S), Verb (V), Direct Object (DO), Indirect Object (IO), Object Compliment (OC), Subject Compliment (SC), Adverbial Compliment (AC), Adverbial (A). For instance, the Subject clause characterizes a subject of a text as the starting point of an action, a process or a state.

Table 34 presents examples and corresponding function clauses ([Yourdictionary, 2008]).

Pattern/Function	S	V	IO (O)	DO (O)	SC (C)	OC (C)	AC (C)
SV	Darby	played					
SVC	The fire	was			devastating		
SVA	Jim	went					there
SVO	Jessica	is doing		homework			
SVOO	Richard	will give	the committee	his proposal			
SVOC	The boss	knows		marketing		the best	
SVOA	I	will take		the dog			to the park

Table 34: Examples of grammatical clause patterns

The name of a clause pattern is shown in the most left column. The title row describes the function clause of a phrase. Example sentences are defined in the table rows. For instance, the example *I will take the dog to the park* in the last row describes the clause pattern SVOA defined by the subject clause S (*I*), the verb clause V (*will take*), the direct object clause DO (O) (*the dog*), and the adverbial compliment clause AC (C) (*to the park*).

For a thorough description of grammatical functions, see [Quirk et al., 1985].

A.3 MEANING AND ITS MODIFICATION

An approach to semantic affect sensing should detect linguistic information used for modifying the text meaning. For instance, the meaning of a text can be modified using adverbials (termed dependent on the extent of integration in the sentence structure such as *adjuncts*, *disjuncts*, *conjuncts*). Within the scope of this thesis *adjuncts* (the integrated adverbials) merit special consideration (Figure 55).

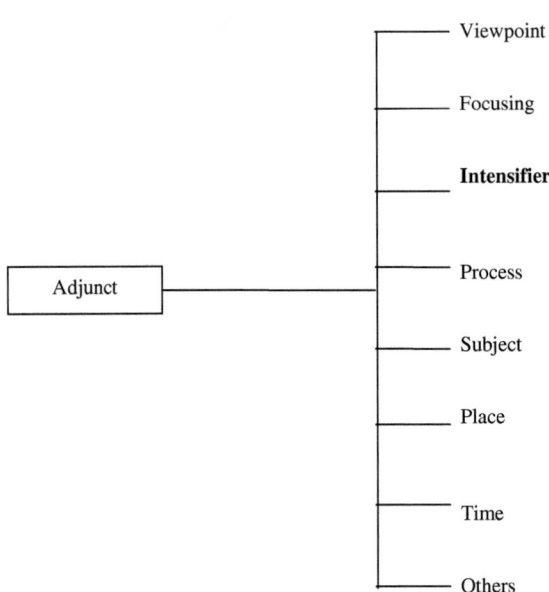

Figure 55: Ontology of adjuncts

The ontology of adjuncts according to [Quirk & Greenbaum, 1988] is described as follows: adjuncts in the *viewpoint* class representing a view of some item, for instance in <u>*Looked at politically*</u>, *it was not an easy problem*; adjuncts in the *focusing* class that indicate that what is being communicated is limited to a part being focused, for instance, the adjunct *especially*; adjuncts in the *intensifier* class, e.g. *definitely*, *completely*, *hardly* that indicate an increase in intensity; adjuncts in the *process* class that define the manner of action, e.g. in the sentence *They treated his friend <u>badly</u>*; adjuncts in the *subject* class relating to the referent of the subject in an active clause, for instance, in the sentence <u>*Resentfully*</u>, *the workers have stood by their leaders*; adjuncts in the *place* class denoting static position or direction, for instance, in the sentence *He lives <u>in a small village</u>*; adjuncts in the *time* class denoting temporal facts, e.g. in the sentence *I'm <u>just</u> finishing my homework*; other adjuncts realized by prepositional phrases or clauses, for instance in *He took the book <u>from me</u>*.

Hence, the most important adjuncts in this thesis belong to the intensifier class (Figure 56).

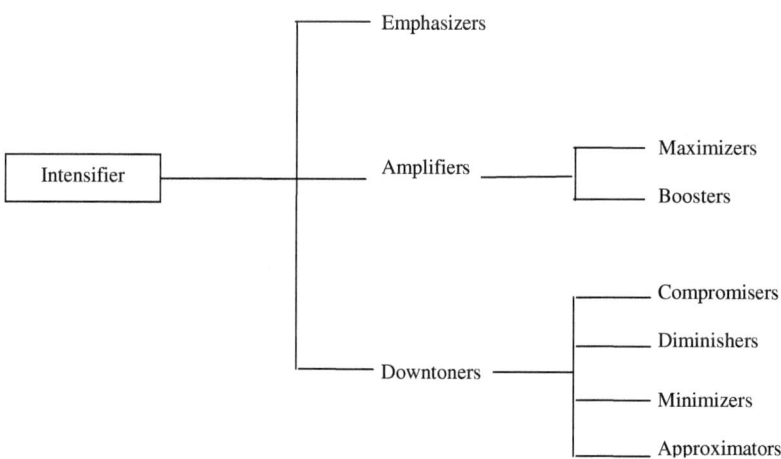

Figure 56: Ontology of intensifiers

Figure 56 describes the following classes of intensifiers:

1. Emphasizers, e.g. *definitely*;

2. Amplifiers: maximizers, e.g. *completely* and boosters, e.g. *very much*;

3. Downtoners: comprimisers, e.g. *kind of*, diminishers, e.g. *partly*, minimizers, e.g. *hardly*, approximators, e.g. *almost*.

The semantics of a text can be modified using different forms of negations:

1. Lexically by inserting particles *not*, or *n't*, as in the sentence *I'm not happy* ([Quirk & Greenbaum, 1988]);

2. By implicit negation, as in the sentence *We came without any excuse* ([Werle, 2002]);

3. By verbal negation with verbs that semantically convey negation as in the sentence *I doubt positive achievements* ([Greenbaum, 1996]).

For simplicity, this thesis gives special consideration only lexical negations.

APPENDIX B: EMOTION RECOGNITION AS A DATA MINING PROBLEM

Statistical analysis of a text independent of its semantics can be organized in phases (Figure 57).

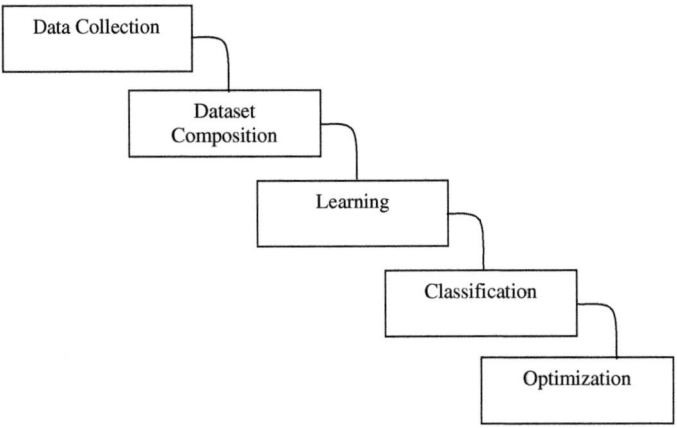

Figure 57: Phases of conventional data mining

Figure 57 shows phases of classification in the conventional data mining processing:

1. *Data collection phase*: collect data for classification (cf. section B.1);

2. *Composition phase*: compose datasets corresponding to the collected data and evaluate necessary features (cf. section B.2):

3. *Learning phase*: train the chosen classifier using the composed datasets (cf. section B.3).

4. *Classification phase*: classify the composed datasets using the trained classifier and yield classification results (cf. section B.4);

5. *Optimization phase*: improve classification results by using approaches to optimizing feature space (cf. section B.5).

B.1 DATA COLLECTION AND INTER-ANNOTATOR AGREEMENT

The data to be classified must be collected. In the case of emotion recognition this data is, for example, a corpus with emotional texts or a corpus with product reviews. The data can be annotated by a human or a group of humans using labels of emotional classes. For instance, a text can be labeled as expressing a positive meaning or a negative meaning. If a group of humans annotates data, individual annotation votes can vary and the provided annotation must be assessed.

An annotation can be assessed using different means, for example, using the inter-annotator agreement that measures how particular annotators agree in their labeling of particular data. The inter-annotator agreement (the Kappa coefficient of agreement among annotators), de facto a standard for assessing annotations of a corpus, is calculated as follows ([Di Eugenio & Glass, 2004])

$$\kappa = \frac{P(A)-P(E)}{1-P(E)} \quad (85)$$

where *P(A)* is the observed agreement among annotators, *P(E)* represents the probability that annotators agree by chance. Assuming that annotators never agree by chance, i.e. the *P(E)*=0, the inter-annotator agreement equals to the observed agreement among annotators $\kappa = P(A)$.

In accordance with [Craggs, 2004], a reliable inter-annotator agreement should be greater than the desirable value of 80%.

B.2 DATASET COMPOSITION

Collected data must be transformed in standard entities, called instances, to be interpreted by data mining algorithms. Instances consist of features (or attributes)[60]. Hereby, extracting[61] and evaluating[62] features (attributes) merit in data mining particular consideration. Feature evaluation can be done differently, for example, the value of a word feature can be the number of occurrences

---
[60] *Feature (or attribute)* in data mining is a significant element of data, e.g. a word in a text.

[61] *Feature extraction* describes the process of identifying significant elements of data, e.g. emotion words in an affective text.

[62] *Feature evaluation* describes a process of assigning numerical values to extracted features, e.g. 0 to a word being absent in a text.

of this word in the analyzed text. An instance can contain a special feature — the class[63] — that is a feature that stores the expected result of classification. The class value can be used for comparison with the calculated value.

Various features influence classification results differently. To assess the influence of features numerically, the information gain measure (IG) can be used. IG determines how homogeneous is collection C relative to attribute a or, in other words, how attribute a contributes to a proper classification of the collection C. IG is defined mathematically as follows:

$$IG(C, a) = \phi(C) - \sum_{v \in V} \frac{|C_v|}{|C|} \phi(C_v) \tag{86}$$

where V is a set of possible values of the attribute a, the subset $C_v = \{c \in C \mid c(a) = v\}$ is a subset of the collection C containing attribute a that has the value v; entropy φ is a auxiliary measure that assesses attribute a. Entropy φ is defined relative to classification classes in the collection C' as

$$\phi(C') = -\sum_{i=1}^{N} p_i \log p_i \tag{87}$$

where N is the number of classes in the collection C', p_i is the probability of class c.

B.3 LEARNING

Based on collected data, particular instances are composed and can be used to train the chosen classifier. Learning can be performed supervised or unsupervised. In the supervised learning, the value of the class feature is supplied manually for each of the instances by a human composer ([Witten & Frank, 2005]). In contrast, unsupervised learning specifies instances without a manually defined class value and this value is defined whilst classification, for example, using probabilistic means.

---

[63] *Class* denotes an outcome of a classification experiment, i.e. a classification result.

B.3.1 SUPERVISED LEARNING

Generally, the classification process consists of two phases: the beginning learning phase (sometimes called training phase) with the corresponding learning subset from the studied dataset and the following testing phase with the corresponding testing subset from the studied dataset. In the supervised learning, the instances in the learning dataset contain the expected class value defined by a human annotator. Correspondingly, the learning phase uses the learning subset of instances in order to adjust particular parameters of the chosen classifier and to maximize hereby the number of instances where the expected class values coincide with the calculated values; the testing phase utilizes the testing subset of instances from the studied dataset to test the trained classifier.

Especially if the amount of classified data is limited, the classification process can use the cross-validation technique. The term *cross-validation* represents an iterational processing where the studied dataset is split in two parts: one part is used for learning; the remaining part is used for testing. After partition, the training part is utilized to learn the chosen classifier; the learned classifier is utilized to calculate classification results using the testing dataset. The classification results are stored and the first iteration step is finished. In the next step, the learning and testing sets are recalculated so that the instances that did not participate in the first testing set are included in the second testing set; the second testing set is classified and the result is stored, and so on. The final classification result is calculated by averaging classification results of the stored results. For instance, in the ten-fold cross-validation the classification result is the sum of classification results of ten parts divided by ten.

Number of learning/testing iterations can be different what influences comprehensibility of classification results: the more realistic the learning/testing partition is, the more realistic are the classification results. Often the ten-fold cross-validation is used in data mining, since it is considered empirically to provide the most credible results of classification.

The cross-validation results may be not realistic, for instance, in the case if the chosen classifier is trained using a learning set that has an unrepresentative choice of the learning and the testing sets. To minimize classification error resulting from the improbable split of learning and testing sets, the compilation of the learning and testing sets can consider the number of instances of a particular class in the testing/learning sets. In other words, the learning and testing sets can be stratified.

Hence, *cross-validation without stratification* describes division of the studied dataset in learning/testing parts without considering the amount of instances of a particular class in the learning/testing sets and the cross-validation sets are chosen fairly randomly. In contrast, *cross-validation with stratification* means that learning/testing partition is performed under consideration of the amount of instances of resulting classes.

B.3.2 UNSUPERVISED LEARNING (CLUSTERING)

If the supervised learning is impossible, the dataset can be composed automatically. In the unsupervised learning, instances contain initially no class values: data mining approaches to unsupervised learning define a method to calculate class values, for example, determine what instances represent the same cluster (group).

The k-means clustering algorithm ([Witten & Frank, 2005]) provides a simple and effective approach to grouping instances in clusters, for example, instances representing emotional texts (Figure 58).

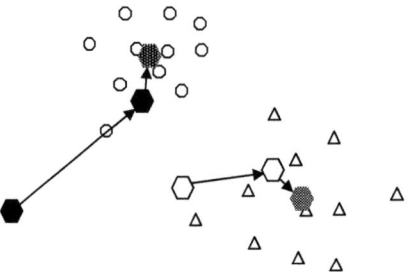

Figure 58: The k-means algorithm

The instances are represented by circles and triangles. The circles represent one cluster, e.g. *negative*, and the triangles represent instances of another cluster, e.g. *positive*.

Figure 58 shows how the k-means algorithm groups particular instances in two clusters. The k-means algorithm is an iterative algorithm. First, the algorithm chooses centroids' position randomly (centers of clusters – also called means) based on their number that is specified in advance (centroids are the diamond-shaped points). Then, all instances' points are assigned to their geometrically closest centroid. Next, the algorithm calculates the ordinary Euclidean distance between the centroids and the cluster points and moves a centroid position so that the distances between new centroids and instances' points are minimized (the arrows show centroids' movements). Iteration continues until the calculated centroid positions do not change (final patterned diamond-shaped points).

B.4 CLASSIFICATION

B.4.1 CLASSIFIER ALGORITHMS

This section describes data mining classifiers that are usually used in opinion mining. Note that the described classifiers implement supervised learning.

Approaches to opinion mining can use the probabilistic NaïveBayes (NB) classifier ([Mitchell, 2007]). NB is a classifier that calculates the probability that an instance belongs to a particular emotional class by applying the Bayes' theorem

$$P(h|D) = \frac{P(D|h)\ P(h)}{P(D)} \qquad (88)$$

where h is a hypothesis, for instance, an example belongs to a particular emotional class, D is the observed example data, for instance, the emotional instance; $P(h|D)$ denotes the probability that h holds if D is *already* observed; $P(h)$ denotes the probability that h holds *before* data D is observed; $P(D|h)$ is the probability of observing D given some world in which h holds. Within this thesis, NB can group emotional texts in a particular emotional class using the probabilities of belonging of particular words of this text to the emotional class.

Approaches to opinion mining can use the support vector machine algorithm (SVM). SVM can be understood at best graphically ([Bennett & Campbell, 2000]). Consider a binary classification task (instances belong to two classes) where each instance to be classified can be visualized as a point in the 2D space. Each dimension is a feature, for example, a feature representing a particular word. In the learning step, the areas in the 2D space are adjusted using a discriminant plane defined by an adjustment function that minimizes misclassification errors. The adjustment function can be given through lines if the adjustment function is linear or through curves if a non-linear adjustment function is used. After adjustment of discriminant planes, the instances to classify are joined together according to the areas defined by convex hulls[64] (Figure 59).

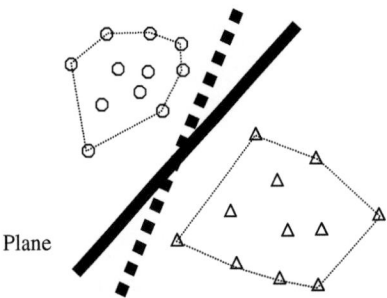

Figure 59: Learning in SVM

Figure 59 illustrates determination of the discriminant planes in the instance space and the corresponding convex hulls (dotted areas). The circles present the instances of one class and the triangles show the instances of another class. The thick lines represent discriminant planes used for determining classes and the thin dotted lines show hypothetical convex hulls.

Up to now, this thesis described classification of instances of two classes. However, instances usually pertain to more than two classes. Hence, a concrete SVM implementation should manage this problem, for example, by combining the calculated convex hulls and present hereby a classification solution for instances of multiple classes. Such implementation can be the SVMlight classifier ([Joachims, 1999]) or SMO in the WEKA toolkit ([Witten & Frank, 2005]).

Approaches to opinion mining can utilize the InfoGain classifier. The InfoGain classifier is a classifier relying on IG. The InfoGain algorithm works as follows: first, it evaluates features from the studied dataset using IG and then classifies the dataset with only those features that exceed a

---

[64] *Convex hull*: in mathematics, a *convex hull* or a *convex envelope* for a set of points X in a real vector space V is the minimal convex set containing X. For a thorough description, see [MathWorld, 2008].

particular value. In this thesis, selected features are those that are evaluated with a rank greater than 0.

Approaches to opinion mining can make use of the ensemble meta-classifier ([Dietterich, 2000]). To perform classification, ensemble meta-classifier combines multiple basis classifiers. Basis classifiers can utilize different classification algorithms, e.g. NB or SVM. The final classification result of the ensemble meta-classifier is based on classification results of the basis classifiers. The conventional approaches to ensemble meta-classifiers are bagging ([Breiman, 1996]) and boosting ([Schapire & Singer, 1999]).

So far, the classifier algorithms were incomprehensible for a human observer. But sometimes it is indispensable to understand the classification process. Rule-based algorithms, e.g. C4.5, can be used for this purpose. C4.5 is a rule-based algorithm that makes classification decisions by utilizing rules in form of a decision tree. In the simplest case, a decision is based on commonsense rules, for example, a decision in the weather forecast domain that it would be rainy if the humidity is high. A rule can be compiled using IG (Figure 60).

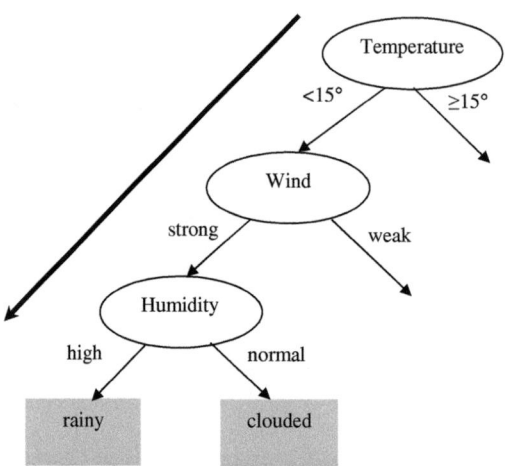

Figure 60: Decision tree for a weather forecast

Figure 60 shows an incomplete decision tree that utilizes information from the weather forecast domain. The ovals show constraints in the decision tree; the arcs are the alternatives of constraint values; the shaded boxes in the last row show the classification outcomes (*rainy*, *clouded*). For instance, the decision tree forecasts rainy weather if a weather forecast predicts a day with the low temperature (<15°), the strong wind, and high humidity (the flow defined by the thick arrow).

Approaches to opinion mining can utilize the Linear Discriminant Analysis classifier (LDA). This classier finds the linear combination of features which best separate two or more classes of instances using statistical means ([Wikipedia, 2008]).

B.4.2 CLASSIFICATION EVALUATION

The composed datasets, for instance, representing a particular emotional corpus can be classified using different classification algorithms, e.g. NB or SVM. Success of classification in data mining is measured traditionally using the *recall* and *precision* measures as follows ([Witten & Frank, 2005]):

$$recall = \frac{I^+}{I}$$
$$precision = \frac{I^+}{I^t} \tag{89}$$

where I^+ is the number of correctly classified instances, I^t is the total number of retrieved instances that the classification algorithm considers to be relevant (either correctly or not), I is the total number of instances of a particular class.

Besides the *recall* and *precision* measure, classification evaluation can be assessed using the *accuracy* measure. However, since calculation of the *accuracy* value can be done differently, its value is assumed within this thesis to be equal to the *precision* measure

$$accuracy \approx precision \tag{90}$$

In order to assess classification plausibly, a measure can be averaged over classes. A *measure averaged over classes* $\overline{M}$ is a data mining measure (*recall, precision, accuracy*) calculated as

$$\overline{M} = \frac{\sum m_c}{N} \tag{91}$$

where m_c is the measure value for instances of class c, N is the number of classes in the studied dataset.

B.5 OPTIMIZING FEATURE SPACE

Classifier algorithms analyze datasets with particular features and calculate classification results. Sometimes, it is possible to improve classification results by optimizing the space of selected features.

There are two conventional data mining methods for feature space optimization, *forward selection* and *backward elimination*, that work fundamentally different according to the way they process an original dataset. The *forward selection* method begins the optimization process with an empty set of features and iteratively adds features from the original dataset to the resulting dataset that amend classification results. In contrast, the *backward elimination* method iteratively deletes features from the original dataset that worsen classification results.

APPENDIX C: AFFECTIVE BEHAVIOUR AS HMMS

C.1 HMMS FOR AFFECTIVE BEHAVIOUR

[Picard, 1997] describes a model for affective behaviour based on Hidden Markov Models (HMM). Generally, a HMM is a probabilistic model represented as a complete directed graph containing states that are connected using conditional probability transitions ([Rabiner, 1989]). A specialized HMM — HMM for affective behaviour — is one that contains affect states and transitions between them. Each state has certain observations that are considered to be characteristic for the state (Figure 61).

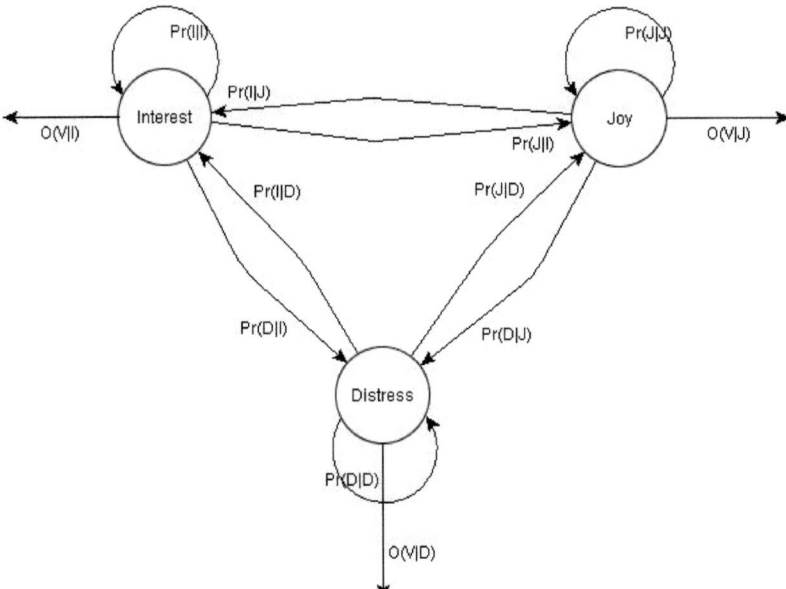

Figure 61: HMM for affective behaviour

The HMM for affective behaviour contains three affect states (*Joy*, *Interest*, *Distress*): the *Pr* arrows are weighted with the conditional probability of transition between two affect states where the initial/final letters in transition labels represent the initial/final letter of the name of the corresponding affect states. For instance, the *Pr(J|D)* transition describes a transition to the affect state ***Joy*** under the condition that HMM is in the affect state ***Distress***. The observations *O* reflect, for example, the voice change in a particular affect state (arrows *O(V|J)*, *O(V|I)*, *O(V|D)*). An observation can be interpreted in the context of this thesis as an experienced emotion that can be detected using an approach to emotion recognition.

Transition probabilities in a HMM can be adjusted using the Baum–Welch algorithm — an iterative procedure that maximizes the probability of a given state sequence by adjusting the probability transitions. Once trained, a computer system that maintains the HMM can perform actions according to the emotional states and state transitions.

C.2 HMMS FOR AFFECTIVE BEHAVIOUR FOR SAL CHARACTERS

The tables below show adjacency matrices of HMMs for affective behaviour in Figure 21. The title row contains names of tail states and the most right column contains names of the head states. A cell value is the probability of the transition from the head state to the tail state.

Poppy (Optimistic and outgoing)

neutral	high_pos	high_neg	low_pos	low_neg	
0,5266	0,198	0,0661	0	0,2093	neutral
0,0482	0,9421	0	0,0097	0	high_pos
0,1058	0	0,8942	0	0	high_neg
0,0007	0	0,3421	0,6572	0	low_pos
0,799	0	0,2009	0	0	low_neg

Spike (Confrontational and argumentive)

neutral	high_pos	high_neg	low_pos	low_neg	
0,5768	0,1086	0,2417	0,0183	0,0547	neutral
0,0971	0,8975	0,0054	0	0	high_pos
0,0296	0	0,9704	0	0	high_neg
0	1	0	0	0	low_pos
0,0137	0	0,0941	0	0,8922	low_neg

Prudence (Pragmatic and practical)

neutral	high_pos	high_neg	low_pos	low_neg	
0,5332	0,1929	0,0001	0,0632	0,2106	neutral
0,2856	0,7142	0	0,0002	0	high_pos
0,0316	0,0001	0,9373	0	0,0309	high_neg
0,0005	0,5292	0,4703	0	0	low_pos
0,1477	0,0738	0,0298	0	0,7487	low_neg

Obadiah (Depressing and gloomy)

neutral	high_pos	high_neg	low_pos	low_neg	
0,5436	0,0265	0,1506	0,2787	0,0006	neutral
0,1653	0,6165	0	0	0,2182	high_pos
0,5647	0	0,4353	0	0	high_neg
0,4795	0	0	0,5205	0	low_pos
0,0454	0,02	0,034	0	0,9006	low_neg

APPENDIX D: SPIN RULES

D.1 GRAMMATICAL SPIN RULES FROM THEORETICAL SOURCES

Table 35 shows SPIN rules from theoretical sources discussed in section 6.2.2.1.

Example	SPIN rules
Interjection *Oh, what a beautiful present!* (299)	*[Word() UH] EmotionalItem(semCat:high_pos)* → *EmotionalPhrase(semCat:high_pos)*
	[Word() UH] EmotionalItem(semCat:low_pos) → *EmotionalPhrase(semCat:high_pos)*
	[Word() UH] EmotionalItem(semCat:high_neg) → *EmotionalPhrase(semCat:high_neg)*
	[Word() UH] EmotionalItem(semCat:low_neg) → *EmotionalPhrase(semCat:high_neg)*
Exclamation *What a wonderful time we've had!* (300a)	*Whquestion() EmotionalItem(semCat:high_pos) Intensifier(orth:"Exclamation symbol")* → *EmotionalPhrase(semCat:high_pos)*
	Whquestion() EmotionalItem(semCat:low_pos) Intensifier(orth:"Exclamation symbol") → *EmotionalPhrase(semCat:high_pos)*
	Whquestion() EmotionalItem(semCat:high_neg) Intensifier(orth:"Exclamation symbol") → *EmotionalPhrase(semCat:high_neg)*
	Whquestion() EmotionalItem(semCat:low_neg) Intensifier(orth:"Exclamation symbol") → *EmotionalPhrase(semCat:high_neg)*
Emphatic *so* and *such I'm so afraid they'll get lost!* (300b)	*The particles so and such are considered during parsing as other intensifiers.*
Repetition *This house is far, far too expensive!* (300c)	*[$W1=Word() $P1=POS()] [$W2=Word() $P2=POS()] EmotionalItem(semCat:high_pos) !equalString($W1,$W2)* → *EmotionalPhrase(semCat:high_pos)*
	[$W1=Word() $P1=POS()] [$W2=Word() $P2=POS()] EmotionalItem(semCat:low_neg) !equalString($W1,$W2) → *EmotionalPhrase(semCat:high_neg)*
	[$W1=Word() $P1=POS()] [$W2=Word() $P2=POS()] EmotionalItem(semCat:high_neg) !equalString($W1,$W2) → *EmotionalPhrase(semCat:high_neg)*
	[$W1=Word() $P1=POS()] [$W2=Word() $P2=POS()] EmotionalItem(semCat:low_neg) !equalString($W1,$W2) → *EmotionalPhrase(semCat:high_neg)*

Example	SPIN rules
Intensifying adverbs and modifiers *We are utterly powerless.* (301);	*Like 300b this grammatical means is already processed by general SPIN rules (intensifiers).*
Emphasis *How ever did they escape?* (302);	*Whquestion() Intensifier() EmotionalItem(semCat:high_pos)* → *EmotionalPhrase(semCat:high_pos)*
	Whquestion() Intensifier() EmotionalItem(semCat:low_pos) → *EmotionalPhrase(semCat:high_pos)*
	Whquestion() Intensifier() EmotionalItem(semCat:high_neg) → *EmotionalPhrase(semCat:high_neg)*
	Whquestion() Intensifier() EmotionalItem(semCat:low_neg) → *EmotionalPhrase(semCat:high_neg)*
Intensifying a negative sentence *She didn't speak to us at all* (303a);	*Like 300b and 301, this grammatical means is considered by general grammatical SPIN rules like intensifiers.*
A negative noun phrase beginning with *not a We arrived not a moment too soon.* (303b);	*[Intensifier(orth:"not a") * Noun()]* → *EmotionalPhrase(semCat:low_neg)*
Fronted negation *Never have I seen such a crowd of people!* (303c)	*FRONTED_NEGATION* → *Intensifier(orth: "Fronted negation")*
Exclamatory and rhetorical questions *Hasn't she grown!* (304, 305)	*Exclamatory and rhetorical questions are identified using syntax of the analyzed text.*

Table 35: Grammatical SPIN rules from theoretical sources

The *SPIN rules* column shows the utilized SPIN rules; an example the rules apply to is listed in the *Example* column.

D.2 GRAMMATICAL SPIN RULES FROM EMPIRICAL SOURCES

Table 36 shows grammatical SPIN rules from empirical examples discussed in section 6.2.2.2. The *SPIN rules* column show the utilized SPIN rules. An example the rules apply to is listed in the *Example* column.

Example	SPIN rules
I am so happy.	*Intensifier() EmotionalItem(semCat:low_pos)* → *EmotionalPhrase(semCat:high_pos)* *Intensifier() EmotionalItem(semCat:high_pos)* → *EmotionalPhrase(semCat:high_pos)* *Intensifier() EmotionalItem(semCat:low_neg)* → *EmotionalPhrase(semCat:high_neg)* *Intensifier() EmotionalItem(semCat:high_neg)* → *EmotionalPhrase(semCat:high_neg)*
I am very happy.	*Intensifier() EmotionalItem(semCat:low_neg)* → *EmotionalPhrase(semCat:high_neg)* *Intensifier() EmotionalPhrase(semCat:high_neg)* → *EmotionalPhrase(semCat:high_neg)* *Intensifier() EmotionalItem(semCat:low_pos)* → *EmotionalPhrase(semCat:high_pos)* *Intensifier() EmotionalItem(semCat:high_pos)* → *EmotionalPhrase(semCat:high_pos*
I am not happy.	*Negation() EmotionalItem(semCat:low_pos)* → *EmotionalPhrase(semCat:low_neg)* *Negation() EmotionalItem(semCat:high_pos)* → *EmotionalPhrase(semCat:low_neg)* *Negation() EmotionalItem(semCat:low_neg)* → *EmotionalPhrase(semCat:high_neg)* *Negation() EmotionalItem(semCat:high_neg)* → *EmotionalPhrase(semCat:high_neg)*
I am not very happy.	*Negation() Intensifier() EmotionalItem(semCat:low_pos)* → *EmotionalPhrase(semCat:low_neg)* *Negation() Intensifier() EmotionalItem(semCat:high_pos)* → *EmotionalPhrase(semCat:low_neg)* *Negation() Intensifier() EmotionalItem(semCat:low_neg)* → *EmotionalPhrase(semCat:high_neg)* *Negation() Intensifier() EmotionalItem(semCat:high_neg)* → *EmotionalPhrase(semCat:high_neg)*

Example	SPIN rules
I am not happy at all.	*Negation() Intensifier() Intensifier() EmotionalItem(semCat:low_pos)* → *EmotionalPhrase(semCat:high_pos)* *Negation() Intensifier() Intensifier() EmotionalItem(semCat:high_pos)* → *EmotionalPhrase(semCat:high_pos)* *Negation() Intensifier() Intensifier() EmotionalItem(semCat:low_neg)* → *EmotionalPhrase(semCat:high_neg)* *Negation() Intensifier() Intensifier() EmotionalItem(semCat:high_neg)* → *EmotionalPhrase(semCat:high_neg)*
I am happy.	*EmotionalItem(semCat:$T)* → *EmotionalPhrase(semCat:$T)*

Table 36: Grammatical SPIN rules from empirical examples

D.3 SCENARIO-DEPENDENT SPIN RULES

Table 37 shows the scenario-dependent SPIN rules discussed in section 6.2.1.2 that are used in the proposed approach to affect sensing. The *SPIN rules* column shows the utilized SPIN rules. A corresponding example sentence the rules apply to is listed in the *Example* column.

Example	SPIN rules
It is an extremely good film	*Intensifier() EmotionalItem(semCat:low_pos) Concept()* → *EmotionalPhrase(semCat:low_pos)* *Intensifier() EmotionalItem(semCat:high_pos) Concept()* → *EmotionalPhrase(semCat:high_pos)* *Intensifier() EmotionalItem(semCat:low_neg) Concept()* → *EmotionalPhrase(semCat:low_neg)* *Intensifier() EmotionalItem(semCat:high_neg) Concept()* → *EmotionalPhrase(semCat:high_neg)*
At least, it was a good film	*Intensifier() Intensifier() EmotionalItem(semCat:low_pos) Concept()* → *EmotionalPhrase(semCat:low_pos)* *Intensifier() Intensifier() EmotionalItem(semCat:high_pos) Concept()* → *EmotionalPhrase(semCat:high_pos)* *Intensifier() Intensifier() EmotionalItem(semCat:low_neg) Concept()* → *EmotionalPhrase(semCat:low_neg)* *Intensifier() Intensifier() EmotionalItem(semCat:high_neg) Concept()* → *EmotionalPhrase(semCat:high_neg)*

Example	SPIN rules
It is not a very bad film	*Negation() Intensifier() EmotionalItem(semCat:low_pos) Concept()* → *EmotionalPhrase(semCat:high_pos)*
	Negation() Intensifier() EmotionalItem(semCat:high_pos) Concept() → *EmotionalPhrase(semCat:high_pos)*
	Negation() Intensifier() EmotionalItem(semCat:low_neg) Concept() → *EmotionalPhrase(semCat:high_neg)*
	Negation() Intensifier() EmotionalItem(semCat:high_neg) Concept() → *EmotionalPhrase(semCat:high_neg)*
A good film	*EmotionalItem(semCat:low_pos) Concept()* → *EmotionalPhrase(semCat:low_pos)*
	EmotionalItem(semCat:high_pos) Concept() → *EmotionalPhrase(semCat:high_pos)*
	EmotionalItem(semCat:low_neg) Concept() → *EmotionalPhrase(semCat:low_neg)*
	EmotionalItem(semCat:high_neg) Concept() → *EmotionalPhrase(semCat:high_neg)*
Not every film is so good!	*Negation() Concept() Intensifier() EmotionalItem(semCat:low_pos)* → *EmotionalPhrase(semCat:high_pos)*
	Negation() Concept() Intensifier() EmotionalItem(semCat:high_pos) → *EmotionalPhrase(semCat:high_pos)*
	Negation() Concept() Intensifier() EmotionalItem(semCat:low_neg) → *EmotionalPhrase(semCat:high_neg)*
	Negation() Concept() Intensifier() EmotionalItem(semCat:high_neg) → *EmotionalPhrase(semCat:high_neg)*

Table 37: Scenario-dependent grammatical SPIN rules

D.4 APPLICATION FREQUENCY OF SPIN RULES

Table 38 shows SPIN rules (the *SPIN rule* column) and the frequencies of their use for classification of FWF (the *Freq. FWF* column) and BMRC-S (the *Freq. BMRC-S* column). The specified frequencies correspond to classification results in Table 30 and are cumulated for all granularities. For instance, the last rule *EmotionalItem(semCat:$T)* shows frequencies as used for affect sensing in sentences in FWF (173) or for affect sensing in BMRC-S (203) whereas the numbers 173 and 203 correspond to the sum of rule applications of the *whole text* granularity and of the *subsentences*' granularity and of the *phrases*' granularity. The rules that are utilized less than twice are not shown for better readability.

SPIN rule	Freq. FWF	Freq. BMRC-S
[Word() UH] EmotionalItem(semCat:low_pos) → EmotionalPhrase(semCat:high_pos)	3	0
Whquestion() EmotionalItem(semCat:high_pos) Intensifier(orth:"Exclamation symbol") → EmotionalPhrase(semCat:high_pos)	0	55
Whquestion() EmotionalItem(semCat:high_neg) Intensifier(orth:"Exclamation symbol") → EmotionalPhrase(semCat:high_neg)	0	14
Whquestion() EmotionalItem(semCat:low_neg) Intensifier(orth:"Exclamation symbol") → EmotionalPhrase(semCat:high_neg)	0	2
[$W1=Word() $P1=POS()] [$W2=Word() $P2=POS()] EmotionalItem(semCat:low_neg) !equalString($W1,$W2) → EmotionalPhrase(semCat:high_neg)	0	12
[$W1=Word() $P1=POS()] [$W2=Word() $P2=POS()] EmotionalItem(semCat:low_neg) !equalString($W1,$W2) → EmotionalPhrase(semCat:high_neg)	3	5
Whquestion() Intensifier() EmotionalItem(semCat:low_pos) → EmotionalPhrase(semCat:high_pos)	0	4
Whquestion() Intensifier() EmotionalItem(semCat:low_neg) → EmotionalPhrase(semCat:high_neg)	0	4
[be Verb() EmotionalItem(semCat:$T) PassiveVerb()] → PassiveEmotionalPhrase(semCat:$T)	0	6
Negation() EmotionalItem(semCat:low_pos) → EmotionalPhrase(semCat:low_neg)	10	49
Negation() EmotionalItem(semCat:low_neg) → EmotionalPhrase(semCat:high_neg)	14	38
Negation() Intensifier() EmotionalItem(semCat:low_pos) → EmotionalPhrase(semCat:low_neg)	4	0
Negation() Intensifier() EmotionalItem(semCat:low_pos) → EmotionalPhrase(semCat:low_neg)	0	3
Negation() Intensifier() EmotionalItem(semCat:low_neg) → EmotionalPhrase(semCat:high_neg)	0	4
Negation() Concept() Intensifier() EmotionalItem(semCat:low_pos) → EmotionalPhrase(semCat:high_pos)	0	3
Negation() Concept() Intensifier() EmotionalItem(semCat:low_neg)	0	3

SPIN rule	Freq. FWF	Freq. BMRC-S
$\rightarrow$ *EmotionalPhrase(semCat:high_neg)*		
Intensifier() EmotionalItem(semCat:low_pos) $\rightarrow$ *EmotionalPhrase(semCat:high_pos)*	4	9
Intensifier() EmotionalItem(semCat:low_neg) $\rightarrow$ *EmotionalPhrase(semCat:high_neg)*	5	5
Negation() Intensifier() Intensifier() EmotionalItem(semCat:high_pos) $\rightarrow$ *EmotionalPhrase(semCat:high_pos)*	0	2
Intensifier() EmotionalItem(semCat:low_neg) Concept() $\rightarrow$ *EmotionalPhrase(semCat:low_neg)*	2	7
Negation() Intensifier() EmotionalItem(semCat:low_neg) Concept() $\rightarrow$ *EmotionalPhrase(semCat:high_neg)*	0	5
Intensifier() EmotionalItem(semCat:low_pos) %Intensifier() Concept() $\rightarrow$ *EmotionalPhrase(semCat:low_pos)*	3	7
Intensifier() EmotionalItem(semCat:low_neg) $\rightarrow$ *EmotionalPhrase(semCat:high_neg)*	4	8
Intensifier() EmotionalPhrase(semCat:high_neg) $\rightarrow$ *EmotionalPhrase(semCat:high_neg)*	0	5
Intensifier() EmotionalItem(semCat:low_pos) $\rightarrow$ *EmotionalPhrase(semCat:high_pos)*	5	6
Whquestion() Concept() Exception() Concept() $\rightarrow$ *EmotionalPhrase(semCat:low_neg)*	0	4
EmotionalItem(semCat:$T) Concept() $\rightarrow$ *EmotionalPhrase(semCat:$T)*	172	428
EmotionalItem(semCat:$T) $\rightarrow$ *EmotionalPhrase(semCat:$T)*	173	203

Table 38: Frequencies of use of SPIN rules

D.5 SPIN Rules for Linking Phrases

Table 39 shows SPIN rules for linking phrases. The *Description* column shows a brief description of a group of the utilized SPIN rules, and the *SPIN rules* column – the corresponding SPIN rules.

Description	SPIN rules
Primitive	*phrase_null* → *Phrase(emotCat:null)* *phrase_low_pos* → *Phrase(emotCat:low_pos)* *phrase_high_pos* → *Phrase(emotCat:high_pos)* *phrase_low_neg* → *Phrase(emotCat:low_neg)* *phrase_high_neg* → *Phrase(emotCat:high_neg)* *phrase_neutral* → *Phrase(emotCat:neutral)*
Compression	*Phrase(emotCat:low_pos) Phrase(emotCat:low_pos)* → *Phrase(emotCat:low_pos)* *Phrase(emotCat:high_pos) Phrase(emotCat:high_pos)* → *Phrase(emotCat:high_pos)* *Phrase(emotCat:low_neg) Phrase(emotCat:low_neg)* → *Phrase(emotCat:low_neg)* *Phrase(emotCat:high_neg) Phrase(emotCat:high_neg)* → *Phrase(emotCat:high_neg)* *Phrase(emotCat:neutral) Phrase(emotCat:neutral)* → *Phrase(emotCat:neutral)*
Summarizing	*or(Phrase(emotCat:low_pos), Phrase(emotCat:high_pos))* *or(Phrase(emotCat:low_neg), Phrase(emotCat:high_neg)) Phrase(emotCat:neutral)* → *Result(emotCat:low_neg)* *or(Phrase(emotCat:low_pos), Phrase(emotCat:high_pos))* *or(Phrase(emotCat:low_neg), Phrase(emotCat:high_neg))* → *Result(emotCat:low_neg)* *Phrase(emotCat:high_pos) Phrase(emotCat:neutral)* → *Result(emotCat:high_pos)* *Phrase(emotCat:low_pos) Phrase(emotCat:neutral)* → *Result(emotCat:low_pos)* *Phrase(emotCat:high_neg) Phrase(emotCat:neutral)* → *Result(emotCat:high_neg)* *Phrase(emotCat:low_neg) Phrase(emotCat:neutral)*

Description	SPIN rules
	→ Result(emotCat:low_neg)
	Phrase(emotCat:null) Phrase(emotCat:$T) → Result(emotCat:$T)
Finalizing	Phrase(emotCat:$T) → Result(emotCat:$T))

Table 39: SPIN rules for linking phrases

D.6 SPIN RULES FOR LINKING CLAUSES

Table 40 shows sample SPIN rules for linking clauses. The *Description* column denotes a brief description of a group of SPIN rules, and the *SPIN rules* column contains the corresponding SPIN rules.

Description	SPIN rules
Primitive	superord_null → Superordinate(emotCat:null) subord_null → Superordinate(emotCat:null) superord_neutral → Superordinate(emotCat:neutral) subord_neutral → Subordinate(emotCat:neutral) superord_low_neg → Superordinate(emotCat:low_neg) subord_low_neg → Subordinate(emotCat:low_neg) superord_high_neg → Superordinate(emotCat:high_neg) subord_high_neg → Subordinate(emotCat:high_neg) superord_low_pos → Superordinate(emotCat:low_pos) subord_low_pos → Subordinate(emotCat:low_pos) superord_high_pos → Superordinate(emotCat:high_pos) subord_high_pos → Subordinate(emotCat:high_pos)

Description	SPIN rules
Heterogeneous clauses	*#neutral vs others*
	Superordinate(emotCat:neutral) Superordinate(emotCat:neutral) $\rightarrow$ *Superordinate(emotCat: neutral)*
	Superordinate(emotCat:neutral) Superordinate(emotCat:low_pos) $\rightarrow$ *Superordinate(emotCat: low_pos)*
	Superordinate(emotCat:neutral) Superordinate(emotCat:high_pos) $\rightarrow$ *Superordinate(emotCat: low_pos)*
	Superordinate(emotCat:neutral) Superordinate(emotCat:low_neg) $\rightarrow$ *Superordinate(emotCat: low_neg)*
	Superordinate(emotCat:neutral) Superordinate(emotCat:high_neg) $\rightarrow$ *Superordinate(emotCat: high_neg)*
	#low_neg vs others
	Superordinate(emotCat:low_neg) Superordinate(emotCat:neutral) $\rightarrow$ *Superordinate(emotCat: low_neg)*
	Superordinate(emotCat:low_neg) Superordinate(emotCat:low_pos) $\rightarrow$ *Superordinate(emotCat: low_neg)*
	Superordinate(emotCat:low_neg) Superordinate(emotCat:high_pos) $\rightarrow$ *Superordinate(emotCat: high_neg)*
	Superordinate(emotCat:low_neg) Superordinate(emotCat:low_neg) $\rightarrow$ *Superordinate(emotCat: low_neg)*
	Superordinate(emotCat:low_neg) Superordinate(emotCat:high_neg) $\rightarrow$ *Superordinate(emotCat: high_neg)*
	#high_neg vs others
	Superordinate(emotCat:high_neg) Superordinate(emotCat:neutral) $\rightarrow$ *Superordinate(emotCat: high_neg)*
	Superordinate(emotCat:high_neg) Superordinate(emotCat:low_pos) $\rightarrow$ *Superordinate(emotCat: high_neg)*
	Superordinate(emotCat:high_neg) Superordinate(emotCat:high_pos) $\rightarrow$ *Superordinate(emotCat: high_neg)*
	Superordinate(emotCat:high_neg) Superordinate(emotCat:low_neg) $\rightarrow$ *Superordinate(emotCat: high_neg)*
	Superordinate(emotCat:high_neg) Superordinate(emotCat:high_neg) $\rightarrow$ *Superordinate(emotCat: high_neg)*
	#low_pos vs others
	Superordinate(emotCat:low_pos) Superordinate(emotCat:neutral) $\rightarrow$ *Superordinate(emotCat: low_pos)*
	Superordinate(emotCat:low_pos) Superordinate(emotCat:low_pos) $\rightarrow$ *Superordinate(emotCat: low_pos)*
	Superordinate(emotCat:low_pos) Superordinate(emotCat:high_pos) $\rightarrow$ *Superordinate(emotCat: high_pos)*

Description	SPIN rules
	Superordinate(emotCat:low_pos) Superordinate(emotCat:low_neg) $\rightarrow$ *Superordinate(emotCat: low_neg)*
	Superordinate(emotCat:low_pos) Superordinate(emotCat:high_neg) $\rightarrow$ *Superordinate(emotCat: high_neg)*
	Superordinate(emotCat:high_pos) Superordinate(emotCat:neutral) $\rightarrow$ *Superordinate(emotCat: high_pos)*
	Superordinate(emotCat:high_pos) Superordinate(emotCat:low_pos) $\rightarrow$ *Superordinate(emotCat: high_pos)*
	Superordinate(emotCat:high_pos) Superordinate(emotCat:high_pos) $\rightarrow$ *Superordinate(emotCat: high_pos)*
	Superordinate(emotCat:high_pos) Superordinate(emotCat:low_neg) $\rightarrow$ *Superordinate(emotCat: low_neg)*
	Superordinate(emotCat:high_pos) Superordinate(emotCat:high_neg) $\rightarrow$ *Superordinate(emotCat: high_neg)*
	Subordinate(emotCat:neutral) Subordinate(emotCat:neutral) $\rightarrow$ *Subordinate(emotCat: neutral)*
	Subordinate(emotCat:neutral) Subordinate(emotCat:low_pos) $\rightarrow$ *Subordinate(emotCat: low_pos)*
	Subordinate(emotCat:neutral) Subordinate(emotCat:high_pos) $\rightarrow$ *Subordinate(emotCat: low_pos)*
	Subordinate(emotCat:neutral) Subordinate(emotCat:low_neg) $\rightarrow$ *Subordinate(emotCat: low_neg)*
	Subordinate(emotCat:neutral) Subordinate(emotCat:high_neg) $\rightarrow$ *Subordinate(emotCat: high_neg)*
	Subordinate(emotCat:low_neg) Subordinate(emotCat:neutral) $\rightarrow$ *Subordinate(emotCat: low_neg)*
	Subordinate(emotCat:low_neg) Subordinate(emotCat:low_pos) $\rightarrow$ *Subordinate(emotCat: low_neg)*
	Subordinate(emotCat:low_neg) Subordinate(emotCat:high_pos) $\rightarrow$ *Subordinate(emotCat: high_neg)*
	Subordinate(emotCat:low_neg) Subordinate(emotCat:low_neg) $\rightarrow$ *Subordinate(emotCat: low_neg)*
	Subordinate(emotCat:low_neg) Subordinate(emotCat:high_neg) $\rightarrow$ *Subordinate(emotCat: high_neg)*
	Subordinate(emotCat:high_neg) Subordinate(emotCat:neutral) $\rightarrow$ *Subordinate(emotCat: high_neg)*
	Subordinate(emotCat:high_neg) Subordinate(emotCat:low_pos) $\rightarrow$ *Subordinate(emotCat: high_neg)*
	Subordinate(emotCat:high_neg) Subordinate(emotCat:high_pos) $\rightarrow$ *Subordinate(emotCat: high_neg)*

Description	SPIN rules
	Subordinate(emotCat:high_neg) Subordinate(emotCat:low_neg) → *Subordinate(emotCat: high_neg)*
	Subordinate(emotCat:high_neg) Subordinate(emotCat:high_neg) → *Subordinate(emotCat: high_neg)*
	Subordinate(emotCat:low_pos) Subordinate(emotCat:neutral) → *Subordinate(emotCat: low_pos)*
	Subordinate(emotCat:low_pos) Subordinate(emotCat:low_pos) → *Subordinate(emotCat: low_pos)*
	Subordinate(emotCat:low_pos) Subordinate(emotCat:high_pos) → *Subordinate(emotCat: high_pos)*
	Subordinate(emotCat:low_pos) Subordinate(emotCat:low_neg) → *Subordinate(emotCat: low_neg)*
	Subordinate(emotCat:low_pos) Subordinate(emotCat:high_neg) → *Subordinate(emotCat: high_neg)*
	Subordinate(emotCat:high_pos) Subordinate(emotCat:neutral) → *Subordinate(emotCat: high_pos)*
	Subordinate(emotCat:high_pos) Subordinate(emotCat:low_pos) → *Subordinate(emotCat: high_pos)*
	Subordinate(emotCat:high_pos) Subordinate(emotCat:high_pos) → *Subordinate(emotCat: high_pos)*
	Subordinate(emotCat:high_pos) Subordinate(emotCat:low_neg) → *Subordinate(emotCat: low_neg)*
	Subordinate(emotCat:high_pos) Subordinate(emotCat:high_neg) → *Subordinate(emotCat: high_neg)*
Homogeneous clauses	*Superordinate(emotCat:neutral) Subordinate(emotCat:neutral)* → *Result(emotCat: neutral)*
	Superordinate(emotCat:neutral) Subordinate(emotCat:low_pos) → *Result(emotCat: low_pos)*
	Superordinate(emotCat:neutral) Subordinate(emotCat:high_pos) → *Result(emotCat: high_pos)*
	Superordinate(emotCat:neutral) Subordinate(emotCat:low_neg) → *Result(emotCat: low_neg)*
	Superordinate(emotCat:neutral) Subordinate(emotCat:high_neg) → *Result(emotCat: high_neg)*
	Superordinate(emotCat:null) Subordinate(emotCat:neutral) → *Result(emotCat: neutral)*
	Superordinate(emotCat:null) Subordinate(emotCat:low_pos) → *Result(emotCat: low_pos)*
	Superordinate(emotCat:null) Subordinate(emotCat:high_pos) → *Result(emotCat: high_pos)*

Description	SPIN rules
	Superordinate(emotCat:null) Subordinate(emotCat:low_neg) → *Result(emotCat: low_neg)*
	Superordinate(emotCat:null) Subordinate(emotCat:high_neg) → *Result(emotCat: high_neg)*
	Superordinate(emotCat:low_neg) Subordinate(emotCat:neutral) → *Result(emotCat: low_neg)*
	Superordinate(emotCat:low_neg) Subordinate(emotCat:low_pos) → *Result(emotCat: low_neg)*
	Superordinate(emotCat:low_neg) Subordinate(emotCat:high_pos) → *Result(emotCat: high_neg)*
	Superordinate(emotCat:low_neg) Subordinate(emotCat:low_neg) → *Result(emotCat: low_neg)*
	Superordinate(emotCat:low_neg) Subordinate(emotCat:high_neg) → *Result(emotCat: high_neg)*
	Superordinate(emotCat:high_neg) Subordinate(emotCat:neutral) → *Result(emotCat: high_neg)*
	Superordinate(emotCat:high_neg) Subordinate(emotCat:low_pos) → *Result(emotCat: high_neg)*
	Superordinate(emotCat:high_neg) Subordinate(emotCat:high_pos) → *Result(emotCat: high_neg)*
	Superordinate(emotCat:high_neg) Subordinate(emotCat:low_neg) → *Result(emotCat: high_neg)*
	Superordinate(emotCat:high_neg) Subordinate(emotCat:high_neg) → *Result(emotCat: high_neg)*
	Superordinate(emotCat:low_pos) Subordinate(emotCat:neutral) → *Result(emotCat: low_pos)*
	Superordinate(emotCat:low_pos) Subordinate(emotCat:low_pos) → *Result(emotCat: low_pos)*
	Superordinate(emotCat:low_pos) Subordinate(emotCat:high_pos) → *Result(emotCat: high_pos)*
	Superordinate(emotCat:low_pos) Subordinate(emotCat:low_neg) → *Result(emotCat: low_neg)*
	Superordinate(emotCat:low_pos) Subordinate(emotCat:high_neg) → *Result(emotCat: high_neg)*
	Superordinate(emotCat:high_pos) Subordinate(emotCat:neutral) → *Result(emotCat: high_pos)*
	Superordinate(emotCat:high_pos) Subordinate(emotCat:low_pos) → *Result(emotCat: high_pos)*
	Superordinate(emotCat:high_pos) Subordinate(emotCat:high_pos) → *Result(emotCat: high_pos)*

Description	SPIN rules
	Superordinate(emotCat:high_pos) Subordinate(emotCat:low_neg) → *Result(emotCat: low_neg)*
	Superordinate(emotCat:high_pos) Subordinate(emotCat:high_neg) → *Result(emotCat: high_neg)*
Simple sentences	*Superordinate(emotCat:neutral)* → *Result(emotCat: neutral)*
	Superordinate(emotCat:low_neg) → *Result(emotCat: low_neg)*
	Superordinate(emotCat:high_neg) → *Result(emotCat: high_neg)*
	Superordinate(emotCat:low_pos) → *Result(emotCat: low_pos)*
	Superordinate(emotCat:high_pos) → *Result(emotCat: high_pos)*

Table 40: SPIN rules for linking clauses

APPENDIX E: PRELIMINARIES OF DATA FUSION

Data fusion defines a method of combining data from different sources (different modalities) aiming, for example, at improvement of classification results ([Mitchell, 2007]). In emotion recognition, these data sources can be lexical, acoustic, or visual. For instance, lexical samples (emotional texts in the lexical affect sensing) can be analyzed together with acoustic samples (emotional utterances in the acoustic modality). The task of data fusion lies in calculating a common result that considers information from participating modalities.

Typically, two conventional ways of data fusion are distinguished: a low-level fusion, sometimes called multi-sensor data fusion, and a high-level fusion, commonly called feature fusion. The low-level fusion concerns a fusing method under special consideration of hardware issues, for instance, fusing sensor data. The high-level fusion fuses data from different data sources that is already transformed in data mining instances.

[Hall & McHullen, 2004] describe such examples of low-level fusion as ocean surveillance, law enforcement, remote sensing, automated monitoring of equipment, medical diagnosis, and robotics. Applications of high-level fusion can be found in fusing data mining instances created on the basis of the lexical and acoustic data.

In this thesis, the high-level feature fusion is examined thoroughly although approaches from the low-level data fusion play a supplementary role. There are 2 main approaches to the high-level feature fusion: feature-level fusion (sometimes called early fusion), and decision-level fusion (Figure 62).

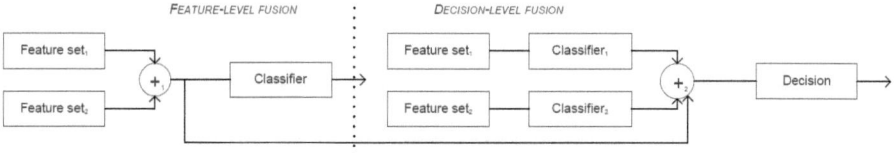

Figure 62: Types of high-level feature fusion

In Figure 62, 2 modalities (modality 1 and modality 2) are considered for fusion. In the feature-level fusion, *Feature set₁* from modality 1 and *Feature set₂* from modality 2 are joined together ($+_1$) in a dataset that is classified by a particular classifier *Classifier*, e.g, SVM, yielding a result of emotion recognition. The decision-level fusion calculates a fusion result by utilizing data from different modalities separately. For this purpose, unimodal classifier *Classifier$_1$* analyzes *Feature set$_1$*; unimodal classifier *Classifier$_2$* analyzes *Feature set$_2$*. Afterwards, the final result of emotion recognition is calculated as combination of results of separate modalities (+$_2$).

Feature-level fusion merges features from different modalities and is fairly self-explanatory, but decision-level fusion requires further discussion. Decision-level fusion can be performed in different ways: statistically, using posterior probabilities of classification outcomes and semantically, using consensus patterns in the majority vote.

The posterior probabilities are the outcome probabilities yielded by the unimodal statistical classifiers: a statistical classifier analyzes an instance and calculates a probability that this instance belongs to a particular class. For instance, *Classifier$_1$* in Figure 62 classifies the instance *I* and calculates a probability vector V_1=(*class$_1$*:<u>0.6</u>, *class$_2$*:0.4, *class$_3$*:0.0) where a pair represents a class name and its probability. A maximal probability value of 0.6 corresponds to *class$_1$* from V_1. *Classifier$_2$* classifies the same emotional instance *I* and yields a probability vector V_2=(*class$_1$*:0.3, *class$_2$*:0.2, *class$_3$*:0.5). A maximal probability value of 0.5 corresponds to *class$_3$* from V_2. And here is a dilemma: different modalities classify the same instance differently as *class$_1$* or *class$_3$*. What should be chosen as an outcome of emotion recognition? What modality and the corresponding probability vector is more important for the final classification outcome, V_1 or V_2?

There are different answers to this question according to the chosen criteria of fusing probabilities of outcomes. The fusion result can be defined by the maximum, or the average, or the product of posterior probabilities. For instance, fusing as maximum is utilized by calculating the maximum value in vectors V_1 and V_2 (probability 0.6) and the resulting outcome of emotional classification is *class$_1$*. The average of vectors V_1 and V_2 is (*class$_1$*:0.45=[0.6+0.3]/2, *class$_2$*:0.3=[0.4+0.2]/2, *class$_3$*:0.25=[0+0.5]/2) and the resulting outcome of emotional classification is *class$_1$*. The product vector from vectors V_1 and V_2 is (*class$_1$*:0.18=[0.6*0.3], *class$_2$*:0.08=[0.4*0.2], *class$_3$*:0.0=[0*0.5]) and the resulting outcome of emotional classification is *class$_1$*. In this case, all criteria (*maximum*, *product*, *average*) indicate *class$_1$* as an outcome of classification and a consensus could be reached. However, it is not always possible.

A consensus can be reached alternatively using the majority vote. Possible variants of the majority calculation can be borrowed from the literature about the low-level fusion ([Kuncheva, 2004]). Accordingly, low-level fusion joins outputs of particular modalities by maintaining different consensus patterns in calculating majority vote as unanimity, simple majority and plurality (Figure 63).

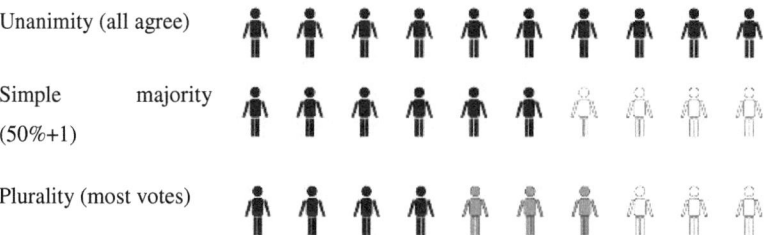

Unanimity (all agree)

Simple majority (50%+1)

Plurality (most votes)

Figure 63: Consensus patterns in the majority vote

Each manikin represents a different output of a unimodal classifier: the black, grey, and white manikins. The unanimity vote assumes an equal output of all unimodal classifiers as a final result; the simple majority vote considers majority vote of outputs of unimodal classifiers as a final result; the plurality vote calculates a final result as the most frequent vote in the unimodal outputs. Hence, a final result in all consensus patterns corresponds to the "black" vote.

APPENDIX F: ACHIEVEMENTS

F.1 PUBLICATIONS

1. Alexander Osherenko, Elisabeth André. Differentiated Semantic Analysis in Lexical Affect Sensing. Proceedings of ACII 2009. 2009.

2. Alexander Osherenko, Elisabeth André, Thurid Vogt. Affect Sensing in Language: Studying Fusion of Linguistic and Acoustic Features. Proceedings of ACII 2009. 2009.

3. Alexander Osherenko. Deducing a Believable Model for Affective Behavior from Perceived Emotional Data. Proceedings of International Workshop on Computational Aspects of Affectual and Emotional Interaction (CAFFEi 2008).

4. Alexander Osherenko. Lexical Affect Sensing: Word Spotting Revisited. Emotional Computer Systems and Interfaces. Proceedings of The Third International Conference on Cognitive Science. Moscow. 2008.

5. Alexander Osherenko. Towards Semantic Affect Sensing in Sentences. Proceedings of AISB 2008.

6. Alexander Osherenko and Elisabeth André. Lexical Affect Sensing: Are Affect Dictionaries Necessary to Analyze Affect? In Proceedings of Affective Computing and Intelligent Interaction (ACII), Springer, 2007.

7. Alexander Osherenko. Affect Sensing using Lexical Means: Comparison of a Corpus with Movie Reviews and a Corpus with Natural Language Dialogues. Workshop on Emotional Corpora (LREC 2006).

8. Chunling Ma, Alexander Osherenko, Helmut Prendinger, and Mitsuru Ishizuka. A chat system based on emotion estimation from text and embodied conversational messengers. AMT. 2005.

F.2 REPRINTS

Chinese University of Hong Kong. Alexander Osherenko and Elisabeth André. Lexical Affect Sensing: Are Affect Dictionaries Necessary to Analyze Affect?

San Jose State University (NASA). Alexander Osherenko and Elisabeth André. Lexical Affect Sensing: Are Affect Dictionaries Necessary to Analyze Affect?

F.3 DEMO

EmoText: Applying Differentiated Semantic Analysis in Lexical Affect Sensing. Proceedings of ACII 2009. URL: http://emotext.informatik.uni-augsburg.de. Last Accessed: 2.07.2009.

F.4 PROJECTS

The EU integrate project CALLAS. URL: http://www.callas-newmedia.eu. Last Accessed: 2.07.2009.

EU FP7 CyberEmotions. URL: http://www.cyberemotions.eu. Last Accessed: 2.07.2009.

BIBLIOGRAPHY

[Andreevskaia et al., 2006a] Andreevskaia, A., Bergler, S. 2006. *Mining WordNet For a Fuzzy Sentiment: Sentiment Tag Extraction From WordNet Glosses.* Proceedings EACL-06, the 11rd Conference of the European Chapter of the Association for Computational Linguistics. pp. 209–216.

[Andreevskaia et al., 2006b] Andreevskaia, A., Bergler, S. 2006b. *Semantic Tag Extraction from WordNet Glosses.* Proceedings of LREC-06, the 5th Conference on Language Resources and Evaluation.

[Austin, 1976] Austin, J.L. 1976. *How to do things with words. The William James Lectures delivered at Harvard University in 1955.* Second Edition. Edited by Urmson, J.O., Sbisa, M. Harvard University Press.

[Balahur & Montoyo, 2008] Balahur A., Montoyo, A. 2008. *Applying a culture dependent emotion triggers database for text valence and emotion classification.* Proceedings of AISB 2008. University of Aberdeen.

[Banerjee & Pedersen, 2003] Banerjee S., Pedersen, T. 2003. *The Design, Implementation, and Use of the Ngram Statistics Package.* Proceedings of the Fourth International Conference on Intelligent Text Processing and Computational Linguistics, Mexico City.

[Bartl & Doerner, 1998] Bartl, C., Doerner, D. 1998. *Comparing the behaviour of PSI with human behaviour in the biolab game.* Ritter, F.E., Young, R.M. (eds.). Proceedings of the Second International Conference on Cognitive Modeling, Nottingham, Nottingham University Press.

[Batliner et al., 2003] Batliner, A., Fischer, K., Huber, R., Spilker, J., Nöth, E. 2003. *How to Find Trouble in Communication.* Speech Communication. 40. pp. 117–143.

[Batliner et al., 2006] Batliner, A., Burkhardt, F., van Ballegooy, M., Nöth, E. 2006. *A Taxonomy of Applications that Utilize Emotional Awareness.* Erjavec, Tomaz ; Gros, Jerneja Zganec (eds.) : Language Technologies, IS-LTC 2006 (Fifth Slovenian and First International Language

Technologies Conference Ljubljana, Slovenia October 9 - 10, 2006). Ljubljana, Slovenia : Infornacijska Druzba (Information Society). pp. 246–250.

[Bednarek, 2006] Bednarek, M. 2006. *Evaluation in Media Discourse. Analysis of a Newspaper Corpus.* Continuum.

[Bennett & Campbell, 2000] Bennett, K. P., Campbell, C. 2000. *Support Vector Machines: Hype or Hallelujah?* SIGKDD Explorations, 2/2. pp. 1–13.

[Bhatia, 2004] Bhatia, V. K. 2004. *Worlds of written discourse.* London, New York. Continuum.

[Bhatia & Gotti, 2006] Bhatia, V. K., Gotti, M. (eds.) 2006. *Explorations in Specialized Genres.* Peter Lang.

[Biber et al., 1999] Biber, D., Johansson S., Conrad, S., Finnegan, E. 1999. *Longman grammar of spoken and written English.* Pearson Education Limited.

[BNC, 2008] *The BNC Frequency List.* 2008. URL: http://www.kilgarriff.co.uk/BNC_lists/all.al.gz. Last accessed: 6.06.2008.

[Bratman, 1987] Bratman, M. E. 1987. *Intention, Plans, and Practical Reason.* CSLI Publications.

[Breiman, 1996] Breiman, L. 1996. *Bagging Predictors, Machine Learning,* 24/2. pp. 123–140.

[Breazeal, 2002] Breazeal, C. L. 2002. *Designing Sociable Robots. Intelligent Robotics and Autonomous Agents.* MIT Press.

[Budanitsky et al., 2001] Budanitsky, A., Hirst, G. 2001. *Semantic distance in WordNet: An experimental, application-oriented evaluation of five measures.* Workshop on WordNet and Other Lexical Resources, Second meeting of the North American Chapter of the Association for Computational Linguistics. Pittsburgh.

[Budd, 1985] Budd, M. 1985. *Music and the Emotions.* Routledge.

[Busso et al., 2004] Busso, C., Deng, Z., Yildirim, S., Bulut, M., Lee, C. M., Kazemzadeh, A., Lee, S., Neumann, U., Narayanan, S. 2004. *Analysis of emotion recognition using facial expressions, speech and multimodal information.* Proceedings of the 6th international Conference on Multimodal Interfaces. ICMI '04. ACM, New York. pp. 205–211.

[Cambridge, 2008] *Cambridge Dictionary.* 2008. URL: http://dictionary.cambridge.org/. Last accessed: 6.06.2008.

[Cambridge, 2006a] *Cambridge Phrasal Verbs Dictionary.* Second Edition. 2006. Cambridge University Press.

[Cambridge, 2006b] *Cambridge Idioms Dictionary.* Second Edition. 2006. Cambridge University Press.

[Campbell et al., 2006] Campbell, N., Devillers, L., Douglas-Cowie, E., Aubergé, V., Batliner, A., Tao, J. 2006. *Resources for the Processing of Affect in Interactions.* Proceedings of the 4th International Conference of Language Resources and Evaluation (LREC Genoa).

[Chambers et al., 2004] Chambers, N., Tetreault, J., Allen, J. 2004. *Approaches for Automatically Tagging Affect.* Shanahan, J. G., Wiebe, J., Qu, Y. (eds.), Proceedings of the AAAI Spring Symposium on Exploring Attitude and Affect in Text: Theories and Applications.

[Choi & Cardie, 2008] Choi, Y., Cardie, C. Learning with Compositional Semantics as Structural Inference for Subsentential Sentiment Analysis. ACL, 2008, pp. 793–801.

[Chung & Pennebaker, 2007] Chung, C., Pennebaker, J. 2007. *The psychological function of function words.* K. Fiedler (Ed.), *Social communication: Frontiers of social psychology.* New York: Psychology Press. A summary of recent findings concerning the links between pronouns, prepositions, and other function words with markers of social and personality processes. pp. 343–359.

[Coltheart, 1981] Coltheart, M. 1981. *The MRC Psycholinguistic Database.* Quarterly Journal of Experimental Psychology, 33A. pp. 497–505.

[Connexor, 2008] *The Connexor Parser.* URL: http://www.connexor.com/. 2008. Last accessed: 6.06.2008.

[Companions, 2009] *Companions Project.* URL: http://www.companions-project.org. 2009. Last accessed: 2.07.2009.

[Cornelius, 1996] Cornelius, R.R. 1996. *The science of emotion. Research and tradition in the psychology of emotion.* Prentice Hall.

[Cowie et al., 2000] Cowie, R., Douglas-Cowie, E., Savvidou, S., McMahon, E., Sawey, M., Schröder, M. 2000. *'FEELTRACE': An instrument for recording perceived emotion in real time.* Proceedings of the ISCA Workshop on Speech and Emotion, Northern Ireland. pp. 19–24.

[Craggs, 2004] Craggs, R. 2004. *Annotating emotion in dialogue – issues and approaches.* 7th Annual CLUK Research Colloquium.

[Dautenhahn et al., 2002] Dautenhahn, K., Bond, A.H., Canamero, L., Edmonds, B. (eds.) 2002. *Socially intelligent robots. Creating Relationships with Computers and Robots.* Kluwer Academic Publishers.

[Dave et al., 2003] Dave, K., Lawrence, S., Pennock, D.M. 2003. *Mining the peanut gallery: Opinion extraction and semantic classification of product reviews.* Proceedings of WWW-03, 12th International Conference on the World Wide Web. Budapest, HU: ACM Press. pp. 519–528

[Di Eugenio & Glass, 2004] Di Eugenio, B., Glass, M. 2004. *The kappa statistic: a second look.* Comput. Linguist. 30, 1. pp. 95–101.

[Diederich et al., 2000] Diederich, J. Kindermann, J., Leopold, E., Paass, G. 2000. *Authorship attribution with Support Vector Machines.* Applied Intelligence.

[Dietterich, 2000] Dietterich, T. G. 2000. *Ensemble Methods in Machine Learning.* Lecture Notes in Computer Science, Springer Verlag, vol. 1857. pp. 1–15.

[Dörner, 2001] Dörner, D. 2001. *Bauplan für eine Seele.* Rowohlt Taschenbuch.

[Eco, 1988] Eco, U. 1988. *On Truth.* A Fiction. Meaning and Mental Representations. Eco, U. (ed.), Marco Santambrogio, and Patrizia Violi. Indiana University Press.

[Ekman, 1993] Ekman, P. 1993. *Facial expression of emotion.* American Psychologist, 48. pp. 384–392.

[Ekman, 1999] Ekman, P. 1999. *Basic emotions.* Dalgleish, T., Power, M. (eds.). Handbook of Cognition and Emotion. Sussex, U.K.: John Wiley & Sons, Ltd.

[Engel, 2006] Engel, R. 2006. *SPIN: A Semantic Parser for Spoken Dialog Systems.* Proceedings of the Fifth Slovenian And First International Language Technology Conference (IS-LTC 2006).

[EmoText, 2009] *EmoText — Emotional Text Analyzer.* URL: http://emotext.informatik.uni-augsburg.de. Last accessed: 11.03.2009.

[Epinions, 2008] *Reviews from Epinions.* URL: epinions.com. Last accessed: 6.06.2008.

[Esuli et al., 2006] Esuli, A., Sebastiani, F. 2006. *SentiWordNet: A Publicly Available Lexical Resource for Opinion Mining.* Proceedings of LREC-06, the 5th Conference on Language Resources and Evaluation.

[Fayyad & Irani, 1992] Fayyad, U., Irani, K. 1992. *On the handling of continuous-valued attributes in decision tree generation.* Machine Learning 8. pp. 87–102.

[Feke, 2003] Feke, M. S. 2003. *Effects of Native-Language and Sex on Back-Channel Behaviour.* Proceedings of the First Workshop on Spanish Sociolinguistics. Lotfi Sayahi (ed). Somerville, MA: Cascadilla Proceedings Project. pp. 96–106.

[Fellbaum, 1998] Fellbaum, C. (ed.). 1998. *WordNet: An Electronic Lexical Database.* MIT Press.

[Finn & Kushmerick, 2006] Finn, A. & Kushmerick, N. 2006. *Learning to classify documents according to genre.* Journal of the American Society for Information Science and Technology (JASIST), Special Issue on Computational Analysis of Style, 57/11.

[Forsyth & Holmes, 1996] Forsyth, R. S., Holmes, D. I. 1996. *Feature finding for text classification.* Literary and Linguistic Computing, 11(4). pp. 163–174.

[Fries, 1996a] 1996. Fries, N. *Grammatik und Emotionen.* Zeitschrift für Literaturwissenschaft und Linguistik. 26. LiLi. pp. 37–69

[Fries, 1996b] Fries, N. 1996. *Sprache und Emotionen.* Bergisch Gladbach, Lübbe.

[Fries, 2007] Fries, N. 2007. *Die Kodierung von Emotionen in Texten: Grundlagen.* JLT - Journal of Literary Theory, 1/2. pp. 293–337.

[Fussell, 2002] Fussell, S. R (ed.). 2002. *The verbal communication of emotions. Interdisciplinary perspectives.* Lawrence Erlbaum Associates, Publishers.

[GAF, 2002] Geneva Emotion Research Group. 2002. *Genfer Appraisal Fragebogen. Format, Entwicklung und Einsatzmöglichkeiten.*

[Gotti, 2003] Gotti, M. 2003. *Specialized Discourse. Linguistic Features and Changing Conventions.* Peter Lang.

[Graham et al., 1992] Graham, R.L., Knuth D. E., Patashnik, O. 1992. *Concrete Mathematics.* Addison-Wesley Publishing Company. Reading, Massachusetts.

[Graesser 2005] Graesser, A.C., Chipman, P., Haynes, B.C., & Olney, A. 2005. *AutoTutor: An intelligent tutoring system with mixed-initiative dialogue.* IEEE Transactions in Education, 48. pp. 612–618.

[Greenbaum, 1996] Greenbaum, S. 1996. *The Oxford English Grammar.* Oxford University Press.

[Hall & McHullen, 2004] Hall, D. L., McMullen, S. A. H. 2004. *Mathematical Techniques in Multisensor Data Fusion.* Artech House Publishers.

[Hirst & St-Onge, 1998] Hirst, G., St-Onge, D. 1998. *Lexical chains as representation of context for the detection and correction of malapropisms.* In [Fellbaum, 1998], pp. 305–332.

[Hillier, 2003] Hillier, H. 2003. *Analysing Real Texts: Research Studies in Modern English Language.* Palgrave Macmillan.

[Hunston & Thompson, 2000] Hunston, S., Thompson G. (eds.) 2000. *Evaluation in Text.* Oxford University Press.

[IMDB, 2008] *Internet Movie Database.* 2008. URL: www.imdb.com. Last accessed: 6.06.2008.

[Jadex, 2009] *Jadex BDI Agent System*. 2009. URL: http://jadex.informatik.uni-hamburg.de. Last accessed: 9.07.2009.

[Jahr, 2000] Jahr, S. 2000. *Emotionen und Emotionsstrukturen in Sachtexten. Ein interdisziplinärer Ansatz zur qualitativen und quantitativen Beschreibung der Emotionalität von Texten.* Walter de Gruyter.

[Janney, 1996] Janney, R. W. 1996. *Speech and Affect. Emotive Uses of English.* [No publisher].

[Joachims, 1999] Joachims, T. 1999. *Making Large-scale SVM Learning Practical. Advances in Kernel Methods - Support Vector Learning.* B. Schölkopf and C. Burges and A. Smola (eds.), MIT Press.

[John et al., 1991] John, O. P., Donahue, E. M., & Kentle, R. L. 1991. *The "Big Five" Inventory: Versions 4a and 5b.* Tech. rep., Berkeley: University of California, Institute of Personality and Social Research.

[Jones & Sutherland, 2008] Jones, C., Sutherland, J. 2008. *Acoustic Emotion Recognition for Affective Computer Gaming.* In: [Peter & Beale, 2008], pp.209–219.

[Izard, 1977] Izard, C.E. 1977. *Human Emotions.* Plenum Press, New York, New York.

[Kamps & Marx, 2002] Kamps, J., Marx, M. 2002. *Words with attitude.* In Hendrik Blockeel and Marx Deneker (eds.), BNAIC'02: Proceedings of the 14th Belgian-Netherlands Conference on Artificial Intelligence. pp. 449–450.

[Kamps et al., 2004] Kamps, J., Marx, M., Mokken, R. Rijke, M. 2004. *Using WordNet to measure semantic orientation of adjectives.* Proceedings of LREC-04, 4th International Conference on Language Resources and Evaluation, IV. pp. 1115–1118.

[Kantor, 1977] Kantor, J. R. 1977. *Psychological linguistics.* The Principia Press.

[Kilgarriff, 1997] Kilgarriff, A. 1997. *Putting Frequencies in the Dictionary.* International Journal of Lexicography 10 (2). pp 135–155.

[Kim & André, 2006] Kim, J., André, E. 2006. *Emotion recognition using physiological and speech signal in short-term observation.* Perception and Interactive Technologies.: LNAI 4201. Springer. pp. 53–64.

[Kipp, 2003] Kipp, M. 2003. *Gesture Generation by Imitation - From Human Behaviour to Computer Character Animation.* PhD Thesis. Saarland University.

[Kjell, 1994] Kjell, B. 1994. *Authorship determination using letter pair frequency features with neural network classifiers.* Literary and Linguistic Computing, 9(2). pp. 119–124.

[Klein & Manning, 2003] Klein, D., Manning, C. D. 2003. *Accurate Unlexicalized Parsing.* Proceedings of the 41st Meeting of the Association for Computational Linguistics. pp. 423–430.

[Kollias, 2007] Kollias, S. 2007. *ERMIS Project.* URL: http://www.image.ntua.gr/ermis/. Last accessed: 6.06.2008.

[Kuncheva, 2004] Kuncheva, L. I. 2004. *Combining Pattern Classifiers.* JohnWiley and Sons Ltd, Hoboken, New Jersey.

[Langenmayr, 1997] Langenmayr, A. 1997. *Sprachpsychologie.* Hogrefe, Göttingen.

[Leacock & Chodorow, 1998] Leacock, C. and M. Chodorow. 1998. *Combining local context and WordNet similarity for word sense identification.* In: [Fellbaum, 1998]. pp. 265–284.

[Lee, 1999] Lee, L. 1999. *Measures of Distributional Similarity.* 37th Annual Meeting of the Association for Computational Linguistics. pp. 25–32.

[Leech et al., 1994] Leech, G., Garside, R., Bryant, M. 1994. *CLAWS4: The tagging of the British National Corpus.* Proceedings of the 15th International Conference on Computational Linguistics (COLING 94). Japan: Kyoto. pp. 622–628.

[Leech & Svartvik, 2003] Leech, G. N., Startvik, J. 2003. *A communicative grammar of English.* Third edition. Longman.

[Levin, 1993] Levin, Beth. 1993. *English verb classes and alternations. A preliminary investigation.* The University of Chicago Press. Chicago and London.

[Lin, 1998a] Lin, D. 1998. *An information-theoretic definition of similarity.* Proceedings of the 15th International Conference on Machine Learning. Morgan Kaufmann, San Francisco CA.

[Lin, 1998b] Lin, D. 1998. *Dependency-based Evaluation of MINIPAR.* Proceedings of Workshop on the Evaluation of Parsing Systems, Granada, Spain.

[Liu, 2007] Liu, B. 2007. *Web Data Mining: Exploring Hyperlinks, Contents and Usage Data.* Springer.

[Liu et al., 2003] Liu, H., Lieberman, H., Selker, T. 2003. *A Model of Lexical affect Sensing Using Real-World Knowledge.* Proceedings of IUI-03, the 8th international conference on intelligent user interfaces. Miami, US: ACM Press. pp. 125–132.

[dos Lucas et al., 2007] dos Lucas, P., Aylett, R., Cawsey, A. 2007. *Affective adaptation of synthetic social behaviour.* Proceedings of ACII 2007.

[Mairesse et al., 2007] Mairesse F., Walker, M., Mehl, M., Moore, R. 2007. *Using Linguistic Cues for the Automatic Recognition of Personality in Conversation and Text.* Journal of Artificial Intelligence Research (JAIR), 30. pp. 457–500.

[Marcus et al., 1993] Marcus, M., Santorini, B., Marcinkiewicz, M. 1993. *Building a Large Annotated Corpus of English: The Penn Treebank.* Computational Linguistics, 19(2). pp. 313–330.

[Marsella & Gratch, 2002] Marsella, S., Gratch, J. 2002. A step toward irrationality: using emotion to change belief. In *Proceedings of the First international Joint Conference on Autonomous Agents and Multiagent Systems: Part 1* (Bologna, Italy, July 15 - 19, 2002). AAMAS '02. ACM, New York, NY, pp. 334–341.

[Maslov, 1943] Maslov, A. 1943. *A Theory of Human Motivation.* Psychological Review 50. pp. 370–396.

[MathWorld, 2008] *MathWorld.* URL: http://http://mathworld.wolfram.com/. Last accessed: 6.06.2008.

[Max-Neef, 1991] Max-Neef, M.A. 1991. *Human Scale Development.* Apex Press, New York and London.

[McCrae & Costa, 1999] McCrae, R. R., Costa, P. T. 1999. A *five-factor theory of personality.* Handbook of personality: Theory and research (2nd ed). Pervin L.A., John O.P. (eds.). pp. 139–153.

[Mehl et al., 2001] Mehl, M., Pennebaker, J., Crow, M., Dabbs, J., Price, J. 2001. The Electronically Activated Recorder (EAR): A device for sampling naturalistic daily activities and conversations. Behaviour Research Methods, Instruments, and Computers, 33. pp. 517–523.

[Mello et al, 2008] D'Mello, S. K., Craig, S. D., Witherspoon, A., Mcdaniel, B., Graesser, A. 2008. Automatic detection of learner's affect from conversational cues. *User Modeling and User-Adapted Interaction* 18, 1-2. pp. 45-80.

[Merriam-Webster, 2007] *Merriam-Webster Dictionary.* 2007. URL: www.m-w.com. Last accessed: 6.06.2008.

[Mitchell, 1997] Mitchell, T. M. 1997. *Machine Learning.* 1st. McGraw-Hill Higher Education.

[Mitchell, 2007] Mitchell, H.B. 2007. *Multi-Sensor Data Fusion: An Introduction.* Springer.

[MRQE, 2008] *MPQE – Movie Review Query Engine.* 2008. URL: http://www.mrqe.com. Last accessed: 9.08.2008.

[Murray, 1991] Murray, D. E. 1991. *Conversation for Action. The Computer Terminal as Medium for Communication.* John Benjamins Publishing Company.

[Myrick & Erney, 1984] Myrick, R. D. & Erney, T. 1984. *Caring and Sharing: Becoming a Peer Facilitator.* Educational Media Corporation.

[Neviarouskaya et al., 2007] Neviarouskaya, A., Prendinger, Ishizuka, M. *Lexical affect Sensing for Social and Expressive Online Communication, Affective Computing and Intelligent Interaction.* Proceedings of ACII2007, Lisbon, Portugal. Springer LNCS 4738. pp. 218–229.

[NielsenBuzzMetrics, 2008] *The Nielsen BussMetrics company.* URL: http://www.nielsenbuzzmetrics.com/. Last accessed: 6.06.2008.

[Oberlander & Nowson, 2006] Overlander, J., Nowson, S. *Whose Thumb Is It Anyway? Classifying Author Personality from Weblog Text.* ACL.

[Ortony et al., 1988] Ortony, A., Clore, G.L., Collins, A. 1988. *The Cognitive Structure of Emotion.* Cambridge University Press.

[Osgood et al., 1957] Osgood, C. E., Suci, G. J., Tannenbaum, P. H. 1957. *The Measurement of Meaning.* University of Illinois Press.

[Osherenko, 2006] Osherenko, A. 2006. *Affect Sensing using Lexical Means: Comparison of a Corpus with Movie Reviews and a Corpus with Natural Language Dialogues.* Proceedings of the Workshop on Emotional Corpora on LREC 2006.

[Osherenko, 2008] Osherenko, A. 2008. *Deducing a Believable Model for Affective Behaviour from Perceived Emotional Data.* Proceedings of International Workshop on Computational Aspects of Affectual and Emotional Interaction (CAFFEi 2008).

[Osherenko & André, 2007] Osherenko, A. André, E. 2007. *Lexical Affect Sensing: Are Affect Dictionaries Necessary to Analyze Affect?* Proceedings of Affective Computing and Intelligent Interaction (ACII 2007). Springer.

[Pang et al., 2002] Pang, B., Lee, L., Vaithyanathan, S. 2002. *Thumbs up? Sentiment Classification using Machine Learning Techniques.* Proceedings of EMNLP-02, the Conference on Empirical Methods in Natural Language Processing. Association for Computational Linguistics. pp. 79–86.

[Pang & Lee, 2004] Pang, B., Lee, L. 2004. *A Sentimental Education: Sentiment Analysis using Subjectivity Summarization based on Minimum Cuts.* Proceedings of ACL-04, 42nd Meeting of the Association for Computational Linguistics. Barcelona, ES: Association for Computational Linguistics. pp. 271–278.

[Pennebaker & King, 1999] Pennebaker, J. W., King, L. A. 1999. *Linguistic styles: Language use as an individual ifference.* Journal of Personality and Social Psychology, 77. pp. 1296–1312.

[Pennebaker et al., 2001] Pennebaker, J.W., Francis, M.E., Booth, R.J. 2001. *Linguistic Inquiry and Word Count (LIWC): LIWC2001.* Mahwah, NJ: Erlbaum Publishers.

[Pennebaker et al., 2003] Pennebaker, J.W., Mehl, M.R., Niederhoffer, K. 2003. *Psychological aspects of natural language use: Our words, our selves.* Annual Review of Psychology, 54. pp. 547–577.

[Beale & Peter, 2008] Beale, R., Peter, C. (eds.). 2008. *Affect and Emotion in Human-Computer Interaction, From Theory to Applications.* Lecture Notes in Computer Science, Vol. 4868, Springer.

[Picard, 1997] Picard, R. W. 1997. *The affective computing.* The MIT Press.

[Planalp, 1996] Planalp, S. *Varieties of Cues to Emotion in Naturally Occurring Situations.* Cognition & Emotion, Volume 10, Issue 2, Mar 1996. pp. 137–154.

[Planalp, 1999] Planalp, S. 1999. *Communicating Emotion: Social, Moral, and Cultural Processes (Studies in Emotion and Social Interaction).* Cambridge University Press.

[Quirk et al., 1985] Quirk, R.; Greenbaum, S.; Leech, G., Svartvik, J. 1985. *A Comprehensive Grammar of the English Language.* Longman.

[Quirk & Greenbaum, 1988] Quirk, R., Greenbaum, S. 1988. *A University Grammar of English.* Longman Publishing Group; Abridged Edition.

[Rabiner, 1989] Rabiner, L.R. 1989. *A tutorial on hidden markov models and selected applications in speech recognition.* Proceedings of the IEEE, 77 (2). pp. 257–286.

[Rada et al., 1989] Rada, R., H. Mili, E. Bicknell, Blettner, M. 1989. *Development and application of a metric on semantic nets.* IEEE Transactions on Systems, Man, and Cybernetics, 19. pp. 17–30.

[Ramyaa & Rasheed, 2004] Ramyaa, C., Rasheed, K. 2004. *Using Machine Learning Techniques for Stylometry.* Proceedings of International Conference on Machine Learning; Models, Technologies and Applications (MLMTA'2004).

[Read, 2004] Read, J. 2004. *Recognising affect in text using pointwise-mutual information*. Masters thesis, University of Sussex. URL: http://www.informatics.sussex.ac.uk/users/jlr24/papers/read-us04.pdf. Last accessed: 6.06.2008.

[Reelviews, 2008] *Reelviews Movie Reviews*. URL: http://www.reelviews.net/. Last accessed: 6.06.2008.

[Resnik, 1995] Resnik, P. 1995. *Using information content to evaluate semantic similarity in a taxonomy*. Proceedings of the 14th International Joint Conference on Artificial Intelligence. Morgan Kaufmann. pp. 448–453.

[Riloff & Phillips, 2004] Riloff, E., Phillips, W. 2004. *An Introduction to the Sundance and AutoSlog Systems*. Technical Report UUCS-04-015, School of Computing University of Utah.

[Riloff et al., 2006] Riloff, E, Patwardhan, S., Wiebe, J. 2006. *Feature Subsumption for Opinion Analysis*. Proceedings of EMNLP-06. Conference on Empirical Methods in Natural Language Processing. Sydney. Association for Computational Linguistics. pp. 440–448.

[Schapire & Singer, 1999] Schapire, R.E., Singer, Y. 1999. *Improved Boosting Algorithms Using Confidence-Rated Predictors*. Machine Learning, 37(3). pp. 297–336.

[Scherer et al., 2001] Scherer, K. R., Schorr, A., Johnstone, T. 2001. *Appraisal processes in emotion*. Oxford University Press.

[Schmid, 1994] Schmid, H. 1994. *Probabilistic Part-of-Speech Tagging Using Decision Trees*. Proceedings of the Conference on New Methods in Language Processing. Manchester, UK.

[Schröder, 2004] Schröder, M. 2004. *Dimensional emotion representation as a basis for speech synthesis with non-extreme emotions*. Proceedings of Workshop on Affective Dialogue Systems Kloster Irsee, Germany. pp. 209–220.

[Schröder, 2008] Schröder, M., Cowie, R., Heylen, D., Pantic, M., Pelachaud, C., Schuller, B. 2008. *Towards responsive Sensitive Artificial Listeners*. Proceedings of Fourth International Workshop on Human-Computer Conversation. Bellagio, Italy.

[Schuller et al., 2005] Schuller, B., Müller, R., Lang, M., Rigoll, G. 2005. *Speaker independent emotion recognition by early fusion of acoustic and linguistic features within ensembles.* Proceedings of INTERSPEECH-2005. pp. 805–808.

[Searle, 1969] Searle, J. R. 1969. *Speech Acts.* Cambridge University Press.

[Singh, 2002] Singh, P. 2002. *The public acquisition of commonsense knowledge.* Proceedings of AAAI Spring Symposium. Palo Alto, CA, AAAI. pp. 1223–1237.

[Sperber & Wilson, 2004] Sperber, D., Wilson, D. 2004. *Relevance Theory.* G. Ward and L. Horn (eds.) *Handbook of Pragmatics.* Oxford: Blackwell. pp. 607–632.

[Stone et al., 1966] Stone, P. J., Dunphy, D. C., Smith, M.S., Ogilvie, D. M. 1966. *The General Inquirer: A Computer Approach to Content Analysis.* MIT Press.

[Strapparava & Mihalcea, 2007] Strapparava, C. Mihalcea, R. 2007. *SemEval-2007 Task 14: Affective Text.* Proceedings of the Fourth International Workshop on Semantic Evaluations. Prague, Association for Computational Linguistics. pp. 70–74.

[Swales, 2002] Swales, J. M. 2002. *On Models in Applied Discourse Analysis.* Research and Practice in Professional Discourse. Candlin Ch. N. (ed.). Macquarie University. City University of Hong Kong Press.

[Swan, 2005] Swan, M. 2005. *English Language Usage.* Third edition. Oxford University Press.

[Taboada et al., 2006] Taboada, M., Anthony, C., Voll, K. 2006. *Methods for Creating Semantic Orientation Databases.* Proceeding of LREC-06, the 5th International Conference on Language Resources and Evaluation. pp. 427–432.

[Tajadura-Jiménez & Västfjäll, 2008] Tajadura-Jiménez, A., Västfjäll, D. 2008. *Auditory-Induced Emotion: A Neglected Channel for Communication in Human-Computer Interaction.* In [Beale & Peter, 2008]. pp.63–74.

[Thorne, 1997] Thorne, S. 1997. *Mastering advanced English usage.* Palgrave Macmillan.

[Truong & Raaijmakers, 2008] Truong, K. P., Raaijmakers, S. 2008. *Automatic Recognition of Spontaneous Emotions in Speech Using Acoustic and Lexical Features.* Machine Learning for Multimodal Interaction. Springer. pp. 161–172.

[Turney, 2001] Turney, P.D. 2001. *Mining the Web for synonyms: PMI-IR versus LSA on TOEFL.* Proceedings of the Twelfth European Conference on Machine Learning (ECML2001). Freiburg, Germany. pp. 491–502.

[Turney, 2002] Turney, P. 2002. *Thumbs Up or Thumbs Down? Semantic Orientation Applied to Unsupervised Classification of Reviews.* Proceedings of ACL-02, 40th Annual Meeting of the Association for Computational Linguistics. Philadelphia, US: Association for Computational Linguistics. pp. 417–424.

[Uzuner & Katz, 2005] Uzuner, Ö., Katz, B. 2005. *Style vs. Expression in Literary Narratives.* Proceedings of the Twenty-eighth Annual International ACM SIGIR Conference (SIGIR 2005).

[Valitutti et al., 2004] Valitutti, A., Strapparava, C., Stock, O. 2004. *Developing Affective Lexical Resources.* PsychNology Journal. 2/1. pp. 61–83.

[Vogt et al., 2008a] Vogt, T., André, E., Bee, N. 2008. *EmoVoice — A Framework for Online Recognition of Emotions from Voice.* PIT '08: Proceedings of the 4th IEEE tutorial and research workshop on Perception and Interactive Technologies for Speech-Based Systems. Springer.

[Vogt et al., 2008b] Vogt, T., André, E., Wagner, J. 2008. *Automatic Recognition of Emotions from Speech: A Review of the Literature and Recommendations for Practical Realisation.* In: [Beale & Peter, 2008], pp.75–91.

[Vygotskij, 1996] Vygotskij, L.S. 1996. *Die Lehre von Emotionen: Eine psychologiehistorische Untersuchung.* Übersetzt von Gudrun Richter. Wissenschaftlich bearbeitet und mit einer Einführung von Alexandre Métraux. LIT.

[Walker & Prytherch, 2008] Walker, S., Prytherch, D. 2008. *How Is It for You? (A Case for Recognising User Motivation in the Design Process).* In: [Beale & Peter, 2008], pp.130–141.

[Werle, 2002] Werle, A. 2002. *A Typology of Negative Indefinites.* Mary Andronis, Erin Debenport, Anne Pycha & Keiko Yoshimura (eds.) Papers from the 38th Meeting of the Chicago Linguistic Society, vol. 2: CLS 38-2: The Panels. Chicago: Chicago Linguistic Society. pp. 127–143.

[Wertsch, 1985] Wertsch, J V. 1985. *Vygotsky and the social formation of mind.* Harvard University Press.

[Whissell, 1989] Whissell, C.M. 1989. *The dictionary of affect in language.* Plutchik, R., Kellerman, H. (eds.): *Emotion: Theory, Research, and Experience.* New York: Academic Press. pp. 113–131.

[Whitelaw et al., 2005] Whitelaw, C., Garg, N., Argamon, S. 2005. *Using Appraisal Taxonomies for Sentiment Analysis.* Proceedings of MCLC-05, the 2nd Midwest Computational Linguistic Colloquium.

[Wiebe, 1994] Wiebe, J. M. 1994. *Tracking point of view in narrative.* Computational Linguistics 20 (2). pp. 233–287.

[Wiebe et al., 2004] Wiebe, J., Wilson, T., Bruce, R., Bell, M., Martin, M. 2004. *Learning Subjective Language.* Computational linguistics, 30(3). pp. 277–308.

[Wiebe & Riloff, 2005a] Wiebe, J., Riloff, E. 2005. *Creating Subjective and Objective Sentence Classifiers from Unannotated Texts.* Proceeding of CICLing-05, International Conference on Intelligent Text Processing and Computational Linguistics. Lecture Notes in Computer Science, vol. 3406. Mexico City, MX: Springer. pp. 475–486.

[Wiebe et al., 2005b] Wiebe, J., Wilson, T., Cardie, C. 2005. *Annotating expressions of opinions and emotions in language.* Proceedings of Language Resources and Evaluation (formerly Computers and the Humanities), 39/2-3. pp. 165–210.

[Wikipedia, 2008] *Wikipedia.* 2008. URL: http://en.wikipedia.org/. Last accessed: 6.06.2008.

[Witten & Frank, 2005] Witten I. H. & Frank E. 2005. *Data Mining: Practical Machine Learning Tools and Techniques.* Second Edition. Morgan Kaufmann.

[Wooldridge, 2002] Wooldridge, M. 2002. *Introduction to MultiAgent Systems*. John Wiley and Sons.

[Yi et al., 2003] Yi, J., Nasukawa, T., Bunescu, R:, Niblack, W. 2003. *Sentiment Analyzer: Extracting Sentiments about a Given Topic using Natural Language Processing Techniques*. Proceedings of ICDM-03, the 3ird IEEE International Conference on Data Mining. Melbourne, US: IEEE Computer Society. pp. 427– 434.

[Yourdictionary, 2008] *Yourdictionary*. 2008. URL: http://www.yourdictionary.com/. Last accessed: 6.06.2008.

[Yu & Hatzivassiloglou, 2003] Yu, H., Hatzivassiloglou, V. 2003. *Towards Answering Opinion Questions: Separating Facts from Opinions and Identifying the Polarity of Opinion Sentences*. Proceedings of EMNLP-03, 8th Conference on Empirical Methods in Natural Language Processing. Collins, Michael, Steedman, Mark (eds.). pp. 129–136.

[Zagat, 2008] *ZAGAT: Ratings & Reviews for New York, Los Angeles, San Francisco, Philadelphia and Restaurants Everywhere*. 2008. URL: http://www.zagat.com. Last accessed: 9.08.2008.

[Zoll et al., 2006] Zoll, C., Enz, S., Schaub, H., Aylett, R., Paiva, A. *Fighting Bullying with the Help of Autonomous Agents in a Virtual School Environment*. Proceedings 7th International Conference on Cognitive Modelling (ICCM-06), Lawrence Erlbaum, Trieste, Italy, 2006.

INDEX

accuracy 213
adjunct 201
adverbial 201
affect segment 61
affect sensing 42
agreeableness cf. *Big Five Personality trait, agreeableness*
amplifier cf. *intensifier, amplifier*
antipodean 1
ANVIL 60
attribute cf. *feature*
authorship attribution cf. *document, authorship attribution*
AutoSlog 31
back-channeling 13
backward elimination 213
Bag-of-Words 81
Big Five Personality trait 51
   agreeableness 51
   conscientiousness 51
   emotional stability 51
   extraversion 51, 52
   openness to experience 52
bigram 32
binary relation features 174
British National Corpus (BNC) 81
C4.5 211
class cf. *feature, class*
collocation cf. *phrase, collocation*
conjunct 201
conjunction 169, 200
conscientiousness cf. *Big Five Personality trait, conscientiousness*
convex hull 210
coordinator cf. *phrase, linking* or *sentence, linking*
copula cf. *word, copula*
cross-validation 207
DAL cf. *Whissell's Dictionary of Affect*
desirable inter-annotator agreement 75
dialogue exchange 81
disambiguation 47
disjuncts 201
document
   authorship attribution 49
   negative 43
   non-topic 43
   positive 43
   topic 43
downtoner cf. *intensifier, downtoner*
E/A data 60
Ekman emotions cf. *emotion, Ekman emotions*, cf. *emotion, Ekman emotions*
Ekman vector 21
emoticon 38
emotion 1
   Ekman emotions 21, 30
   Izard emotions 21, 37
   positive 51
emotion word cf. *word, emotion word*
emotional phrase cf. *phrase, emotional*
emotional sentence cf. *sentence, emotional*
emotional stability cf. *Big Five Personality trait, emotional stability*
emphasizer cf. *intensifier, emphasizer*
ensemble meta-classifier 211
EQI 26
extraction patterns (EP) 31
extraversion cf. *Big Five Personality trait, extraversion*
feature 205
   class 206
   evaluation 205
   evaluation as frequency vector 44
   evaluation as presence values 44, 45
   evaluation as reciprocal frequency vector 84
   extraction 205
FEELTRACE 60
figurative expression cf. *phrase, figurative expression*
forward selection 213
frequency vector cf. *feature, evaluation*
function word cf. *word, function word*
General Inquirer (GI) 24
   ambiguous words 25
genre 80
granularity features 174
hapax legomena cf. *word, hapax legomena*
inflected word cf. *word, inflected*, cf. *word, inflected*

intensifier 202
   amplifier 203
   downtoner 203
   emphasizer 203
   valence shifter 42
interaction dynamics 197
Internet Movie Database (IMDB) 59
Izard emotions cf. *emotion, Izard emotions*, cf. *emotion, Izard emotions*
Izard vector 21
lemma cf. *word, lemma*
lemmatization cf. *word, lemmatization*
Levin verbs 26
lexical feature cf. *word, lexical feature*
LIFO 104
linear discriminant analysis classifier (LDA) 212
Linguistic Inquiry and Word Count (LIWC) 25
Maslov's theory of human needs 42, 54
measure averaged over classes 213
metaphor 17
modality 10, 196
Multi-Perspective Question Answering (MPQA) 34
NaïveBayes (NB) 209
Neef's theory of human needs 42
negation 203
negative document cf. *document, negative*
news headlines 39
N-gram 34
non-topic document cf. *document, non-topic*
objective sentence cf. *sentence, objective*
openness to experience cf. *Big Five Personality trait, openness to experience*
opinion 1
Osgood's dimensions cf. *word, Osgood's dimensions*
phrase
   adjective phrase 199
   adverb phrase 199
   collocation 35
   emotional 30
   figurative expression 20
   linking 200
   noun phrase 199
   verb phrase 199
phrase combination 160, 163
PMI-IR 29
POS tagging 25
positive document cf. *document, positive*
positive emotion cf. *emotion, positive*

precision 212
presence values cf. *feature, evaluation*, cf. *feature, evaluation*, cf. *feature, evaluation*
priority queue 102
question word 148
recall 212
reciprocal frequency vector cf. *feature, evaluation as reciprocal frequency vector*
Rochester Marriage Counseling Corpus 60
Sensitive Artificial Listener corpus (SAL) 60
sentence
   emotional 30
   grammatical function 200
   linking 200
   objective 34
   subjective 34
SMO 210
stemming cf. *word, stemming*
stopword cf. *word, stopword*
stratification 208
STRIPS 17
subjective sentence cf. *sentence, subjective*
subjectivity 35
subordinator cf. *phrase, linking* or *sentence, linking*
subsentence combination 151, 160, 162
support vector machine (SVM) 209
SVMlight 210
Switchboard 59
text piece cf. *sentence*
theory of pragmatic relevance 42, 54
topic document cf. *document, topic*
TreeTagger 138
unigram 32, cf. *word, unigram, word, unigram*
usability testing 31
valence shifter cf. *intensifiers*
Wall Street Journal (WSJ) 36
what-word 149
Whissell's Dictionary of Affect (DAL) 26
wh-word cf. *phrase, linking* or *sentence, linking*
word
   copula 83
   emotion word 24
   function word 50
   hapax legomena 35
   inflected 25, 26
   lemma 26
   lemmatization 44
   lexical feature 81
   Osgood's dimensions 14
   question word 148

stemming 44
stopword 26
tagwords 51
unigram 81
what-word 149
word spotting 41
word spotting cf. *word, word spotting*
WordNet-Affect 29

```
...und das hat mit ihrem Singen die
Lorelei getan.
        Heine «Lorelei»
```